BEYOND EMPIRICISM

STUDIA PAEDAGOGICA

New Series
34

Editorial Board
Prof. Dr. E. De Corte (Chairman)
Prof. Dr. A. De Munter
Prof. Dr. M. Depaepe
Prof. Dr. B. Maes
Prof. Dr. G. Vandemeulebroecke

Studia Paedagogica

BEYOND EMPIRICISM
ON CRITERIA FOR EDUCATIONAL RESEARCH

Edited by Paul SMEYERS and Marc DEPAEPE

Leuven University Press
2003

With the support of
K.U. Leuven Commissie voor Publicaties

© 2003 Universitaire Pers Leuven / Leuven University Press / Presses Universitaires de Louvain
Blijde Inkomststraat 5, B-3000 Leuven

All rights reserved. Except in those cases expressly determined by law, no part of this publication may be multiplied, saved in an automated datafile or made public in any way whatsoever without the express prior written consent of the publisher.

ISBN 90 5867 325 1

D / 2003 / 1869 / 50

NUR: 847

TABLE OF CONTENTS

Foreword   7

Introduction (Paul Smeyers and Marc Depaepe)   9

I   ***Educational Research as a Social Discourse***
(Section Editor Nicholas Burbules)

Six stories in search of a character? "The philosopher" in an educational research group   27
David Bridges, University of East Anglia, Norwich, U.K.

The importance of new technologies in promoting collaborative educational research   41
Nicholas Burbules, University of Illinois at Urbana-Champaign, U.S.A. and Bert Lambeir, KULeuven, Belgium

Constructing the Eden of our earthly existence. Empiricism and the history of educational research in Belgium before the second World War   53
Marc Depaepe and Angelo Van Gorp, KULeuven, Belgium

From colonialism to globalisation: Performativity in New Zealand education   65
James D. Marshall, Michael Peters, and Ruth Irwin, University of Auckland, New Zealand

II   ***Educational Research as a Discursive Practice***
(Section Editor Thomas Popkewitz)

Journals and the making of experts and educational knowledge. Exploring a Portuguese pedagogical journal (1921-1932)   81
Luís Miguel Carvalho, Technical University of Lisbon, Portugal

From schools of thinking to genres of writing. New roles for philosophy of education   93
Bas Levering, Utrecht University, The Netherlands

The disciplinary terrains of soul and self-government in the first map of the educational sciences (1879-1911)   105
Jorge Ramos do Ó, University of Lisbon, Portugal

Educational research and constituting the American School at the turn of the 20th century   117
Thomas S. Popkewitz, The University of Wisconsin-Madison, U.S.A.

	Research and revelation: What really works? Richard Smith, University of Durham, U.K.	*129*
	Ideas in their historical context: The case of German "Geisteswissenschaftliche Pädagogik" as a national grammar Daniel Throehler, Pestalozzianum, Zürich, Switzerland	*141*

III Educational Research: Epistemological Issues
(Section Editor Wouter van Haaften)

Self-understanding and self-determination:
An unfamiliar look at the philosophy of education — *155*
Jan Bransen, KUNijmegen, The Netherlands

The concept of truth in educational theory — *167*
Stefaan Cuypers, KULeuven, Belgium

Experiencing knowledge: Some philosophical insights for educational research — *181*
Kathleen Coessens, VUB, Belgium

Wittgenstein and Cavell: Reappraising scepticism in educational theory — *195*
Stefan Ramaekers, KULeuven, Belgium

Causality and (in-)determinism in educational research — *207*
Paul Smeyers, KULeuven, Belgium

IV Educational Research: Ethical Considerations
(Section Editor Lynn Fendler)

Theorising educational practices: The politico-ethical choices — *221*
Michael A. Peters, University of Glasgow, U.K.

Personal autonomy, authenticity and the intrinsic valuation of nature — *237*
Dirk Willem Postma, KULeuven, Belgium and KUNijmegen, The Netherlands

Equal recognition: Identity politics and the idea of a social science — *247*
Paul Standish, University of Dundee, U.K.

Ethical problems of community in educational research — *257*
Lynn Fendler, Michigan State University, U.S.A.

FOREWORD

This book is one of the results of the discussions that have taken place in a Research Community convened under the title *Philosophy and History of the Discipline of Education. Evaluation and Evolution of the Criteria for Educational Research*, subsidized by the FWO-Vlaanderen. Convinced that collaboration between research groups from the Flemish part of Belgium and from around the world could play a vital part in responding to the desperate need for systematic reflection on the criteria for educational research, the editors of this book took the initiative and applied in 1998 to the Fonds voor Wetenschappelijk Onderzoek Vlaanderen. Thus academics from the Katholieke Universiteit Leuven, the Vrije Universiteit Brussel and the Universiteit Gent, together with scholars from the Humboldt Universität zu Berlin, the Katholieke Universiteit Nijmegen, the University of Auckland, the University of Lisbon, the University of Dundee, the University of Wisconsin-Madison, the University of Illinois at Urbana-Champaign and Stanford University formed a Research Community. Since then several other centers have become involved, with meetings in 2000, 2001 and 2002 in Leuven. The researchers are united in the belief that there is a place within the discipline of education for "foundational" approaches – not to answer any need for a (new) foundation, but rather to enable the systematic study of educational practice from a discipline-orientated perspective. The level of discussion that these meetings generated surpassed our expectations, resulting not only in a deepened understanding of educational research but also providing the opportunity for many Flemish doctoral students to participate in discussion with leading scholars in philosophy and history of education. The essays in this collection reflect the different topics that were addressed. They bear witness to the belief that educational theory must go beyond empirical educational research if it is to provide a real understanding of the human practice that education is. This belief is reflected in the title of this book: *Beyond Empiricism: On Criteria for Educational Research*.

In compiling this collection we are grateful for the assistance we have had from the section editors: Nicholas C. Burbules, Tom Popkewitz, Wouter van Haaften and Lynn Fendler. Special thanks are due to Paul Standish for his help with the introduction and also to Betty Vanden Bavière for the care she has shown in preparing the text for the publisher. Finally, we want explicitly to acknowledge the financial support of the FWO-Vlaanderen in the establishment of this Research Community.

P.S. & M.D.

INTRODUCTION

Paul Smeyers and Marc Depaepe

The issues that are discussed nowadays in the discipline of education, and the particular ways in which they are dealt with, need to be understood as part of the history of the subject. Moreover, changes have taken place in terms of the kind of research that is pursued under the title "educational sciences", or, to put this more broadly, in educational theory. From the 1960s onwards the so-called realistic turn in academic pedagogy tends to have led in the direction of the empiricists. In postmodern times, however, philosophers and historians of education have questioned this empiricist emphasis, with an eye for the deconstruction of its founding claims and myths. Historians and sociologists of educational science such as Tom Popkewitz (1997) and Lynn Fendler (2003) have shown that, since the nineteenth century, the "elusive science" of education (Condliffe Lagemann, 2000) functioned as a discourse – as a technology of power – that regulated processes of social inclusion and exclusion, contributing to the normalizing and disciplining of the masses. The sick, the mentally ill, prisoners, workers, soldiers and school children were not only measured and observed: they were also classified in groups that, as it were, formed living graphs. Becoming ever more refined, this strategy of control, found expression in quasi-uniform school architecture, in the technology of a learning conversation heavily guided by the teacher, in the separation of special education from ordinary (or "normal") education, and so on. To borrow the title of Ian Hacking's inspirational essay (1996), these practices might aptly be called "the taming of chance". But first and foremost, of course, the scene of education has itself changed.

There was a time when education and schooling were not readily seen as "essentially contested concepts", when, following Kant, education was understood as the "means" to become human – and, that is to say, rational. This was itself a reaction to an earlier period, characterized by the inculcation of values and the uncritical learning of facts or bodies of information, and where discipline was understood as obedience to authority. With the Enlightenment, rationality becomes the proper end of what a human being is. This is not to say that this results in a means-end reasoning: in becoming free from one's inclinations and passions, one realizes one's true nature – that is one puts oneself under the guidance of reason. Thus, liberal education, along these lines, is concerned with the initiation of the learner into forms of thought and understanding that are part of the cultural heritage. In their strongest formulation these norms were thought to be stable and valid, moreover, for all cultures. In the German tradition, where, at least initially, this academic endeavor flourished particularly, the concept of education also encompasses child-rearing as well as more formal schooling. It was against this overall understanding of becoming human that child-centered theory was directed. For its protagonists child-rearing could not properly be characterized by activities pursued by adults in order to bring children to adulthood. From this position the educator (the parent or the teacher) is, first of all, the adviser to the child, and the facilitator of what she or he really wants. It is the child, it is argued, who is from the very beginning responsible for the learning process. It is hardly the case that this either was or is seen as unproblematic. It is doubtful, for instance, whether it is possible for an individual to discover within herself what she really wants, and furthermore it is not clear how parents could possibly avoid initiating their children into the values that they live by. But beyond this "internal debate", the change in the content of education as an academic study (i.e. child-rearing and schooling) is due now to a radical pluralism that has swept the world. This is in itself part of a wider crisis of rationality. The question whether reason, and reason alone, can decide what should be done, and if, moreover, rational thinking is even possible at all, are at the heart of the matter. This is reflected in philosophy of education itself.

However, in the English-speaking world after World War Two philosophy of education initially identified itself in terms of the traditional approach of a rational endeavor. Scheffler's *The Language of Education* (1960) stimulated considerable discussion on the concept of teaching while Peters' analysis of the concept of education (*Ethics and Education*, 1966) provided an example of conceptual analysis that came to serve as something of a paradigm. In their work analytic philosophers of education claimed that they were attempting to clarify the criteria used in the use or application of concepts by clarifying the rules or conditions under which concepts were used or applied. Borrowing the notion of language as rule-governed activity from the work of the later Wittgenstein – though improperly adapting this because ultimately they were searching for foundations, and for necessary and sufficient conditions – they pursued a research program of analysis and clarification. This first came under attack from sociologists of education and then from the general vocational thrust of education in Margaret Thatcher's Britain. In North America, whilst the gains made by the analytic approach were not abandoned, attempts were made to broaden the field. Philosophers of education sought legitimacy in the ideas of general philosophers – for example, in Rawls, Marx, the phenomenologists and the Frankfurt school, and writers such as Illich and Freire were fervently discussed. In more recent years attention turned to Apple, Giroux and McLaren, whose works were widely published and discussed. Though not all of this contested ground has been relinquished, clearly the general interest nowadays has shifted to thinkers such as Rorty, Derrida, Lyotard and Foucault. A strong and sustained critique of foundationalism has emerged.

To some extent the inspiration for more recent trends has, on the one hand, been sought in Wittgenstein's anti-foundationalism. From that position education can be conceived as a dynamic initiation into a "form of life". Here parents are seen as the first educators, and it is from this responsibility that the responsibility of the state concerning schooling can be derived. Parents offer the child the truths by which they live: what moves them, what appeals to them, what they understand as "human being", the way of life in which they hope that the child will come to participate. What falls outside our actions and our language is not intelligible and thus cannot be justified. Only through educational practice, an initiation into those actions and that language, will it become clear "what is there for us" and "what is valuable for us". For Wittgensteinian epistemology and ethics, there is no either/or. It is always language-and-the-world, always the individual-and-the-others.

What is labeled postmodern educational theory focuses on a particular aspect of the present *Zeitgeist*. A profound objection to modernity has always been that the modern technical genius for finding effective means to ends has diverted attention too much from serious consideration of our chosen or implicit ends themselves, whether ethical, economic or educational. Under the "postmodern condition", as Lyotard has described it, the obsession with efficiency and effectiveness has finally parted company altogether with controversial, political questions of what we should be trying to achieve. All kinds of business and activity are measured and ranked against each other, with ever less concern for the rationale for doing so. Thus, performativity obscures differences, requiring everything to be commensurable with everything else, so that things can be ranked on the same scale and everyone can be "accountable" against the same standards. This in turn entails the disvaluing, and perhaps the eradication, of what cannot be ranked. Schools and pupils are now required to "speak their truth" (in Foucauldian phrase) on pain of punishment. This they are to do in the methodical and routine terms of examinations and tests, and, moreover, in a form acceptable to management. Despite this drive to "optimize the system's performance" under centralized control, there has also been a countervailing tendency toward dispersal and differentiation. Such variety would, supposedly, empower consumers by giving them a wider range of choice in the marketplace. In itself this apparent contradiction is easily related to historic trends in modernity: to secularization and bureaucratization in the sphere of culture, and rationalization and liberalization in the sphere of society. What are new are the terms in which these processes have come to be understood and celebrated. Power has moved elsewhere – to consumers rather than producers, or at any rate to those (advertising agencies, marketing consultants and "facilitators" of all kinds) who have the expertise to manipulate consumer choice and sell educational products just like any others. The family, too, suffers bewilderment in its attempts to educate the young. Like teachers, parents find themselves the objects of suspicion and distrust. An ethos of care sits uneasily with the emphasis on children's rights and, above all, on the individual child's right to choose. The family is scrutinized for its outcomes: how are your chances of good examination results, or your earning potential, affected by being brought up by a single parent? Children in this position may be compensated by being offered, in that most revealing phrase, "quality time" by the parent who has left, as if this improved the child's opportunity of turning into a quality product (by the standards of quality control). The courses of relevant experts in parenting skills will help obscure the fact that bringing up children is not really regarded as valuable in a society dominated by economic rationality. In their efforts to resist this contemporary malaise, philosophers and historians of education have turned to a number of writers (such as Derrida, Lyotard, Foucault, Rorty).

Mainstream educational research, on the other hand, dominated by the paradigm of "real research", has also undergone an interesting evolution, as exemplified by renewed discussion about research methods, particularly about the respective merits of quantitative and qualitative approaches. A number of historians and sociologists of educational sciences have demonstrated that the preference in the social and behavioral sciences for what was seen as a superior quantitative approach rested not just on developments within these disciplines but also and equally on external changes associated with the social context in general and with the dominance, in particular, of meritocratic values with the rise of the neo-liberal society (see e.g., Depaepe 1993). At the same time some of the work of certain philosophers of education over the last two decades (see Blake, Smeyers, Smith, & Standish, 1998, 2000, and 2003) has exposed (*à la Kant*) the naivety of thinking dominated by the means-end schema. To a greater and greater extent, the idea of an applied science in which, educational intervention is a simple consequence of understanding is being abandoned in favor of a theory of development that is realized in the intervention itself. In line with this, one sees an evolution in which the innovative role of pedagogical research can be emphasized again. Thus, "utopian" perspectives acquire a new legitimacy: the integration of empirical and philosophical research, of quantitative and quantitative methods forces itself upon us once again.

However, although qualitative methods are now regarded with more respect than ever before, this does not mean that the debate has terminated. There is still the general suspicion that in one way or another what is offered by social science research, including qualitative research, cannot adequately satisfy the need for knowledge. What looms behind this may be captured by the following false assumption: not understanding everything is equated with not understanding anything. What is longed for is something similar to the law-like explanation and "prediction" of the natural sciences, or so some would have it. This desire parallels that of philosophers for whom philosophy has to amount to valid reasoning warranted by methods of conceptual analysis (necessary and sufficient conditions) and logical rules of induction and deduction, or for whom it must offer an overarching metaphysical system. One author who vigorously attacked these positions was Ludwig Wittgenstein. So it is no wonder that some have found in his work ways of exposing the shortcomings of certain types of research in the social sciences.

According to Wittgenstein, in the *Geisteswissenschaften*, the human "sciences", one must try to understand human conduct in order to comprehend the reasons for our actions. The understanding that is offered has to be of the same kind as the understanding involved in the "practice" in question, involving the descriptions of everyday language. It must always go back to the understanding of the practitioners. He also advises us *to refrain from formulating theories*, because they are not capable of bringing forward the heterogeneity of cases and always presuppose more homogeneity than in fact can be found. He also suggests that not everything is explainable or understandable and draws our attention to different kinds of understanding. It becomes important then to ask such questions as "What is important for a human being?" and "What is there that may be relevant without necessarily being useful for something else?" The important difference between understanding and explaining, according to Wittgenstein, can be indicated by the difference in the effects they have upon those involved:

> *Compared with the impression that the description makes on us, the explanation is too uncertain. Every explanation is an hypothesis. But an hypothetical explanation will be of little help to someone, say, who is upset because of love. It will not calm him.*
> (Wittgenstein, 1979, p. 63)

Researchers in the human sciences may find themselves bewildered by this. The tasks of research are to be found in interpretation, meaning, so Wittgenstein seems to say, that one must "place things side by side". It goes without saying that academic psychology nowadays, still very much operating along Popperian lines, will find it hard to come to terms with such a program, just as it could not digest it half a century ago. But even in circles of educational researchers who have come to accept the legitimacy of both quantitative and qualitative research designs, this will be found to be problematical. What is the point of these descriptions, it will be asked, if not to generate a theoretical approach that is useful for the examination of future cases? Are we to take it that all theory is superfluous then?

There is also a more general concern for such researchers because the view in question holds that instead of "crystalline purity" we need first a better understanding of the nature of the problem we are dealing with; we need this before the proper method(s) for its research can be determined. It will only be possible to outline the contours of a *social* science if one understands, and takes seriously, what the word "social" really means This entails that, before one can characterize *educational* research, one must elaborate what one understands by "education". Yet it seems that, in the absence of a deeper understanding of why educational research is necessarily different from that of the natural sciences, there will continue to be attempts to rephrase problems in more positivist terms in order to have "results". Such results, it is supposed, enable one to deal better with (i.e. to manipulate and predict) the problems that education presents. Of course, unless one understands the nature of education in terms of *human activity* (and the over-hasty pursuit of "results" can obscure the nature of this), it will be impossible to understand the nature of educational research. In his characterization of what we should do Wittgenstein says:

> *This is how philosophers should salute each other: "Take your time!"*. (Wittgenstein, 1998, 91e)

Within qualitative research, more particularly in the field of "narrative inquiry", it is specifically the distinction made by Polkinghorne (1995) between an "analysis of narratives" and "narrative analysis" that is of some relevance here. In an "analysis of narratives" one looks for common features in different cases in order to define them within a broader category. By pointing at features that different experiences have in common, one can construct cognitive conceptual frameworks. The purpose of the paradigmatic analysis is not only to discover and to describe categories, but also to describe the relationships between categories. In "narrative analysis", the data are mostly not in a narrative form. The information comes from different sources: the researcher arranges events and actions by showing how they contribute to the evolution of a plot. The plot is the thematic line of the narrative, the narrative structure that shows how different events contribute to a narrative. The writing of it involves an analytical development, a dialectic between the data and the plot. The resulting narrative must not only fit the data but also bring out an order and a significance that were not apparent in the data as such. The result is not so much an account of the actual happening of events from an objective point of view as the result of a series of constructions. Where in the "analysis of narratives" the narratives are the source of knowledge, the narrative in "narrative analysis" is the result of the research.

A parallel can be drawn between this contrast and the contrast that exists between educational theory and its counterpart in empirical educational research. On the one hand, philosophy of education is getting more and more empirical in the sense that it pays greater attention to the ways in which we actually speak in the context of particular practices. (A radical distinction between rationality-as-such and what we say in a particular discourse is, in general, no longer accepted.) The nature of this commitment can also be captured by the term "embedded rationality" (as referring to a particular culture or historical period or discourse). On the other hand, empirical research that can be "accepted" within the context of education has in recent times become more and more "philosophical": there is less and less a strict distinction between the *a priori* and the *a posteriori* and between what "is the case" (facts) and what "ought to be the case" (values). Thus values are as much discussed as factual statements about data. As in philosophy, where less attention is given to distinguishing between different schools or methods or movements with their different conceptions of the task of philosophy (at least, strict distinctions have been softened), in empirical research the idea that the different aspects of a particular case have to be considered at the same time and in relation to each other is gaining influence. This *rapprochement* between philosophical and empirical research opens a new prospect and challenge for the future, but it also generates a number of questions.

If our aim is to enhance discussion about the criteria for educational research, many issues are implicated – not least the all-encompassing question of why we should bother to spell out criteria, why, in other words, it is important for those working in this business to set down requirements for such a quality label. As must be plain, we choose these words carefully, as we think that they indeed have the right connotations in educational discourse nowadays. Why do we think we need a justification, to whom do we find the need to offer one, and last but not least why do we – does anyone – want to engage in *this* kind of research? What is ultimately the point of it? Even if this already seems to overburden us with questions, let us add some more: In general, what is science for? What kind of science is helpful then? What is education for? What kind of education is helpful? Is this meta-discourse meaningful? And moreover, and in connection with all of these, how do we know – the question *par excellence* – the truth or the cogency of the presuppositions, the general philosophical intuitions that form the basis of each and every answer?

In our own context these general questions come down to three:

1. Do we need a justification *for ourselves*, as it were – for the particular kind of position we take *vis-à-vis* that of others working in history of education or philosophy of education?
2. Do philosophy and history of education need a justification within the context of educational research? In other words, are they just history and phi-

losophy "of" education (like the history and philosophy "of" other human activities), or do they have a special "educational" function on their own?
3. And finally, does educational research need to be justified to educational practitioners and policy-makers, as well as within society at large?

A positive answer to these questions will, furthermore, require some kind of specification as to what such a justification might look like, i.e. what criteria will need to be met. And let us acknowledge that, of course, this way of conceptualizing the matter puts it at a meta-level. Clearly we are interested in the contours of particular answers to substantive questions, as we think that most of us have given up on the idea that it is fruitful or even possible to distinguish conclusively between method (or form) and content, or between external and internal criteria for that matter. But there may still be some value in distinguishing these questions from each other in view of our ponderings on criteria for research.

* * *

The contributors to this collection attempt to say something about where we are now concerning these matters and where we think we should be going. The chapters are organized into four sections where educational research is discussed respectively as a social discourse, as a discursive practice, in relation to epistemological issues, and in the light of questions of ethics.

In the section "Educational Research as a Social Discourse" the chapters examine the changing contexts of social discourses and practices that accompany, and frequently drive, changes in the methods and aims of educational research.

Bridges and MacLure look at the composition of research groups as a factor in shaping attitudes and approaches toward interdisciplinary collaboration. They recount six case studies from the UK, each of them including philosophers or philosophically inclined researchers along with more empirically oriented scholars. The core question they address is whether there is any distinctive contribution a philosopher can make in such interdisciplinary settings. At the same time, they also explore ways in which the philosopher might be involved more directly in research activities (such as ethnographic observations) for which philosophical training may or may not have prepared them. Like the other authors in this section, Bridges and MacLure question the appropriateness of models of research collaboration drawn from the physical sciences for interdisciplinary studies in the social sciences, including in education.

Burbules and Lambeir also explore the question of interdisciplinary collaboration but through a different lens, examining in what ways new information and communication technologies can support and foster new forms of collaborative inquiry. They emphasize three dimensions of research that are changed by these new technologies: changes in writing and publication practices, changes in forms of data gathering and analysis, and changes encountered when engaging research in global networks that bring together vastly diverse cultural and national groups. While Burbules and Lambeir explore a range of research areas in which these changes are having an impact, their main concern is with educational research.

Depaepe and Van Gorp examine the research careers and influence of four leading educational scholars in Belgium during the first half of the Twentieth Century. These scholars all shared an interest in "pedology", a presumably more scientific approach to the study of teaching and learning. They each brought with them models of inquiry imported from the natural and medical sciences and, through their own associations, each had influence upon the others. Depaepe and Van Gorp suggest that the evolution of the views of these scholars over time owed as much to their relationships and the interlocked nature of their careers, as to the development of their intellectual thought *per se*. They shared, above all else, an emancipatory view of the power of science, even though their actual impact tended in fact to reinforce a "well-ordered, rationally managed and scientifically supported society".

Marshall, Peters and Irwin examine the shifting national educational research policies in New Zealand over a number of administrations, government commissions and reports. The argue that, in spite of wide-ranging differences in ideology, the inexorable trend has been an increase in the discourses of scientism, efficiency and usefulness in the shaping of criteria for government-funded research – a trend crystallizing in what Jean-François Lyotard called a culture of performativity as a policy imperative.

A theme running across the chapters in these sections is the international context in which educational research theories and practices evolve in response to shifting policies, values and discourses. The second section, "Educational Research as a Discursive Practice", focuses on the assemblage of ideas, institutions and cultural connections in which the criteria and evaluation of educational research are formed. The notion of *discourse* is used to connote the centrality of "thought", speech and "reason" as constitutive elements in the production of social and cultural life.

The first two chapters of this section consider historically the systems of reason that order, classify and govern the objects "seen" and acted on in schooling and its research. Popkewitz and Do O explore the pedagogical sciences as historically relating two seemingly opposite registers of modernity: social administration and the production of the autonomous individual in the 19th and early 20th centuries. Do O focuses on the French Compayré Moment to explore psychopedagogical concerns with the soul and the internal structuring and governing of subjectification. Popkewitz examines the U.S. educational sciences as an assemblage of cultural practices that order, differentiate and regulate the inner characteristics and capabilities (in other words, the soul) of the child. These analyses enable an understanding of the educational sciences as inscription devices that function as intellectual tools to map the interior of the self, rendering the characteristics of the individual visible and amenable to government.

The next two chapters focus historically on the formation of national systems of pedagogical research as they relate to global educational discourses. Carvalho's chapter examines the formation of Portuguese pedagogical journals. His concern is with overlapping practices that relate the globalization of discourses about the child and science in the late 19th century/early 20th century to the formation of national school systems and professionalized teachers who feel *at home* both in the local and the global. Tröhler's chapter discusses the argument against Dewey's pragmatism and its notion of the citizen in the development, within German educational sciences, of the *geisteswissenshaftliche Pädagogik*. It is argued that this pedagogy embodied a conception of *Geist* – or, otherwise put, a new conception of human being – drawn from the values of the German Protestant philosophical tradition, in the light of which education retains an autonomy from social, economic and political contexts. The resulting goal of the autonomy of the individual, encapsulated, so the author argues, in the notion of *Bildung* during the 1920s Weimar Republic, embodied a skepticism toward democracy.

The last two chapters of this section focus on a philosophically oriented discussion of the problematic of educational research. Levering examines genres of writing and narrative inquiry. He traces the heritage of Dutch philosophy of education as part of the German tradition of *geisteswissenshaftliche Pädagogik*, discussed earlier in Tröhler's analysis. Levering argues that contemporary traditions of educational research suffer from the "chronic disease named moldability-optimism", the belief that research can mold or engineer the individual, a notion already traced above in the idea of pedagogical research as governing the soul. Levering draws distinctions between grand and small narratives and between theory and praxis to explicate different genres in research. In Smith's chapter, current policy efforts to base school quality, effectiveness and improvement upon evidence-based research are examined. Smith argues that, while this particular empirical conception of statistical and quantitative research methods is supposed to identify what works in school, it may in fact work against school improvement and the quality of education.

In sum, the chapters in this section offer a variety of intellectual approaches to the investigation of the object, theories, methods and findings of educational research. They consider the "thought", ideas and knowledge of education not merely as expressions of human purpose and intent to improve the world of schooling, but as historically formed principles that order, differentiate and divide the objects of reflection and action.

The contributions to the third section, "Educational Research: Epistemological Issues", focus on various issues in educational research that invoke knowledge claims. The first two may be seen as representative of opposing views concerning the more general questions of skepticism and perspectivism. The next two papers deal with different aspects of knowledge acquisition – in the individual knower and in the context of educational research. The last paper addresses philosophical problems of personal identity and self-knowledge, leading to some reflections about the relation between general philosophy and philosophy of education.

Cuypers notes a pervading skepticism about truth in much work in philosophy of education nowadays. In fact, the notion of truth is itself considered irrelevant to thinking about education by many postmodernist authors, and it, together with rationality as an educational ideal, has come under fire. However, part of the educational enterprise will always be the instruction by specialists who place both themselves and their students under the norms of truth and rational inquiry, going beyond shifting interpretations from different perspectives. Cuypers argues that the usual postmodernist challenges can indeed be met. First, the metaphysical vulnerability admittedly inherent in the correspondence theory of truth can be avoided by drawing on Tarsky's semantic truth-theory. Second, foundationalism in epistemic justification can be avoided by way of a persistent policy of fallibilism. Third, the perspectivistic dangers of this policy can be fended off on the strength of a realist theory of knowledge invoking Popper's notion of verisimilitude.

Ramaekers strikes out in the opposite direction, taking David Carr's concerns about postmodernist forms of skepticism and perspectivism as his target. Like Cuypers, Carr wants to hold on to the possibility of cross-cultural canons of rationality, knowledge and truth, without which, he claims, a concept of education as initiation would be empty. Carr also rejects foundationalism and defends fallibilism and a minimal realism. Ramaekers, in what may perhaps be seen as a typical postmodernist gesture, does not so much refute Carr's arguments but shifts the attention to a different notion of skepticism. In view of the diversity of perspectives in our ever-growing multicultural world,

Ramaekers argues, the classical quest for certainty can no longer be a fruitful approach for educational theory. In the light of this, he proposes a reappraisal of skepticism itself. This is inspired by Cavell's interpretation of the work of the later Wittgenstein, according to which education as initiation is not so much seen as initiation into knowledge but rather as an initiation into a community. What is important here is not so much epistemic agreement about the truth of propositions but rather our existential agreement in what we say and do in the language community. On this view, the notion of skepticism is broadened, having primarily to do with our forms of attunement to one another and our forms of agreement in ordinary language use.

Coessens presents a phenomenological analysis of experiencing as a general and fundamental mode of human existence, and in particular of knowing as one of its basic instantiations. As knowledge is central to human culture and being, and as education is for a large part concerned with the transmission of knowledge, she investigates precisely what it means for a potential knower to attain knowledge. After drawing attention to several aspects of experiencing in general, Coessens describes what is involved in the process of experiencing knowledge, as opposed to experiencing being and experiencing meaning, a task she undertakes with reference to the theories of Merleau-Ponty and Dewey. Her account is illustrated with an analysis of how processes of knowledge-experiencing are involved in such seemingly simple practices as hammering and story-telling.

Smeyers argues that the concept of causality seems to pervade our thinking about ourselves and others, about our environment, even about the entire universe we live in. Not only physicists and engineers but also social scientists have since the Enlightenment been preoccupied with finding causes in order to be able to manipulate particular outcomes. Here, for many, to explain an event is to identify its antecedents, i.e., its causes. He notes that two problems remain unresolved, however: first, in many cases one does not have enough facts to be able to construct an explanation and so one can never be sure that a new condition will not be revealed; second, the inferential conception suffers from the fact that it seriously misconstrues the nature of the subsumption of facts under laws, i.e. the temporal asymmetry reflected by inferences is precisely the opposite to that exhibited in explanation. He, therefore, argues that the covering law conception has to take a different form, and furthermore that, given the impossibility of predicting precise outcomes with absolute certainty, what we do will always invoke some kind of *practical reasoning*.

Bransen shows how the philosophy of mind can gain from paying attention to how education contributes to human life. In particular, we can thus better understand certain metaphysical problems concerning personal identity and certain epistemological problems about self-knowledge. Human nature is temporal. Human beings go through changes that in many ways result not only from various forms of natural development but from their being educated. Second, who we are is in part dependent not only upon our sensitivity to who we are but also upon who we think we should be and should become; in other words, human nature is always also characterized by a normatively significant self-relatedness. Is it necessary, therefore, to develop a notion of personal identity that can incorporate and do justice to these crucial features of temporality, change and normative self-relatedness that are, in important ways, constituted by education. In this way philosophy of education is not to be considered as merely a form of "applied" philosophy as opposed to "pure" philosophy: it rather makes a crucial contribution to philosophy itself.

The final section, "Educational Research: Ethical Considerations" consists of critical examinations of the relationship between self and other. In a post-empiricist spirit, neither the self nor the other is assumed to have an essential nature. Rather, the analyses in these chapters examine various ways of constituting the ethical subject. In some cases, the analyses challenge traditional assumptions about the relationship between ethics and ontology. In other cases, the analyses highlight historically specific power relations that construct possibilities for subjectivity.

Focusing on the relationship between the self and the other, Standish draws on Charles Taylor and Emmanuel Levinas to consider, first, the politics of identity and, second, the idea of a social science. Standish argues that certain understandings of identity politics foreclose ethical relations by constructing totalizing, and therefore limited, orientations toward the other. The danger of identity politics is that, in its ontological recognition of others, it covers over the possibility of an ethical orientation towards the Other, in Levinassian terms – that is, a relation that is not to be understood in terms of defining characteristics and their recognition. Given the necessity mentioned above of a proper understanding of the social in social science, Standish argues that educational research that does not take this complexity into account must be unsound.

Educational research is full of debates about the relation between theory and practice. In his chapter, Peters suggests that, although we readily use the term "practice" in educational research (e.g., "communities of practice", "reflective practitioner"), we are not clear about what we mean when we say "practice". To address this, Peters examines various philosophical treatments of practice, highlighting the elusiveness of practice in theories of educational research. This essay extends Hubert Dreyfus' and Stephen Turner's analyses of practice to examine intellectual traditions that derive from Marx,

Heidegger, Bourdieu and Freire. Finally, Peters addresses the need to theorize practice in order to contribute to understandings of teaching. Concerning our inadequate theorization of practice, Peters asks, "How do we educate beginning or novice teachers in the practice of teaching when there is no viable model of transmission?"

In his contribution to the ethics of educational research, Postma draws our attention to the intrinsic value of nature. Problematizing commonplace notions of liberal autonomy and authenticity, Postma critiques certain fundamental assumptions of modern educational projects. He writes: "The listening attitude inherent to our recognition of intrinsic value contrasts strongly with the imperative of active choice that is at the heart of the liberal ideal of personal autonomy.... Paradoxically, we thereby seem to seclude ourselves from the very sources of authentic identification, among them, the silence, beauty and inspiration we find in our natural environment". In this way, Postma's analysis suggests that, in order to fulfill its ethical mandate, educational research must take the intrinsic value of nature into account.

To historicize a widely used concept in educational research, Fendler analyses three influential traditions that have contributed to common understandings of the term "community". She suggests that Third Way thinking, labor-union solidarity and emotional attachment have shaped current assumptions in research about community. Community building serves, in some cases, to forge identity and facilitate empowerment. Fendler suggests, however, that these discourse practices simultaneously effect exclusion and assimilation. Drawing from Nikolas Rose and Chantal Mouffe, the chapter cautions that "the rhetoric of community can serve as sheep's clothing for the wolves of exclusion, normalization and antagonism".

References

Blake, N., Smeyers, P., Smith, R., & Standish, P. (1998). *Thinking again: Education after postmodernism*. New York: Bergin & Garvey.
Blake, N., Smeyers, P., Smith, R., & Standish, P. (2000). *Education in an age of nihilism*. London: Falmer Press.
Blake, N., Smeyers, P., Smith, R., & Standish, P. (Eds.). (2003). *The Blackwell guide to the philosophy of education*. Oxford: Blackwell.
Condliffe Lagemann, E. (2000). *An elusive science: The troubling history of education research*. Chicago: The University of Chicago Press.
Depaepe, M. (1993). *Zum Wohl des Kindes? Pädologie, pädagogische Psychologie und experimentelle Pädagogik in Europa und den USA, 1890-1940*. Weinheim: Deutscher Studien Verlag.
Fendler, L. (2003). Teacher reflections in a hall of mirrors: Historical influences and political reverberations. *Educational Researcher, 32*(2), 16-25.
Hacking, I. (1996). *The taming of chance*. New York: Cambridge University Press.

Peters, R.S. (1966). *Ethics and education*. London: Allen & Unwin.

Popkewitz, T. (1997). Educational sciences and the normalization of the teacher and the child: Some historical notes on current USA pedagogical reforms. *Paedagogica Historica, 33*, 387-412.

Polkinghorne, D. (1995). Narrative configuration in qualitative analysis. *International Journal of Qualitative Studies in Education, 8*, 5-23.

Popkewitz, T. (1997). Educational sciences and the normalization of the teacher and the child: Some historical notes on current USA pedagogical reforms. *Paedagogica Historica, 33*, 387-412.

Scheffler, I. (1960). *The language of education*. Springfield, IL: Thomas.

Wittgenstein, L. (1979). Remarks on Frazer's Golden Bough. In C. Luckhardt (Ed.), *Wittgenstein: Sources and perspectives* (pp. 61-81). Hassocks: The Harvester Press.

Wittgenstein, L. (1998). *Culture and value* (P. Winch, Trans.; edited by G.H. von Wright in collaboration with H. Nyman; revised edition by A. Pichler). Oxford: Blackwell.

I. EDUCATIONAL RESEARCH AS A SOCIAL DISCOURSE
(Section Editor Nicholas Burbules)

SIX STORIES IN SEARCH OF A CHARACTER? "THE PHILOSOPHER" IN AN EDUCATIONAL RESEARCH GROUP

David Bridges
with notes in response by
Maggie MacLure

Introduction

My concern is with the relationship of the philosopher to the empirical and applied domain: How does one engage philosophically within "a research group"? In addressing this question I will discuss six research groups with which I have some experience and reflect on the different roles that philosophers have played in their work. Maggie MacLure's thoughtful comments in response to an earlier version of this paper will appear in the text in italics.

The language of "the research group" is a very familiar one in the natural science research community, in which it is attached to a particular scale of research projects (often associated with considerable investment in capital equipment), the prospect of at least medium-term continuation of funding, and a particular organisational structure with a clearly segmented division of labour. This model has been more rare in educational research, and it has been asked whether educational research would be more productive or effective if it was organised in something closer to the natural science pattern. But it remains to be asked: What are the consequences for educational research – which voices and perspectives will be suppressed and which will be promoted – if the scientific research group becomes the preferred or even the required form for organising educational research? With this caution in mind, let me turn to some particular examples, to sites of practice, to see what they might reveal about the role of the philosopher in educational research groups.

The "Cambridge Group" of Philosophers of Education

I have only once belonged to something which self-consciously referred to itself as a research group. In a recent piece of autobiographical writing (Bridges, 2003) I recalled it in these terms:

> *The London Institute experience was important, but increasingly Cambridge provided its own intellectual stimulus, because Richard Pring and Hugh Sockett had come to the Cambridge Institute*

of Education as research fellows and Peter Scrimshaw had joined Charles Bailey and myself at Homerton. John Elliott, initially working on the Humanities Curriculum Project, was also living in Cambridge – and we were all working on higher degrees in philosophy of education. We would meet for seminars, food and wine in each others' houses and all travel to the London seminars in Hugh Sockett's minibus....With growing self-confidence we concluded after a visit to Dillons bookshop that we could write rubbish no worse than that which we found on the shelves there, and the "Cambridge Group", as we came to think of ourselves, contracted with Hodder and Stoughton for a series of books on philosophy of education (Elliott & Pring, 1975; Bridges & Scrimshaw, 1975; Sockett, 1979). Paul Hirst moved from London to join us at the Cambridge Department of Education, soon to be joined by Terry McLaughlin and at Homerton by Mike Bonnett, and was hugely supportive to our own initiatives and became part of an increasingly strong and capable team.

It may be useful to consider some of the features of this group:
- a number of people talking in a broadly similar academic language;
- physical and social proximity (perhaps less important today than it was then);
- reciprocity of interest and mutual support in pursuing individual objectives;
- a succession of common projects (notably in publishing and in the development of philosophy of education in Cambridge);
- a sense of our difference from others – notably in this case the main base of philosophy of education at the London Institute. Rightly or wrongly we saw ourselves as much more closely aligned with contemporary debates and development around the school curriculum. We also self-consciously adopted a different mode of discussion to the sharply antagonistic mode fashionable in London.

What is interesting in terms of the comparison with the scientific model of the research group is that we had no formal structure to support this group, no funding, and we operated without a hierarchy – or with several hierarchies, because we were in the happy position of acknowledging the different strengths of individual members of the group even though this did not entirely prevent an element of competition between us. Were our instincts right in seeking something non-hierarchical – is this something to do with "the management of talent" as it is sometimes expressed? Is this question essentially an empirical one (experience and observation indicate that specified conditions produce certain observable effects), or is it possible to derive such views of the social organisation and ethos of a research group from an understanding of the nature of research itself?

This in turn raises the question of the ethical obligations people owe toward one another when they are working in a research group. It seems to me that research groups work under a complementary obligation of mutual criticism and support: personal and practical support in overcoming difficulties in the research process but also political solidarity when faced with attempts to censor or distort or otherwise undermine the integrity of the outcomes of research and the research process. For the moment, however, the point I want to make here is that a research group is not just a unit for the organisation of research production: it is a group of people joined in a network of mutual obligations which are created by the epistemological and social conditions which give the group integrity.

The Farmington Trust Moral Education Project

My next example will be the Farmington Trust Moral Education Project (Wilson, Williams, & Sugarman, 1967) which, innovatively in those days, brought together a philosopher, a psychologist and a sociologist to propose a way forward for moral education in schools. The philosopher was John Wilson, who subsequently wrote about philosophy and educational research in terms which have led him and me into a quite extended debate (Wilson, 1994; Bridges, 1997; Wilson, 1998; Bridges, 1998). His view, still firmly rooted in conceptual analysis, represents a lot of what I have been reacting against, which is why it provides a convenient starting point.

The project was established in the days when educational theory was increasingly defined in the UK in terms of the foundation disciplines of philosophy, sociology, psychology and history of education. At a time when each of these was emphatically defining itself in terms of its differences from the others, it was quite adventurous to set up an educational research and development project which was structurally interdisciplinary. Wilson (the philosopher) Williams (the psychologist) and Sugarman (the sociologist) had to establish a *modus operandi* as a research group in the absence of many clear precedents. What is especially pertinent to my purposes here is the role taken by the philosopher. Wilson saw his job as providing the conceptual mapping of the territory, or, to borrow a different metaphor, the conceptual architecture of moral education. Moral education, in his view, could only be articulated upon some clear sense of what it was to be "moral" and of the knowledge and understanding which were the components of moral choice and action (Wilson, Williams, & Sugarman, 1967).

This conception of the role of the philosopher as conceptual architect has not just remained an historical curiosity. As late as 1994 Wilson was still defining philosophy in these narrow conceptual terms: "That is all that 'philosophy', in the sense in which I am using the word, requires: it is a practice, a discipline of thought, devoted to getting clear about words and concepts and the logical implications that they carry" (Wilson, 1994, p. 4 his underlining). Philosophers are specialists in this task who act as consultants to researchers proper: "There is no real alternative to educational researchers themselves taking on this task... of working out the meaning and concepts with which their research is concerned. Enough philosophers (not just me) are around to help them with this if required: there is certainly some professional expertise here, though most intelligent researchers can do a lot for themselves, once they get the hang of it" (ibid., p. 6).

While I share the view that more care and clarity in the use of language and concepts could benefit a lot of research writing (and indeed some philosophical writing), Wilson's view that this is all that philosophy can contribute to research is damagingly misleading. First, it fails to do justice to the richness of philosophical writing on moral, epistemological and political issues. Second, it is rather patronising toward people who are not philosophers but who can be perfectly clear about their language and concepts without the assistance of philosophers. Third, it ignores all the literature about language and meaning which renders problematic the idea that there is a simple clarification of *the* meaning of a word which is to be had. Finally, the process of conceptual analysis comes heavily laden with theory, which is not without its ideological baggage. The processes of *defining, prescribing or negotiating* the meaning of terms themselves reflect different kinds of power relations between the "analyst" and other members of the linguistic community.

But if I am not happy with Wilson's view of the role of the philosopher in the context of multi-disciplinary educational research (see also Bridges, 2003), what are the alternatives?

The Social Science Research Council School Accountability Project

Between 1979 and 1981 I was a member of a research team working on a research project directed by John Elliott on school accountability. It was constructed around the idea of a self-accounting school, which at the time seemed to offer an alternative model of accountability to the more bureaucratic and centrally driven models which were on the political horizon and of course rapidly came to dominate the political and educational agenda. There were five of us in the team: John Elliott, who had some background in philosophy of education, but was at that time one of the main driving forces in the field of action research; Dave Ebbutt, who was also extensively involved in action research; Rex Gibson, a sociologist; Jennifer Nias, a social psychologist; and myself a philosopher with, as it turned out usefully, a previous incarnation as a historian.

The project was unequivocally founded on empirical work, on case studies of six schools conducted over an eighteen-month period. We would be looking at the way in which these schools, all of which presented themselves as wishing to be accountable to their communities, communicated with and related to parents, governors, local employers, the local press and any other segments of their communities. This would require analysis of documentary evidence, observation or participant observation of some events and a wide range of interviews. We each produced substantial case studies based on this material and, out of these case studies, a collection of analytic papers addressing issues raised from reading across them.

In one sense my training and identity as a philosopher were entirely submerged in my role in this group as an apprentice ethnographer. Given that I had very little previous experience and no training in this kind of work, I was largely pre-occupied with the social processes involved in ethnographic research. My most useful resource was my earlier historical training, and the comfort of Lawrence Stenhouse's notion of research as "contemporary history". I realised that what I was collecting would constitute (for example, in the form of transcripts of interviews) a large volume of textual or documentary evidence on people's perceptions of events and relationships. As an historian, I had some idea how to handle such material.

But no empirical research, least of all this kind of ethnographic research, is theoretically or ideologically neutral: nor did we set out to purge it of such impurities. On the contrary, the field research was conducted in a context of intense political and educational debate about school accountability – debates which were explicit in the schools in which we were working and the conversations we had with participants. In regular meetings in the research teams, too, we were constantly discussing the issues which were arising out of our individual cases. Inevitably, of course, these discussions were informed by the theoretical and analytic frameworks each of us brought to the work. We did not necessarily label these with our particular disciplines; nor did we observe rigid disciplinary boundaries in the ideas and material we referenced.

In the analytic papers which came out of the project (Elliott, Bridges, Ebbutt, Gibson & Nias, 1981), we could indulge our particular interests more freely. Rereading the ones I wrote today, I recognise a distinctive philosophical flavour interwoven with the evidential reporting: in the attention given to contrasting views of the purpose of education; in the reference to the moral obligations of teachers to their children; in the interrogation of the discourse about, for example, an "adaptable" workforce; about the location of "the world of work"; in the analysis of the relationship between accountability, communication and control; and most vividly, perhaps, in my ideologically transparent discussion of "the rational professional and professional autonomy".

These reflections lead me to two observations. First, and not for the first time (see Bridges, 1997, 1999), I am driven to observe that biographical stories about the forms of enquiry through which people come to particular ideas or hypotheses are not necessarily congruent with the logical stories we are obliged to construct to provide the "proper" epistemological foundation for those ideas or hypotheses. What I might think or write because of my philosophical background might be something which someone else might as easily arrive at from, for example, a sociological background.

Second, and by extension, there are a whole variety of intellectual habits, dispositions and indeed virtues which are shared across the academy; there is, especially across the social sciences, an abundance of common literary reference; there are overlapping methods and methodologies; and any social science programme worth its salt will take students at least some way into the epistemological and ethical problems underlying its practice. In the course of the study of any one of these disciplines one is likely to encounter a substantial body of literature and thought which is also addressed in another. One's identity as "a philosopher" or "a sociologist" is something which, for many of us working in education, is something imposed on us or selected from a range of possibilities, and does not reflect the actual heterogeneity of our intellectual roots and resources. It seems to me to follow from this that we have to question the idea that there is someone present in a research group who can satisfactorily be categorised as "the philosopher."

> *Your reflections helped me think about the nature of interdisciplinarity. For me, there is (to put it crudely) a "good" and a "bad" version. The bad one (and the one promoted, I think, by funding bodies in the UK) thinks of interdisciplinary research as a coming together of a bunch of "characters" with very distinct (and intact) disciplinary identities – a sociologist, a psychologist, a philosopher etc. The assumption seems to be that new knowledge will emerge as a kind of accumulation (or fusion perhaps) of the perspectives of each individual. But I suspect that when interdisciplinarity does "work", it does so for the reasons that you point to in your discussion of the Cambridge Accountability project. That is, new knowledge emerges when people <u>lose</u> some part of their discrete professional/ occupational identities, in the process of working on some common purpose.*

> *I'd go further, and argue that the productive potential of interdisciplinary projects isn't (or isn't just) that you provide more "angles" on an issue or problem – but rather, that the various disciplines infect and unsettle one another. So, sociological certainty gets pricked by philosophical challenge; psychological notions of the self get complicated by social or philosophical ones, and so on. Isn't such a commitment to unsettling itself an instance of (some kind of) philosophical attitude?* (Maggie MacLure)

A Multi-Disciplinary Project on Classroom Discussion

This project brought together a group of some twenty educational researchers at one stage or another in a five year programme of work directed by Jim Dillon of the University of California, Riverside. It culminated in a book published under the title *Questioning and Discussion: A Multi-Disciplinary Study* (Dillon, 1988). Dillon produced six transcripts of discussion in American High School classrooms, provided a little information about the context of each discussion, and invited a team of scholars from different disciplinary backgrounds to provide analyses from the perspective of their particular disciplinary or sub-disciplinary orientation. Philosophical perspectives of slightly different kinds were provided by C.J.B. Macmillan, William Knitter and myself, and Dennis O'Brien also contributed to our discussions.

This example raises again for me the question of what a philosopher can do when faced with empirical data – in this case a set of transcripts. The (philosophical) task of course gets easier as soon as we get commentaries from different perspectives upon the data; we can then begin to unpack the methodological or epistemological assumptions underlying the different accounts and interpretations. (Of course, as just noted, so can people who are not philosophers.) But how does a philosopher deal with primary data?

> *"How does a philosopher deal with primary data?" you ask. Why is there a problem? I detect an old, unchallenged binary opposition here. Is it that transcripts and speech seem "spontaneous", "raw", un-wrought, un-thought – i.e. self-evident, and therefore (somehow) impervious to philosophical interventions? You write that the analytic task became "easier" once there were commentaries on those transcripts, which then offered up assumptions that could be "unpacked". But isn't the "primary" data textual too? Can't it be philosophically "unpacked" to disclose interpretative strategies, or "epistemological" assumptions, or identity claims on the part of the speakers? Or would I be speaking like a*

discourse analyst in making such a suggestion? (Maggie MacLure)

Drawing on work I had done for my doctoral thesis (Bridges, 1979, 1988), my chapter derived (or claimed to derive) the criteria of quality from an analysis of the functions of discussion in the refinement and enrichment of understanding. In one sense the philosophical work was fairly quickly dispatched as I went on to explore the ways in which the features of discussion that I had identified were or were not exhibited in the evidence. Macmillan had a slightly more subtle approach, but was essentially engaged in the same task of examining the transcripts against certain criteria. He had developed with Jim Garrison what they called an "erotetic" concept of teaching (Macmillan & Garrison, 1983) which asserts that "when a teacher is teaching what he [sic] is doing is attempting to answer the students' questions about the subject matter." (Macmillan, 1988, p 90). Knitter had the philosophically more obvious task of providing a meta-analysis of the other analyses (Knitter, 1988).

But here I am left with an empirically grounded report of what these philosophers did, faced with a set of transcripts of classroom discussion, but without much confidence that I can extract from this any general theory of what the role of the philosopher, *qua* philosopher, ought to be in such circumstances.

The Centre for Applied Research in Education

All the cases I have illustrated so far are research groups formed temporarily in connection with particular projects, though these teams had been drawn from or went on to constitute much more longstanding networks of professional friends and colleagues. This next illustration is of a different order. The Centre for Applied Research in Education at the University of East Anglia is one of the longest established educational research centres in the UK, having been established in 1970 by Lawrence Stenhouse. It established its reputation as the driving force in the UK for the development of action research; for its sophistication of approaches to educational evaluation, notably through MacDonald's work in "democratic evaluation"; and through its development and teaching of qualitative methods of enquiry and engagement with methodological issues in educational research. My own association with the Centre goes back to its very early days, though it was not until my appointment to a Chair at UEA in 1990 that I became routinely involved in its work.

There is much that could be said about CARE as a research group, but I want to make a single point here. None of the staff whom I joined in CARE would have identified themselves as philosophers with the exception of John Elliott (and even he would have said something else about himself first). Yet I have rarely encountered a centre in which there was a greater enthusiasm for what I would identify as philosophical ideas. Its participants were constantly wrestling with the status of research knowledge and professional knowledge; with problems of inference and generalisability; with what Helen Simons dubbed "the science of the singular" (Simons, 1980); with the ethical issues associated with insider and outsider research; with the politics of contract research and issues of intellectual property; with the ontology of classrooms; and with the very nature of education and educational processes.

Philosophically animated research groups (and CARE is just one of many) do such things as: question the status of the knowledge and evidence that they produce; reflect on the nature of the "self" and its involvement in the generation of research knowledge; explore relationships between language (or discourse) and reality; interrogate notions of ethics, democracy, authenticity, authority, experience, generalisation etc. And importantly, they do it routinely, as part of whatever else it is that they also do.

I think that, in some respects, the prospects for this kind of philosophically animated educational research are better now than ever. After all, social and educational research is already "infected" with philosophical ideas. The poststructural or postmodern "turn" has involved a blurring of the boundaries between disciplines that previously considered themselves intact and "pure" – literature, philosophy, anthropology, education, psychoanalysis, etc. And philosophy has been central to this dissemination (in Derrida's sense) of ideas and practices that formerly were (or tried to be) more "disciplined". Continental philosophical traditions - hermeneutics, phenomenology, critical theory, existentialism etc – have made a huge contribution to the development of post-paradigmatic "Theory". But this has been at the expense of the former "purity" of those individual traditions.

Not everybody thinks this is a good thing, of course. There is continued resistance to the spread of this philosophical/literary/psychoanalytic/linguistic virus, from those who want to stay more emphatically within the old disciplinary categories. (Maggie MacLure)

The example of CARE illustrates a different construction of "the role of the philosopher in an educational research group". In one sense it renders "the philosopher" redundant for the best possible reason – because serious and informed engagement with philosophical issues in educational research becomes part and parcel of the professional practice of the entire research group. But the sad thing has been that this community of discourse has not been adequately joined (in the UK anyway) to the community of discourse populated by people who identify themselves as philosophers of education. They have occupied different journals, attended different conferences, read and referred to different books and only rarely joined in common debate.

> *The kind of inter- (or post-) disciplinary provocation we are both interested here can probably only work amongst members of a discourse community - i.e., people who, as you suggest, are bound together by ties of history, purpose, custom, loyalty, obligation and a sense of difference and who are also bound together by the kinds of texts they produce, consume and value. As you note, the differences between the putative communities of qualitative researchers and philosophers of education are also, in a fundamental way, textual. Their respective members "have occupied different journals, attended different conferences, read and referred to different books and only rarely joined in common debate".*
>
> *A key question, for this present forum, then, would be whether it can establish goals that are sufficiently inclusive to allow for the opening up of a new discursive "space" for productive engagements of research/philosophy/education. I am not sure how general those shared goals would need to be in order to allow everyone to be counted in. Personally, I would be comfortable within a discourse community whose philosophical (and indeed educational) intentions inclined towards scepticism, critique, provocation and resistance to simplification. I would be less sure about joining a community whose philosophical inclinations were to arbitrate, discriminate, evaluate, settle educational questions, or offer "masterful" interpretations.* (Maggie MacLure)

The European Education Research Association (EERA) Philosophy of Education Network and Network Convenors Group

My last example is intended as a reminder of changes which have taken place in the way in which research collaborations can operate. The very language of "networks" has assumed a new significance over this period in indicating groups which are uncontained by any spatio-temporal limitations; groups which are multi-centered and have multiple connections one with another.

There is no membership list for the EERA Philosophy of Education Network, though its broadest identity is probably in the people who have asked to be on its e-mail list and who consequently receive from time to time notices of conferences, calls for papers, pleas for help, job vacancies and just an occasional prompt to take part in an e-mail discussion. It also exists for a few days each year as a network programme at the EERA annual conference. The network has five convenors located in different countries of Europe, who have to correspond regularly, in particular to arrange the conference programme and to meet occasional demands for the EERA Secretariat. Recently they have taken to staying at the same hotel for the conference so that they get a chance to get to know each other and enjoy informal exchange. Some exchange visits and possible research collaborations are beginning to take place out of this activity.

The network is a loose group that has had limited outcomes in terms of generating, as distinct from the presenting, research. It is a reminder, however, of the ways in which contemporary research groups can operate:
- across geographical divides;
- in loose-knit as well as tightly knit configurations (with "lurkers" as well as active participants);
- in virtual space and without direct face-to-face contact;
- in a multi-layered, multi-media, multi-dimensional learning and research environment (see Burbules & Callister, 1999).

This arrangement is not without its problems however. The sort of research group practices made possible by developments in ICT and web-based communications require some capacity to communicate, some common language. Beyond this they require what Hunt has referred to as "the discipline of a discipline ... the rules of conduct governing an argument within a discipline... the rules of conduct [which] make a community of arguers possible" (Hunt, 1991, p. 104 and see also Popkewitz, 1984). Perhaps another route for philosophers to take is to examine more closely the discipline, the rules of conduct or the discourse requirements which make such research groups possible.

Summary and Conclusion

It might be helpful in conclusion to pull out some of the issues raised in this chapter which might provide a focus for further discussion:

i the question of whether attempts to structure research under "research groups" represents an imposition of a model of research production drawn from one part of the academy onto other parts to which it is less suited;

ii questions to do with the social order of research groups and the sort of principles which support the research endeavour;

iii questions to do with the mutual ethical obligations which underpin relations within a research group;

iv questions to do with the role of "the philosopher" in an interdisciplinary or multi-disciplinary research group;

v questions to do with what anyone qua philosopher can make of empirical data;

vi questions of "non-philosophers" who seem to be doing philosophical work and of "philosophers" whose intellectual role and resources cannot be reduced to the philosophical;

vii questions to do with how philosophers and those in the research community who would not define themselves in these terms can engage more effectively together;

viii questions to do with the conditions which "make a community of arguers possible" within a research group.

References

Bridges D. (1979). *Education, democracy and discussion.* Slough: NFER/Nelson. Re-printed (1988) University Press of America

Bridges, D. (1988). A philosophical analysis of discussion. In J. Dillon (Ed.), *Questioning and discussion: A multi-disciplinary study.* Norwood, NJ: Ablex.

Bridges, D. (1997). Philosophy and educational research: A reconsideration of epistemological boundaries. *Cambridge Journal of Education, 27,* 177-190.

Bridges, D. (1998). On conceptual analysis and educational research: A response to John Wilson. *Cambridge Journal of Education, 28,* 239-241.

Bridges, D. (1999). Writing a research paper: Reflections on a reflective log, *Educational Action Research, 7,* 221-234.

Bridges (2003). *Fiction written under oath? Essays in philosophy and educational research.* Amsterdam: Kluwer.

Burbules, N.C., & Callister, T.A. (1999). Universities in transition: The challenges of new technologies. Paper presented to the *Cambridge Philosophy of Education Conference,* 18 September 1999.

Dillon, J. (1988). *Questioning and discussion: A multi-disciplinary study.* Norwood, NJ: Ablex.

Elliott, J. (1998). *The curriculum experiment: Meeting the challenge of social change.* Buckingham: Open University Press.

Elliott, J., Bridges, D., Ebbutt, D., Gibson, R., & Nias, J., (1981). *School accountability: The SSRC Accountability Project.* London: Grant MacIntyre.

Hunt, L. (1991). History as gesture; or the scandal of History. In J. Arac & B. Johnston (Eds.), *Consequences of theory.* Baltimore: John Hopkins University Press.

Knitter, W. (1988). Review of disciplinary perspectives. In J. Dillon (Ed.), *Questioning and discussion: A multi-disciplinary study.* Norwood, NJ: Ablex.

Macmillan, C.J.B. (1988). An erotetic analysis of teaching. In J. Dillon (Ed.), *Questioning and discussion: A multi-disciplinary study.* Norwood, NJ: Ablex.

Popkewitz, T.S. (1984). *Paradigm and ideology in educational research: The social functions of the intellectual.* London/New York: Falmer.

Simons, H. (Ed.). (1980). *The science of the singular.* Norwich: CARE Occasional Publications.

Wilson, J. (1994). *Philosophy and educational research: first steps.* Paper presented to British Educational Research Association Annual Conference, Oxford.

Wilson, J. (1998). Philosophy and educational research: A reply to David Bridges et al. *Cambridge Journal of Education, 28,* 129-33.

Wilson, J., Williams, N., & Sugarman, B., (1967). *Introduction to moral education.* Harmondsworth: Penguin Books.

THE IMPORTANCE OF NEW TECHNOLOGIES IN PROMOTING COLLABORATIVE EDUCATIONAL RESEARCH[1]

Nicholas C. Burbules and Bert Lambeir

I.

Educational research, like research generally, is becoming more collaborative. Individual researchers still operate quite happily on their own, of course; but there is an increased awareness that a broad-scale understanding of educational issues requires the perspectives and skills of different researchers approaching a problem from multiple sides, especially if the research is expected to have significant policy implications. Research of all varieties is tackling problems of increasing scope, complexity, and – therefore – interdisciplinarity. In a globalized world, more interdependencies are coming to the fore, and more people have a stake in the costs and consequences of large-scale research.

Educational research, in particular, must confront the skepticism that it has often been of relatively poor quality and has had very little effect on changing or improving educational practices. One reason frequently cited for this failure is the tendency of many educational researchers to treat educational problems as site-specific phenomena, abstracted from a larger set of social processes: focusing on a specific classroom or a particular teacher-student relation. Alternatively, focusing on wider contextual influences inevitably raises multidimensional, extremely complex dynamics not amenable to site-specific research categories or methods. On a policy level, this means that interventions to be implemented across a range of social institutions and interactions require research that does not fall within simple disciplinary categories, and that does not frame hypotheses around simple, linear, cause-effect dynamics. Rather, such research would need to be sensitive to the highly complex and interactive ways in which significant social phenomena are overdetermined. Thus, the decision about which categories, methods, and

---

[1] This essay is based on material from four previous papers: Nicholas C. Burbules, "Discipline, Community, and Standards for Educational Research: Implications of New Information and Communication Technologies" and Bert Lambeir, "Co-Labour-Time and the Birth of the Data Generation," both presented at the international symposium on Philosophy and History of the Discipline of Education, at the Catholic University of Leuven (Autumn 2000); Nicholas C. Burbules, "Collaboration and the Standards of Educational Research," presented at the Catholic University of Leuven (Autumn 2002); and Bert Lambeir, "Even More is Not Enough: Doing Educational Research in a Virtual World," presented at the European Conference on Educational Research, Lisbon (Autumn 2002).

frameworks will guide a research project needs to be made in an interdisciplinary context. It is not simply a matter of saying "the methods must fit the problem," because even defining what the problem is already assumes certain constraints on how it will be studied. Deciding what factors are relevant to consider affects the range of possible explanations that can be derived.

In scientific contexts, there is a growing interest in issues of a fundamental, even profound, nature. Scientists across a host of domains have the sense now that they are working with very basic questions about the deep structural workings of phenomena: astronomers hypothesizing about the formation of the universe in its first moments following the "Big Bang"; particle physicists theorizing about the component elements and forces that make up everything in the universe; or the Human Genome Project, which seeks to unravel the underlying code of all human life. Government and institutional funders for such research unquestioningly accept the assumption that research on this scale must be enormously expensive; must be focused and continuous over a long term of effort; and must be collaborative. "Collaboration" in recent years has taken on the force of a mantra in education, government, and business; and in part this is because of the scope, complexity, and interdisciplinarity of the problems being pursued.

Our purpose here is not to argue that social research, and educational research specifically, ought to strive for "scientific" status, or that it can adopt the specific patterns of collaboration typical of scientific research like the Human Genome Project (though it would certainly appreciate such a research budget!). But educational research does share with these other fields of inquiry an intrinsic interest in interactions across many categories of phenomena; and, we are suggesting, especially where educational policy matters are concerned, research that does not operate across a complex range of factors will be inadequate.

To study education is to study a complex reality: every educational situation varies from every other since it includes teachers, students, their relations to each other and to other teachers and students, interaction patterns, different class cultures, shared and divergent experiences, and so on. Hence any specific issue of educational policy or practice almost certainly will entail questions of learning or cognition, of pedagogy, of social institutions, of communication, of cultural dynamics. (Imagine a large-scale study on how to reduce teen pregnancies in school, for example, or reducing dropouts.) It is quite odd then, when educational research wants to address educational reality by trying to draw simple causal inferences about instruction. The requirement to generalize and the overall search for causal explanations lose their meaning when the dynamic nature of educational processes is taken into account. In this respect it becomes doubtful whether educational research can directly cause the improvement of education in a means/ends sense. In ignoring the versatility of education, researchers tend to lose their grip on the reality of the school ground. Furthermore, in trying to objectify educational reality, this approach to educational research (and policy) precludes the opportunity of doing something really new.

Collaboration in the educational domain is important, then, not only because of the scope and interdisciplinarity of the problems under consideration, but because collaborative approaches better reflect the complexity of the situation; they encourage more subtle problem definitions and recognize simple causal assertions as too reductionistic. Moreover, because the people and educational contexts being studied are very diverse, the representativeness of the body of researchers involved with studying a problem (their race, gender, and so forth) is one of the few safeguards that various kinds of blind spots will not fundamentally damage the credibility of the research.

A key factor shaping attitudes toward collaboration in research is the increased incorporation of new information and communication technologies into the processes by which research data are gathered, represented, analyzed, written up, reviewed, shared, criticized, and published. This is our central concern in this essay. In important and sometimes unprecedented ways, these new technologies are not just facilitating collaboration among people, along lines of well-established practice; they are *changing* people's understandings of what collaboration is. Discussions of these new technologies invoke the idea of collaborative spaces and collaborative tools as *sites* of inquiry and creation, and not simply as facilitators or media of collaboration. These ways of rethinking collaboration, we will argue, raise new issues for disciplinary methods and standards of research; for the contexts in which research gets evaluated, and against what aims; for the populations of researchers and the boundaries of who is central, and who is peripheral, to the research community; and for expectations about knowledge and the uses and effects of knowledge upon policies and practices.

II.

The first area we will discuss concerns the processes of writing, representing, and publishing research online, and the new ways in which these support new understandings and practices of collaboration.

(1) Normally, researchers think of collaboration in writing as the process of drafting text, sharing these drafts, reviewing and revising one another's work, and so on, until a consensual version is completed that includes the ideas of many contributors and speaks with the voice of everyone and of no one in particular. Collaboration is viewed as the *process* that

yields a *product* that belongs to them all; the text displays the fruits of their collaboration. New technologies for generating written text, however, invert this relation: the writing space *becomes* the site of collaboration, and the text that is being produced facilitates and instantiates the collaboration.

One example of this new kind of writing space is an "interactive paper" technology developed by Jim Levin and Jim Buell at the University of Illinois (http://cterntl.ed.uiuc.edu/ipp/about.cfm). In this relatively simple form, each author has access to the same textual space online, and each written statement can be the subject of comment, criticism, or elaboration by other writers. The text may begin with something written by one individual; but the additional commentary and amplifications of others may dwarf the original or leave the rudimentary text far behind as the revisions, comments, responses to comments, and responses to responses all grow out of the original text, each in turn potentially generating its own branches and lines of further discussion (of course many online newsgroups or discussion forums have a similar threaded or branching structure).

There are many questions that arise from this basic idea: What kind of "text" is this, and to whom does it belong? Is the result "one" text or many? Is a text generated in this way online significantly different from a conventional text with copious annotations and marginalia? How is it different from a sequential set of texts, each written in response to the one before, but constituting some kind of serial conversation over time? Can a text like this ever be "finished," and would that necessarily be a good thing?

Some online journals have experimented with incorporating something like an interactive paper format, blurring the lines between circulating a draft for reviewer comments and publishing a final version for readerly response. In this context, a journal is not only a delivery medium for disseminating final works, but a forum that uses the works as an occasion for discussion and reformulation of the ideas – here again the textual space is not simply the *product* of collaboration, but the *facilitator* of it.

(2) A second area of new collaborations in writing concerns the fundamental hypertextuality of online text. Early on, this capability was described as "electronic footnotes." But footnotes are still clearly subordinate to a "main" text, and typically operate as optional content included only to elucidate or reference textual content that is regarded as primary. Hypertext goes beyond citational practices to relate multiple texts to each other in many ways; one can link not only to a reference, but to partial or complete texts that become in a sense part of the original text; and this linking relation can be reciprocal and co-equal. Hence, each link, and hence each text, is *embedded*

in the others, in ways that do not necessarily direct a linear sequence of order or priority in which these embedded text segments must be read.

Here, again, the written artifact instantiates a process of collaboration; in this case among authors who may be quite unaware of one another, joined now by a text that, through hyperlinks, creates a new set of relations among ideas by juxtaposing and reassembling text segments written at other times and even for other purposes. Indeed, the new text might contain *nothing but* such assembled segments! This writing form, which one of our colleagues calls "patchwording" (like a quilt), *creates* a collaboration, either through the efforts of a single compiler/editor (is this activity properly termed a kind of *authorship?*); or through the efforts of the authors of these text segments, each building links to the others, perhaps each for no purpose but his or her own, but in the process creating a complex interwoven set of interlinked texts because each is linking to the others, possibly without knowing that those others are also linking to each other, and back to that author as well (see for example "web rings" as one form this can take). The resulting questions echo those of the previous example, in terms of challenges to the idea of "authorship," of what it means to "finish" a text, or in terms of primacy of ownership over this new collaborative text – or if in fact "ownership" (in the sense of copyright, etc.) should even remain an important determination in such cases.

(3) A third aspect of online writing as a collaborative medium concerns the new possibilities of multimedia composition; in one instance simply as a compilation of text, music, images, and so on, that brings together authors/creators in different media to make something together that none could have made alone. But this would simply leave the question at the level of collaboratively *producing* a multimedia text. Beyond this level, as we have said, one should look at the possibilities of multimedia as *creating* a collaborative environment or occasion – where a creative format that allows such interrelating of sound, image, and text *already* defines a collaborative possibility, one that might change views about how these different media sources relate to each other: for example, overturning the traditional academic privileging of text as the medium through which proper research needs to be published by, say, collaboratively producing a documentary video as a form of serious scholarly research.

A step even further than this considers the ways in which multimedia and hyperlinked forms of representation create a context in which different voices, cultural value systems, or researcher perspectives can find simultaneous and co-equal modes of expression. One of the points being stressed in social research, including educational research, today is a suspicion about unquestioned authorial neutrality: Whose voice, whose perspective, is driving the study? Multimedia research can more easily include, for instance, primary qualitative data (say, unedited video or audio tapes from interviews), relatively unfiltered by analysis, along with the author's edited selections and interpretations. This would allow those researched a chance to "speak for themselves." This can also be seen as a kind of "test" of authorial reliability, by allowing readers to check the author(s)' interpretations against their own readings of the primary data (in this sense, *they* become collaborators too!).

As we have been emphasizing, these new forms of writing, representing, and publishing research are not just new tools in the researcher's toolkit; they change the relations among multiple researchers, those researched, and the audience. They decenter a single authorial voice (even a single "collaborative" one), in favor of multiplicity, dynamism, and interpretive openness. Together, they constitute a productive space in which collaboration can happen, but a collaboration shaped by the forms in which it expresses itself – not simply a collaboration directed toward a specific product. Indeed, as we have suggested, certain kinds of collaboration can only happen under these conditions, and certain potential collaborators can only be involved in these ways. Because new forms of writing, representing, and publishing research break open the boundaries of who qualifies to participate in scholarly production, the decision of who will be involved is not even entirely in the hands of the original authors – scholars sometimes have collaborative partners whether they want them or not.

III.

A second dimension of this process concerns new tools of research and data-gathering and the ways in which they also support forms of collaboration that decenter notions of where, how, and among whom research happens.

One example of this change includes new forms of teleconferencing or videoconferencing, and the ways in which they provide opportunities for synchronous, or simultaneous, interaction at a distance. In part, of course, these technologies are simply recreating the conditions in which this same collaboration might have occurred around a single table, face-to-face. But now such interactions can involve potential collaborators who would never be part of immediate, face-to-face collaboration around a single table – people from outlying corners of the globe, disabled people, people without academic credentials, people who cannot afford travel, and so on. This point is not trivial when you consider that one way of changing our views about research collaboration is not only in the *how* of doing it, but in *who* should be included in it. Nor, as we move toward virtual interactive environments that are multisensory and increasingly naturalistic, where participants interact as active personae with each other and with a data environment, it becomes even more clear that the virtual space *is* the site of collaboration, and that it shapes the intentions and actions of the participants.

But this example only scratches the surface of the changes we are discussing here; new information and communication technologies are not just media for talking back and forth. They also make possible gathering data (through remote instruments, like cameras on another planet, or sensors buried deep in a volcano, or images from fiber optic cables inside a medical patient's body) that could never be observed directly. In educational research, we talk about "observation," of course, but normally this is in unavoidably intrusive ways, in particular sites to which researchers can gain personal access; distant video technologies can support other kinds of observation and data-gathering (some of which, however, may raise problems of "surveillance" in the Foucauldian panoptic sense).

Another area of research concerns very complex simulations running on supercomputers that model large-scale processes so that they can be parsed and analyzed in a way that actual phenomena never could; this makes the simulation or model not only an aid to research, but a research environment itself, one that can generate new data which, in turn, can be studied in productive ways. The Human Genome Project, for example, would have been simply unthinkable without enormously fast and powerful computers, a speedy connection among them, and complex modeling technologies. In these sorts of examples the technology establishes an occasion for collaboration around data that are *created* with the technologies, not just *collected* by them. Because these models involve massive amounts of information there is no way they could be studied by single individuals, or even by a simple collaborative group – they require many disciplinary tools. Building and maintaining such data environments can itself be a complex collaborative research task.

For example, to take a case closer to our own field of study, witness the huge Wittgenstein archive at the University of Bergen (http://www.hit.uib.no/wab/). Gathering all of his textual production in one site, and linking it together in a complex hypertext, is both a substantive scholarly endeavor itself, and a space for further scholarly collaboration. It is not just archival or documentary work in the simple sense. In the examples we are describing here, therefore, the very existence of data of a certain scale, of a certain difficulty, of a certain complexity, creates an informational space through which researchers can and must work together to create it and then to make sense of it. The data environment, if you will, compels collaboration; it would not exist without it.

The examples from the natural sciences may seem an inappropriate model for social science research, specifically educational research. We don't have large-scale "models" or "simulations" of learners or learning environments. But even here large data sets can be formed by melding multiple smaller data sets; as with quantitative meta-analyses, sometimes a clearer picture emerges from aggregated particulars. This technique is often termed "data mining," and can be developed in such a way that *visual* representations of the data literally reveal emerging patterns. Data mining can work with information spaces that dwarf ordinary conceptions of statistical analysis or qualitative interpretation. For example, the Shoah project of the Virtual History Foundation involves recording and coding video interviews with every living Holocaust survivor. When those tens of thousands of hours of interviews have been recorded and digitized, how will researchers use them? Are there ways of bridging conventional dichotomies of quantitative and qualitative methods to create tools – by necessity involving some statistical or numerical analyses – that also respect the qualitative nature of the material being studied? Here again, such very large data sets are open-ended exploratory environments that compel collaborative research approaches; and this is an underused approach in educational studies, partly because of the tendencies toward particularism noted at the beginning of this essay.

We have tried to highlight how these kinds of changes in research environments pose challenges to some traditional categories and distinctions of research. We have just shown how the quantitative/qualitative distinction might be questioned. Another is the distinction between gathering data, in a purportedly open-minded empirical fashion, and then only later analyzing and interpreting it. In the kinds of research domains being described here, the design and development of information environments is already a research endeavor, structured by multifaceted efforts not only in developing technologies as tools, but in building into them assumptions about knowledge and the phenomena to be studied that are themselves complex theoretical endeavors. In this sense even the data themselves are, to use a familiar phrase, "theory-laden," but here because the very design of an information space requires collaboration, planning, and original insight; there is no way to collect and archive useable data on this scale without building into the design a set of assumptions about how it will be used, for what purposes, and by whom.

IV.

A third dimension of these information and communication technologies that affects collaborative research is the way that they exist within, and reinforce, an increasingly global context of interaction.

It is clear enough that a global medium allows disparate and far-flung scholars to work together; but there are further effects of doing this. When disparate and far-flung scholars are brought together, other things change; disciplinary standards will need to be re-examined and negotiated; research assumptions and aims may work at cross-purposes; even the choice about the language in which the collaboration will take place has implications for what can be talked about, and by whom. In such instances, the technologies that facilitate collaboration, from one standpoint, also shape and determine the collaborations that can and cannot occur.

These technologies also promote a certain kind of publicity for research that has rarely existed in the past. Data and preliminary results on the Internet can be studied (and criticized) by anyone with access to them; in some cases the data might be used by other scholars for other research purposes; issues of ownership and confidentiality may be at stake. One can argue that it is in the researcher's self-interest to encourage access to, and commentary on, his or her research and results in order to help improve it. Yet other imperatives, obviously, press researchers to keep their data and results private until they are ready to "publish" the work officially (and even after the final publication of their work they may still feel proprietary toward "their" data). Either choice manifests assumptions about the scale of collaboration and who one's collaborators are (as we asked earlier, can strangers who reanalyze one's data be seen as collaborators?). Of course, such choices have to be made even in traditional research environments too; but new information and communication technologies heighten the issue. But there is another side to this global context: When decisions about supporting collaborative research are made by policy makers on the national level, what is their underlying rationale? The tendency of global collaboration in research seems to be another attempt to satisfy the consumer (the policy community) with "useful" information that can support "cost-effective" reforms. Is this not a market-based discourse, characterized by a fundamentally economic rationale? Is the effect of globalizing research, ironically, another way to reduce the scope of what is counted as valuable research? How far will we have to go in "bridging the gap between theory and practice," and what is the price to pay? We have highlighted the benefits of sharing ideas, exchanging data, co-generating theories and explanations, and so on. Clearly, information and communication technologies can play a major role in these activities. But at the same time this might drive a process toward standardization, for example, the standardization of language: Which language will predominate on the network? Moreover, there is a benefit to much social, educational and historical research *because* of their particularity. More general (or "global") social or educational theories may not respect the heterogeneity of cases, especially across wide cultural differences. Hence, the global context of research can be productive and counterproductive simultaneously; technology enables some things and reduces other possibilities. When the latter is at stake, perhaps educational researchers should withdraw from the apparent "problem" at hand, from time to time, to think and eventually think again, about their methods and aims of research.

V.

And here is the overarching import of these observations: these changes in the forms, purposes, and media of collaboration coincide with larger contemporary doubts about the nature of research and research knowledge. Standard assumptions about the objectivity and finality of "facts," about the neutrality and universality of methods, about generalizability, or about the unquestioned good of modernist, predominantly Western, approaches to intellectual production being spread to the rest of the world all come under challenge in this new context.

An exploration and reconsideration of the nature of collaboration brings questions about the methods and aims of research into contact with questions about the contexts of research, and how these contexts act to include *and exclude* prospective participants. When we view the problems and processes of research as themselves structuring the forms of collaboration that can arise in response to them, we avoid the simple instrumentalism of thinking that the form of collaboration can simply be shaped to the question at hand. Sometimes the very definition of the question (and who gets to define it) *is* the problem.

When we realize that new information and communication technologies are vastly opening up the possibilities of what collaboration can look like, and who can be part of it, certain value questions come to the fore. For fields like educational research, which by nature invite interdisciplinary and open-ended questions, the forms of collaboration also express, inevitably, conflicting assumptions about human nature, society, knowledge, and value. What is the relation between the development of interdisciplinary collaborative teams and the standards or criteria of *educational* research?

Interdisciplinary collaboration in the full sense involves scholars from different disciplinary, theoretical, and methodological perspectives who define common questions and investigate them using mixed methods, and who are continually in dialogue with one another about how their different perspectives relate to one another. But interdisciplinary research, if it is to be successful, must overcome certain kinds of barriers. One is an issue of vocabulary: different disciplinary, theoretical, and methodological perspectives often use different terminologies to describe the features of a complex phenomenon, and this is not a simple or trivial problem because these differences in language often reflect deep differences in how the world is conceived. Interdisciplinary collaboration often requires the negotiation, or invention, of a new, shared vocabulary, but this reintroduces the potential problem of language standardization. Interdisciplinary collaboration also requires a reexamination of methods of inquiry, and often involves scholars working with tools that are not professionally their own – what benefits are to be gained, for example, when a non-historian helps sift through archival data, or when an anthropologist helps conceptualize an experimental research design?

Finally, and perhaps most challengingly, interdisciplinary collaboration requires some negotiation around the criteria of evidence and truth that pertain to shared investigations. This is not as simple as, say, delimiting quantitative versus qualitative inquiry, because there are gulfs almost as deep *within* those categories as there are between them, where issues of evidence and truth are concerned. But interdisciplinary collaborations must engage such questions because the very nature of the collaboration requires that two or more persons will look at the same information and come to some agreement about what it means, what it proves, or what it stands for. Turning these differences from a problem into an intellectual resource is a primary challenge here – and needless to say can be a deeply contested one.

But there are other impediments to interdisciplinary collaboration that are also worth noting here. One is the tendency, already discussed, to want to "own" one's data and preserve it for one's own analysis and interpretation. Sharing it may entail that others "get credit," or even more problematically perhaps, others may interpret it in ways that are antithetical to one's own view, or even show it to be mistaken. As we have discussed, the capacities of new information technologies to make possible the "publication" – the making public – of one's data, along with one's analysis or interpretation of it, creates a huge new possibility in the way we view intellectual production, collaboration, and accountability within a community of inquiry. And yet, for reasons that do not need to be belabored, this potential continues to be resisted by many researchers.

The fact that scholars in humanities disciplines especially tend to be more individualistic also creates a significant impediment to collaboration. There are deep issues here about the intellectual and moral significance of formulating and advocating for a *personal* perspective in these disciplines (think of Nietzsche in philosophy for instance; could he have been part of a collaborative team?). We also need to acknowledge the institutional implications and reward systems that often drive scholars into this self-interested mode: the greater weight given to sole-authored publications in many disciplines, for example.

All of this returns us to the question of standards and criteria for educational research, and how these shape or delimit collaborative possibilities. If one accepts that mutual criticism and cross-checking are part of how a community of inquiry advances its knowledge base, then the question arises of how this can happen in interdisciplinary collaborations, where the methods of investigation and of confirmation are often quite diverse. One path is to make these methods of investigation and confirmation an element of reflective discussion and negotiation within the group. But a group may feel, with justification, that it is spending so much of its time hashing through those meta-questions that it never gets on with the substantive issues at hand.

Moreover, the benefits of mutual criticism and cross-checking *within* a community of inquiry need to be supplemented by the benefits of criticism from *outside* that community of inquiry. This may come from those who explicitly do not share the disciplinary, theoretical, or methodological perspectives of those working within it; or it may come from distinct standpoints of political or cultural difference. In either case, it may be the very resistance of such perspectives to the setting of common standards of investigation and of confirmation that makes their criticisms so important; by definition such criticisms must come from the outside.

CONSTRUCTING THE EDEN OF OUR EARTHLY EXISTENCE
Empiricism and the History of Educational Research in Belgium Before the Second World War

M. Depaepe and A. Van Gorp

> *"Science will capture humanity, the world, the cosmos in irrefutable data, and the children will form the first, without doubt, along straight paths, learn to know and possess the truths of their existence; the future will no longer hide any secrets from anybody. In the distant future lies the Eden of our earthly existence"*
> (Schuyten, 1919)

The years between 1890 and 1940 were marked by the growth of empirical research in pedagogy. Within this general trend, different paradigmatic conceptions can be distinguished (see Depaepe, 1992, 1993). hereas "child study" developed in the United States in the direction of "educational psychology", "pedology" (a Greek neologism indicating the "discovery" of a "science of the child") began to evolve in continental Europe into "experimental pedagogy" – an evolution which was particularly noticeable in Belgium, and which is the subject for this paper. Our study is based on four trend-setting figures – Medard Schuyten, Ovide Decroly, Jozef Verheyen and Raymond Buyse – who were conceptually, geographically and chronologically representative of the development of "scientific" educational theory in Belgium before the Second World War (see also Depaepe, 2001). They were instrumental in bringing about the move from pedology to experimental pedagogy and focussing on the explicit and implicit criteria for science it uses. This paper examines the pioneering role pedology played in Belgium and further afield, which explains how the four protagonists were all to a greater or lesser degree influenced by this movement; it concludes by discussing the criteria they used for achieving scientific quality.

The Pedological Dream of Medard Carolus Schuyten (1866-1948)

The pedological movement in Belgium was largely centered around Medard Schuyten in Antwerp, although there were also several active groups in Brussels (Depaepe, 1993, 1997; 1998a). Schuyten's influence appears to have been particularly significant for the development of pedological theory and research. With a background in the natural sciences, Schuyten remained rooted in the positivist mindset that was prevalent during the 19th century.

Schuyten received a permanent commission as a researcher in 1899, and became the Director of the Pedological Department of Antwerp, which included a Laboratory in which pedological research with children from Antwerp took place. In 1905 an educational element was added into this position, leading him to teach chemistry in the industrial school and natural sciences and pedology (and/or psychology) in the newly founded secondary schools for boys and girls.

At the same time he was also a professor in organic chemistry at the "Université nouvelle" in Brussels, and it was at this new university, founded in 1894, that he offered from 1899 on a course in pedology, the first in Belgium. After the First World War the "Université nouvelle" was changed into the "Institut des Hautes Etudes de Belgique", which was primarily aimed at post-graduate studies. Schuyten remained attached to this institute until 1923, when a disagreement with his superiors led to breaking his contract. This disruption in his career can be attributed to his shock at the events of the First World War, including the death of his youngest son, which affected him for the rest of his life and became the eventual cause of a complete split from scientific work.

The first phase of Schuyten's work was closely bound up with his role in the pedological movement. Initially begun as a reaction to the Anglo-Saxon child study, which was said to be too sentimental, naturalist and romantic-religious, the pedology movement presented itself as a more scientific and sophisticated (i.e., positivistic) form of child study. The foundation stones of pedology were lain by the American Oscar Chrisman (1896), who coined the phrase in a PhD thesis in Jena in Germany. Schuyten quickly seized upon this new conceptual direction. He wanted to promote the "scientific study of children and of scientific institutes in general" (Lievevrouw-Coopman, 1903-1904).

In 1902 the *Algemeen Paedologisch Gezelschap* (APG; General Paedological Association) was founded as a scholarly society behind the idea of pedology. In terms of participants this association was far from unsuccessful. The number grew over ten years from eleven to around 150. But in terms of research the Antwerp pedological movement must be described as a one-man show. Pedology nevertheless soon gained an international reputation (see e.g, Monroe, 1901), which helped Schuyten in his attempts to establish an international pedological association, in competition with the French researcher Alfred Binet (see Depaepe, 1987a). The high point of the pedological movement in Belgium was the first (and only) international pedological congress, held in Brussels in 1911 (Depaepe, 1987b). Schuyten, the chairman of the organising committee, was also the deputy chairman of the congress, while Ovide Decroly (see infra) acted as chair.

The point of departure for Schuyten's pedological research was his unhappiness with the way in which educational theories in general were being developed. Education could not advance without undertaking a scientific study of children. He contrasted this with what he called "empiricism" (by which he meant the old ways of dealing with children based on experience and tradition) and the "metaphysical" deviations to which pedagogy had fallen prey. In his opinion, education had to be supported by research in physiology and psychology; most of all, educational theory had to become more mathematical and to "follow the path of other exact sciences...chemistry, physics and the like" (Schuyten, 1900, 1902-1903)

The educational themes studied by Schuyten were extremely divergent and had no common characteristics; however, they were unified by two positivist assumptions: (1) a belief in a universally valid and quantifiable (and therefore rationally and mathematically discoverable) natural law, which controls psychological and physical phenomena; (2) an unconditional belief in the emancipating power of science and, linked to this, the possibility of "rational" and "technical" improvement of the world through scientific research (see also Depaepe, 1985).

But Schuyten's aim of constructing a single pedological method failed. Pedology unsuccessfully tried methods and techniques taken from physiology, psychology, and anthropometry. If a pedological methodology had been developed, it might have acted as the centrifugal force to hold together the movement, but without it there was no cohesion. With the start of the second phase of his work after the First World War, the APG lost its appeal. The organisation resumed its activities in 1922 (it had lain dormant during the war) but Schuyten had already been dismissed and in 1929 the organisation finally disappeared (Depaepe, 1993).

The Pedagogical Charisma of Ovide Decroly (1871-1932)

The fact that the 1911 international pedology congress in Brussels was chaired by Decroly, a renowned Belgian educational reformer, underlines his position in the movement. As one of the leaders of the so-called New Education, Decroly strongly believed in the idea of a research-driven educational reform. Nevertheless, he had a rather different concept of education as a science, in comparison to Schuyten and others.

Like Schuyten, Decroly had a background in the natural sciences (*Hommage*, 1933). So it may not be surprising that Decroly was also won over by the positivistic mentality that was in vogue during the 19th century. This showed through in his studies in medicine at the University of Ghent; he was involved with research during his studies and he later specialized in neurology at the universities of Berlin and Paris.

His specialization brought him to the Brussels polyclinic where he met Jean Demoor, who was behind the founding of the first "special schools" for deprived children in Brussels in 1897. On Demoor's initiative, the contact between the two men led in 1901 to founding the "Institut d'enseignement spécial" which was conceived as a "psychological laboratory" where Decroly could give free rein to his positivistic approach, focussing in particular on experimental methods. Central to the institute was the idea of a "medical" pedagogy, based on not only the physical but also the psychological state of the child. Mental health was dependent on physical health, which in turn was dependent on cerebral health. It is here that Decroly's background as a neurologist clearly shows through (Decroly, 1901, 1903, 1904).

Decroly's ideas about the education of "abnormal" children contained the seeds of a strong commitment to the child (compared with the educational reform movement) and were based on a dissatisfaction with the existing education system, which Decroly termed "anti-social" because it did not prepare for "real life" (See also Depaepe, 1990a; De Wilde, 1992). Decroly (1902) emphasized that the creation of an appropriate education for abnormal children required the accurate delineation of the category of "abnormal". The search for this definition took him to the deep waters of experimental science, and thus to the possibilities offered by pedology.

Initially, Decroly (1905) sought inspiration from Demoor, who believed that the only valid definition of abnormal was when people felt their abnormality hindered them from fitting into the environment in which they were placed. But Decroly sought a more scientific basis for the definition, as can be seen in his overview of "abnormal pedagogy", published together with Demoor (Demoor & De Croly, 1904). In that contribution, the authors state their belief that "the psychology of abnormal children" was a "science under construction", in which a positivistic direction was being taken with a rational methodology. In order to develop a better definition of the abnormal Decroly developed a technique that was starkly reminiscent of the clinical methods from his medical background: research had to go hand-in-hand with an exact diagnosis, which was only of value if it was supported by the individual history of the children, in which both their hereditary and social antecedents were crucial elements. Decroly and Demoor supported their argument by referring their readers to important works such as those of Alfred Binet.

Exploring the paradigms of experimental science provided Decroly with more possibilities for psychological or psychometric tests, which seemed to offer the best chance of developing a scientifically based classification of "abnormability" (see e.g., Besse, 1982). Decroly particularly focussed on the Binet-Simon "échelle métrique d'intelligence", a scale based on research into the anthropometric borders of abnormality. Decroly used, adapted and elaborated the scale, which was developed in 1905 and 1908. In 1910 he published an improved version with Julia Degand. Together with Raymond Buyse, Decroly worked on an overview of existing mental tests and developed tests on his own, of which "l'épreuve de la boîte à ouvrir" (the famous "Decroly's box") was the best known.

From his work with abnormal children, Decroly wondered whether some of his ideas might not be applied to work with normal children. His school for normal children ("l'école pour la vie, par la vie" / the school for life through life) grew to be an educational Mecca of world renown. It was at this point that Decroly's experimental scientific research made room for more practical and experiential research - a programme, however, that constantly was colored by the discourse of the believers. These "Decroliens", to which Jozef Verheyen belonged, were, above all, successful in giving a "language" to the pedagogical charisma of the leader (see Depaepe, Simon, & Van Gorp, 2003).

Experimental Pedagogy as Educational Reform:
Jozef Emiel Verheyen (1889-1962)

After the First World War, with the decline of pedology, a "revival" took place of the philosophical and normative traditions within educational theory. This created a problem for the positivistic, scientific development of pedagogy. It was argued that educational theory was being manipulated by experimental research and that this was only one aspect of education. But the experimentalists seemed to be very flexible. Some of them (like Buyse, see infra) agreed that philosophers had to indicate the norms of education and stressed that their specialization was purely technical; others tried to integrate the normative frameworks in which the discourse of educational reform was embedded.

As an exponent of the "neutral, experimental pedagogy" in Flanders, which found its institutional grounding in the late 1920s at the State University of Ghent, Verheyen belonged to the latter category (Verheyen, 1954; De Clerck, 2002). Since partisanship was forbidden at the University of Ghent, it was, in contrast to the situation at the Catholic University of Louvain, impossible to teach an ideologically framed education, like Catholic pedagogy. So, academics of the Ghent university tried to find refuge in the methodology of "experimental pedagogy" on the one hand and in the child-centeredness of the New Education Movement (the European counterpart of Progressive Education in the United States) on the other hand.

Verheyen was given the task of elaborating an experimental pedagogy at the academic level, based on his experience as a county primary school inspector and his time spent as a student of the educational reforms of Claparède and Decroly. From 1923 to 1928 Verheyen directed an "experimental" school in Zaventem. In 1927 he was appointed as senior research assistant at Ghent: in addition to his responsibilities for the development of a laboratory for experimental pedagogy, he was to be the academic supervisor of a genuine "experimental school", which could be considered as the continuation of the Zaventem experiment. This experimental school had to offer future teachers the possibility of research and give them the opportunity to try out, in practice, ideas from educational reform theories (Depaepe, 1999; Depaepe, Dams, & Simon, 1999). Ultimately, an existing municipal school in a working-class district of Ghent was selected as the experimental or pilot school. Based on a personal empathy for less well-off children, Verheyen also had a scientific motive for this selection: children from the lower classes do not receive any help from their parents with their school work. Research on these children and tests relating to their intellectual development, therefore, should not run the same risks of influence from the family circle, unlike children from higher social classes.

As far as the content of educational innovation is concerned, Verheyen held a great respect for Claparède and for Decroly, whom he labeled the "modern Pestalozzi" (Verheyen, 1961). This commitment was demonstrated in a tendency to take "globality" as a starting point, which shared, ironically, a significant number of characteristics with fascist-style education and with Catholic "totalitarian" educational theory (see e.g., Depaepe, 1998b). Verheyen's list of the four factors which he believed had led to the development of an "academic" science of education reveal his influences: (1) the "wonderful" growth in child- and youth psychology, which he, following Dewey, Claparède and other reformers, labeled a "Copernican revolution"; (2) the interest within medical circles in abnormal children (a tradition where the central figures were Itard, Séguin, Montessori and, of course, Decroly); (3) the continuation of experimental and other methods of positive science in educational theory (in particular Binet, Meumann and Thorndike); and (4) the development of "new schools" by academics.

In reality, however, even the most advanced forms of reform pedagogy remained very tame in their concrete application. Both in school and in society, the limits of the meritocratic worldview were not breached. Verheyen's modernism was always situated within the frame of the socially acceptable, so that the function of the school as a socialization and selection institution was not questioned. The child was expected to embrace the moral code for the general welfare, to abide by the prescriptions of the school community and to learn to train himself/herself in self-control, submission, and disciplined behavior. Hence, while the educational reforms of Verheyen and his partisans discursively stressed their discontinuity with the past, in fact they revealed a yearning for an idyllic rural community that was thought lost, where nothing but peace, quiet, and harmony seemed to prevail (Depaepe et al., 2000; Depaepe, 2002).

Raymond Buyse (1889-1974) and the Critique of the Union of Empirical Research and Educational Reform

Raymond Buyse certainly had stronger roots than Verheyen, and probably even stronger than Decroly, in the pedology movement. After the success of the international pedology congress, Iozefa Ioteyko founded the "Faculté internationale de Pédologie" in 1912, which, due to the war, lasted only until 1914 (Depaepe, 1985, 1993). Buyse was one if its twelve students. He finally graduated in 1919 as a doctor of pedology, after which he worked closely with Decroly. In 1929 Buyse, with Decroly, strongly criticized the so-called "arithmetic fetishism"; he believed that a quantitative approach to human science was not an end in itself but rather a means with which, in a given circumstance, one could arrive at a more rational approach. His cooperation with Decroly, however, could not be ascribed to a common ideological outlook; in fact, there were important philosophical differences which hindered a permanent collaboration on an institutional level. Decroly was a freethinker and Buyse a Catholic. Rather than becoming an assistant of Decroly at the (freethinking) University of Brussels, where Decroly taught child psychology, Buyse had to develop his own career at the (unified) Catholic university of Louvain.

In 1935 Buyse drew the distinction between the experimental pedagogy ("la pédagogie expérimentale") and the experiential pedagogy ("la pédagogie expériencée"), which was how he referred to educational reforms (Buyse, 1935). In contrast to purely scientific experiments, reform pedagogy did not follow the natural scientific paradigm, whereby work was undertaken following well-established variables or at least under as controlled circumstances as possible. For Buyse, experiments in the framework of reform pedagogy meant trying out a highly specified renewal of educational practice. Innovations were not so much the fruit of laboratory research as the creative intuition and experiences of talented educationalists.

By contrast, according to Buyse experimental pedagogy should only be concerned with the neutral, technical side of education, and more particularly, with the neutral, technical side of teaching. Experimental pedagogy therefore should be aimed primarily toward the study of educational teaching processes, teaching methods and means. In Europe, Buyse became a leader of experimental didactics, through which he believed it was possible to embed experimental-scientific research into an ideological and normative framework, such as the Catholicism he supported. He also believed that experimental pedagogy was methodologically dependent on progress in the study of psychology.

Social Factors Behind Individualized Conceptions of Research

Until now we have concentrated almost exclusively on the conceptual framework of the educational science and its internal scientific criteria: in the case of pedology as well as in the case of experimental pedagogy (or didactics), the specialists looked to the natural sciences (biology, chemistry, physics, etc.) as a model. The differences in scope of these claims (pedology made claims as a framework science, while experimental pedagogy reduced its claims to the construction of instrumental knowledge, along with the normative) showed that these trends cannot simply be explained by an intrinsic drive for scientization. Explaining the appeal of the experimental paradigm used by pedology and experimental education, therefore, requires a socio-historical "history of science" approach. As we argued elsewhere (e.g., Depaepe, 1987a, 1993, 1997), the rise of empirical research in education was related to complex social factors and phenomena (intra-scientific as well as extra-scientific), such as the rise of positivism in the 19th century, the institutional growth of an educational market, the professionalisation and academisation of educationalists, the making of a meritocratic society, and the need to justify values through "objective" and "neutral" research. Following Oelkers (1996), we have argued that, in this area, the continuity was much greater than the discontinuity: the same implicit criteria continuously played a role in the outlook of "scientific" pedagogy.

Pedologists were convinced that the acceptance of pedology into the school system and at home would lead to improved education of children and thus to better citizens. Pedologists set themselves a specific social task: through better knowledge of children individually, they can be helped in their choice of profession. Another social factor recognized by pedology was the unconditional belief in the liberating force of science (Depaepe, 1990b). For his part, Buyse was convinced that school could enable anyone to climb the social ladder, without anyone being forced off it. Within experimental education there were similar ideas: for Binet the criterion for good education was that it enabled an individual to fit into his environment. This same idea can be found in Demoor and Decroly's views on abnormal children.

However, this so-called "emancipatory" power of science must be seen in the light of the eugenics movement, which believed that experimental pedagogy was one of the most significant of all sciences because it was concerned with the improvement of the human race and with the management of social capital represented by children. But this striving for "emancipation" in no way implied the elimination of the existing society; hence it could well be wondered whether this striving for increased educational success was not simply a sign of preference for a more rationally ordered (and thus more easily controlled) community, than working toward an emancipatory interest in the child. The stronger emphasis on classification meant, for Decroly and Verheyen, a more child-oriented practice, but at the same time it gave force to a more subtle exercise of power. Research was, in fact, more patronizing than emancipating.

Moreover, drawing similarities between experimental educational research and experimental medicine, as did Buyse, implied that both disciplines were equally valid and therefore worthy of the same academic recognition. The highest demand of the experimental theorists was thus academic recognition and, having achieved this, a desire for individual scientific careers. As far as the four central characters described here are concerned, Decroly, Verheyen, and Buyse each gained a university posting, in Brussels, Ghent and Louvain respectively. For ideological reasons in the context of the war Schuyten refused a professorship at the German-occupied Ghent university and threw away all his chances after the First World War due to his state of mind (Buyse also refused a university position at the university of Brussels for ideological reasons).

Experimentalists presented themselves as world reformers. Their fundamental axiom was that better research on children would make children happier, which would improve their overall productivity, both culturally and economically. A faithful following of educational and pedological recommendations would enable the right person to be put in the right place, socially and industrially. Thus, instead of attacking Western meritocracy, educational theory – even as "reform pedagogy" – retained the positivistic dreams of experimentalism, which were that research into the educational reality in schools could help toward achieving a better life, which meant a well-ordered, rational and scientifically supported life.

Conclusion: Evolution and Evaluation of Criteria for Educational Research?

1. The incorporation of an experimental approach or methodology constituted an essential element in the scientisation of educational research;
2. The preference for the experimental approach or methodology reflected, all in all, an empirical and inductionistic concept of science: sensory observation was considered to be fundamental for all true knowledge;

3. This preference for experimental research led to the primacy of facts over ideas. By means of observations, measurements, and experiments pedologists and experimental pedagogues sought to derive general patterns, universally applicable laws, and theorems;
4. Science was perceived as a horn of plenty from which nothing but progress and blessings would flow;
5. Hence, the distinction between pure and applied sciences was, certainly in the domain of education, a very relative one, determined much more by the desire for the optimalisation of educational practice;
6. Therefore, educational researchers – pedologists as well as experimental pedagogues – presented themselves as unbridled world reformers, constructors of "the Eden of our earthly existence". Experimental pedagogues, however, were less ambitious than pedologists. By arguing that the experimental offered only one approach for pedagogy and at the same time, covered only a limited area of the educational reality, it opened the door to other philosophical and normative approaches in pedagogy;
7. Nevertheless, the possible contribution to status enhancement came from the experimental side, while the old "metaphysical" as well as "empirical" pedagogy was almost constantly threatened with mockery. In experimental pedagogy as well as in pedology, the example of the prestigious medical and natural sciences was never far away. Apparently, the greatest desire of pedologists and experimental pedagogues was academic recognition; behind their call for academisation lurked the desire to build individual scientific careers, knit together in a strong international network;
8. Finally, this ambitious and absorbing adventure, called "scientific pedagogy", did not result in a revolutionary change of the world. It rather wanted to contribute to greater social efficiency, through the realisation of the positivistic dream of a well-ordered, rationally managed, and scientifically supported society. In this sense pedology as well as experimental pedagogy must be qualified as highly modernistic.

Sources and Literature

Besse, J.M. (1982). *Ovide Decroly: psychologue et éducateur*. Toulouse: Privat.
Buyse, R. (1935). *L'expérimentation en pédagogie*. Bruxelles: Lamertin.
Chrisman, O. (1896). *Paidologie. Entwurf zu einer Wissenschaft des Kindes*. Jena: Vopelins.
De Clerck, K. (2002). *75 jaar Pedagogische Wetenschappen aan de Gentse Universiteit*. Gent: Archief Gent.
Decroly, O. (1901). *Institut d'enseignement spécial de Bruxelles pour enfants des deux sexes*. Bruxelles: Polleunis & Ceuterick.
Decroly, O. (1903). Congrès international de l'assistance des aliénés et spécialement de leur assistance familiale, tenu à Anvers du 1er au 7 septembre 1902, sous la présidence d'honneur de M. Van den Heuvel, ministre de la justice / Rapports

et compte rendu des séances publiés par les soins du docteur Fritz Sano, secrétaire général du Congrès. Anvers: La Librairie Néerlandaise.

Decroly, O. (1903). *Institut d'enseignement spécial de Bruxelles. Direction médico-pédagogique.* Renaix: J. Leherte-Courtin.

Decroly, O. (1904). La médico-pédagogie, In *Livre jubilaire dédié à Richard Boddaert, professeur à l'université de Gand, à l'occasion du 70e anniversaire de sa naissance par ses élèves et anciens élèves, 7 octobre.* (Annales de la Société de Médecine de Gand, 84, pp. 119-140). Gand: E. Vanderhaeghen.

Decroly, O. (1905). La classification des enfants anormaux. *Bulletin de la Société de Médecine mentale de Belgique, 122*, 384-419.

Demoor, J., & De Croly, O. (1904). Revue de pédagogie des enfants anormaux. *Année Psychologique, 10*, 317-327.

Depaepe, M. (1985). Science, technology, and paedology. The concept of science at the "Faculté Internationale de Pédologie" in Brussels (1912-1914). *Scientia Paedagogica Experimentalis, 22*, 14-29.

Depaepe, M. (1987a). Social and personal factors in the inception of educational research in education (1890-1914): An explanatory study. *History of Education, 16*, 275-298.

Depaepe, M. (1987b). Le premier (et dernier) congrès international de pédologie à Bruxelles en 1911. *Le Binet Simon, 87* (612), 28-54.

Depaepe, M. (1990a). Soziale Abnormität und moralische Debilität bei Kindern. Ein Diskussionsthema auf internationalen wissenschaftlichen Zusammenkünften am Anfang des Jahrhunderts. *Paedagogica Historica, 26*, 185-209.

Depaepe, M. (1990b). La pédologie comme base d'un monde meilleur. J. Ioteyko et la science de l'enfant au début du XXe siècle. In Y. Fumat, A. Guillain, & P. A. Sigal (Eds.), *Les enjeux éducatifs. Emergence - permanence – recurrence* (pp. 211-235). Montpellier: Publication de la Recherche. Université Paul-Valéry.

Depaepe, M. (1992). Experimental research in education, 1890-1940: Historical processes behind the development of a discipline in Western Europe and the United States. *Aspects of Education. Journal of the Institute of Education. The University of Hull, 42*, 67-93.

Depaepe, M. (1993). *Zum Wohl des Kindes? Pädologie, pädagogische Psychologie und experimentelle Pädagogik in Europa und den USA, 1890-1940.* Weinheim/Leuven: Deutscher Studien Verlag/Leuven University Press.

Depaepe, M. (1997). The heyday of pedology in Belgium (1899-1914): A positivistic dream that did not come true. *International Journal of Educational Research, 27*, 687-697.

Depaepe, M. (1998a). The pedologist Medard Carolus Schuyten: An insane positivist or just a starry-eyed idealist? *Paedaogica Historica, Supplementary Series, 3* (1), 209-229.

Depaepe, M. (1998b). Katholische und nationalsozialistische Pädagogik in Belgien 1919-1955. Ihre ambivalente Beziehung im Spiegel der "Vlaamsch Opvoedkundig Tijdschrift". *Zeitschrift für Pädagogik, 44*, 503-522.

Depaepe, M. (1999). Experimentelle Pädagogik, Reformpädagogik und pädagogische Praxis. Überlegungen über ihre wechselseitigen Beziehungen dar-

Depaepe, M. (2001). La pédagogie. In R. Halleux, J. Vandersmissen, A. Despy-Meyer, & G. Vanpaemel (Eds.), *Histoire des sciences en Belgique, 1815-2000* (Vol. 1, pp. 329-342). Bruxelles: Dexia/ Tournai: La Renaissance du Livre.

Depaepe, M. (2002). The practical and professional relevance of educational research and pedagogical knowledge from the perspective of history: Reflections on the Belgian case in its international background. *European Educational Research Journal, 1,* 360-379.

Depaepe, M., Dams, K., & Simon, F. (1999). "La vie et l'école". Analyse historique du discours rénovateur de Joseph Emile Verheyen. *Education et Recherche. Revue Suisse des Sciences de l'Education, 21,* 9-32.

Depaepe, M. et al. (2000). *Order in progress. Everyday educational practice in primary schools: Belgium, 1880-1970.* Leuven: Leuven University Press.

Depaepe, M., Simon, F., & Van Gorp, A. (2003). The canonization of Ovide Decroly as a "saint" of the new education. *History of Education Quarterly, 43,* 224-249.

De Wilde, Ph. (1992). Eugenetisch pessimisme en pedagogisch optimisme bij J. Demoor. Case-study naar het geneeskundig denken over abnormaliteit, eind negentiende – begin twintigste eeuw. *Pedagogisch Tijdschrift, 17,* 349-369.

Hommage au Dr. Decroly (1933). Saint-Nicolas: Scheerders-Van Kerckhove.

Lievevrouw-Coopman (M.) (1903-1904). Le laboratoire pédologique d'Anvers. *L'Ecole Nationale, 3,* 211.

Monroe, W.S. (1901). Notes on child study in Europe. *Pedagogical Seminary, 7,* 512.

Oelkers, J. (1996³). *Reformpädagogik. Eine kritische Dogmengeschichte.* Weinheim/ München: Juventa.

Schuyten, M. (1900). Voorwoord. *Paedologisch Jaarboek, 1,* viii.

Schuyten, M. (1902-1903). Een kijkje in de pedologie. *Paedologisch Jaarboek, 3-4,* 454.

Schuyten, M. (1911). *La pédologie. Synthèse.* Gand: Vanderpoorten.

Schuyten, M. (1919). Psycho-paedagogische oorlogsnota's. *Paedologisch Jaarboek, 1-128.*

Van Daele, H. (1969). *150 Jaar stedelijk onderwijs te Antwerpen, 1819-1969.* Antwerpen: Stad Antwerpen.

Van Gorp, A., Depaepe, M., & Simon, F. (2003). *Backing the actor as agent in discipline formation: An example of the "secondary disciplinarisation" of the educational sciences, based on the networks of Ovide Decroly (1901-1931).* Manuscript submitted for publication.

Velle, K. (1991). *De nieuwe biechtvaders. De sociale geschiedenis van de arts in België.* Leuven: Kritak.

Verheyen, J.E. (1954). *Het Hoger Instituut voor Opvoedkundige Wetenschappen van de Rijksuniversiteit te Gent. Terugblik en toekomstperspectieven.* Gent: Hoger Instituut voor Opvoedkundige Wetenschappen.

Verheyen, J.E. (1961). *De experimenteerschool van de Rijksuniversiteit te Gent.* Gent: Hoger Instituut voor Opvoedkundige Wetenschappen.

FROM COLONIALISM TO GLOBALISATION:
Performativity in New Zealand Education

James D. Marshall, Michael Peters, and Ruth Irwin

Introduction

In New Zealand the public education system has always been involved in the testing and selection of the young for later professional and technocratic positions in life. The placing of the child at the centre of the curriculum after 1935, in a move toward progressive education by Director General of Education Clarence Beeby, meant that knowledge about the individual child was of paramount importance. Two outcomes of this shift were the expansion and development of Departments of Education within the Universities to develop the testing industry, and the establishment of the New Zealand Council for Educational Research (NZCER) in 1935. Initially, in the mid-1930s, testing and measurement per se were not a major aspect of NZCER's research programme, but they are now part of NZCER's core business. The research upon which the testing and measurement industry was based was essentially psychological and has been characterised as *positivistic* (McCulloch, 1986; Marshall, 1987). Lyotard's concept of *performativity* seems to us a more appropriate characterization today.

The introduction of the Proficiency Examination to New Zealand schools in 1889 was the first major step toward establishing a testing and selection process for entrance to the Public Service. There have been recent major changes in the major National qualifications. Since 1988, there have been a number of "reforms" especially in the area of curriculum (MoE, 1993). All of these should be seen as steps toward education under the effects of globalisation and the knowledge economy and society. Some critics of these changes have seen the post 1988 "reforms" as moves toward what Lyotard termed "performativity", i.e, the subsumption of what had been a very successful state education system to the demands of efficiency and the production of *useful* "knowledge" as a commodity. In these moves we can detect another positivistic turn in the universal application of business technologies and management structures to all forms of institutions including education (see further, Peters, Marshall & Fitzsimons, 1999).

With these "reforms" we have entered a new era of education and educational research. It is not just a revival of vocationalism, although it has that aspect. Instead it involves different ways of conceiving persons – as autonomous choosers – different conceptions of knowledge and education, and particular conceptions of our relationships to technology, the environment and others.

This report on the *History and Philosophy of the Science of Education in New Zealand* then will have three sections:

1. the science of education pre-1930s when, in a colonial setting, most educational ideas were imported, or accepted on the advice of eminent international "experts";
2. the psychologistic phase – 1930s to 1980s, with an accompanying flourishing of the testing industry and experimental methodology;
3. the performativity phase – after the 1988/9 "reforms".

Education in a Colonial Setting

The British Crown assumed Sovereignty in 1840 after the signing with Maori of the Treaty of Waitangi[1] and a long sphere of colonial rule ensued. This situation involved a considerable deferral to Britain on a number of matters, including education. New Zealand was seen as a brave new world by most of the immigrants from Great Britain in the 19th century. They were from the upper working classes and the lower middle classes, and were prepared to work hard because, ambitious and enterprising as they were, they perceived few barriers to success. New Zealand was seen then as a land of opportunity both socially and economically.

Legislation passed in 1877 provided a universal free and compulsory *primary* education for all children – for the indigenous Maori and pakeha (non-Maori). Prior to this there had been special provision for Maori schools – to teach them English and to assimilate them into Western culture (Simon, 2000). Prior to the establishment of Maori schools in 1847 the churches had provided missionary schools for Maori but these were for their own "agendas", namely to civilise and Christianise.

Educational provision varied between the provinces. If some of the early settlers were strong on educational rhetoric they were often tardy on the provision of provincially funded schools. Thus most schools initially were either privately or church provided. Prior to the passing of the 1877 Act only 58% of children in the age group 5-15 were on the school rolls. Furthermore while the 1877 Act provided for a national education system it was some years before all children were able to take advantage – because of needing to travel

---

[1] The interpretation of this Treaty by Maori and Pakeha has had a long and unfortunate history, especially over the meaning of "sovereignty".

considerable distances, preferring to remain working on the farm, etc. This was to be followed by free places in secondary schools for those who passed the Proficiency Exam (1889) in 1903 and this was extended to all, as a right, in 1938.

The education which was provided in the new state schools and in the "private" secondary schools was essentially modeled upon best practice in the English and Scottish systems of education. This was to change with the recession of the 1930s, the coming to power of the first Labour Government, in 1935 and a think tank of prominent thinkers on education. In this group were Clarence Beeby, James Shelley, Sir Thomas Hunter, William Sutch and H.R.Somerset. Their ideas, arising from several deliberations, were represented in practice in NZCER and in the educational bureaucracy from 1935 on by Beeby.

Theory of education was taught mainly in the universities and, until the 1970s, it was also essentially psychologically based. Teacher preparation was undertaken in separate Colleges of Education, with joint appointments between the Colleges of Education and the State Department of Education. Professors of Education at the University were also Principals of the Colleges. Departments of Education in the universities played a pivotal role as a hub for teacher trainees to acquire a liberal education in the universities. This was to cease from 1923 when the colleges assumed a total teaching role and University Departments of Education were left "stranded" in Arts Faculties for nearly a decade. In the now independent Colleges of Education, almost all theory was psychologically based. The first Professors of Education at the University of Auckland were either educational psychologists or developmental psychologists. New Zealand education was also served by a number of visiting experts and expert external advisers, such as the British psychologist Sir Cyril Burt. The first Professor of Sociology was not appointed in a New Zealand university until 1966, and only later philosophers and other contributors to theory.

Unfortunately most of the early historical work on education in this period has occupied an historical "twilight zone" (McCulloch, 1986, p. 10). Gary McCulloch argues that the main function of this historical work was to serve dominant trends and perspectives in education, not to question them. These studies saw the education system as a symbol of (liberal) progress of a free, secular, compulsory and national education system. The very liberal principles upon which it was predicated were left intact. Also "unnoticed" was the position of the indigenous people – Maori – within this "progressing" system. This system was meant to be promoting equality of opportunity for all, but no one had asked if it was achieving such aims. Indeed no research was conducted on this matter until the 1980s (Lauder, Hughes, & Taberner,

1984). Recently the Ministry of Education sponsored a "history" of the reform period in the 1980s and 1990s, which glorifies the reforms instead of submitting them to critical scrutiny.

The Psychologistic Phase: Testing and Measurement

McCulloch (1986) locates educational research within a positivist tradition, identifying the psychological background of many early influential people. A visiting academic was to note the strongly psychological emphasis within education departments (Hearnshaw, 1965). Ray Adams (1985) categorises this emphasis more finely, as being not merely psychological but also *positivistic*, i.e., as "being quantitative, technocratic and reportedly value free". Marshall (1987) reaches similar conclusions on much philosophy of education in New Zealand.

Fitt was to introduce experimental methodology to education in New Zealand. But by the mid-1930s, with the need to know about the individual child, experimental and empirical research and theory blossomed. If this was positivist in its emphasis upon experimentation, it was positivist also in another sense, which was identified in a widely disseminated article by William Renwick, also a Director General of Education. Renwick (1986) attempted to separate "proper" educational research from other research activities such as history and philosophy of education. He argued that *educational research* should examine "learning and teaching in the institutional or organisational settings", where "the essential function…is to help learners and teachers by providing evidence that will assist them, and others, in the evaluation of their educational aims and the usefulness of various means of achieving them." Thereby *critical* evaluation of education, such as the deschoolers or the new sociology of education, was not on the agenda of *educational research*. In Renwick's view, research should be directed at improving established systems, thereby approving them. However, we would stress that such research is not reflective and reflexive upon its own methodology and assumptions. Moreover, as it is directed at improving the performance of the system, without questioning its aims, such research can be seen as an example of *performativity*. Instead, we believe that research should question the givenness of the contexts under study and the definitions of research problems by funding agencies or other sponsors of research – in short, research should be *critical*.

The very structures of our education system are positivistic. Cries of centralism are legion in a structure designed to ensure accountability and control for technocratic ends. The system is partitioned into layers by age with a corresponding division if not fragmentation of responsibilities. There is an *instrumental* approach to knowledge (a point conceded by Renwick, 1986, p.

4), and it is difficult to find in Departmental literature since World War II a concern with "knowledge for knowledge's sake". Knowledge is almost always seen as being instrumental toward the good of society or the good of the individual (see the national curriculum [MoE, 1993])

The structure of government reports also has positivistic features. There is a clear division between facts and values – for example in the separation of the working papers for the Education Development Conference of 1973 into *Aims and Objectives, Teaching and Learning* and *Administration of Education*. These reflect not only a fact/value dichotomy but also a technocratic view of bureaucracy: as if aims and objectives can be separated from administrative structures and organization, and as if aims and objectives were capable of being settled once and for all, or at least at some particular point in time. This is further reflected in the title (and in the content) of the Picot Report of 1988 (MoE, 1988 – one of the major reports which led to the neoliberal "reforms") – entitled "Administering for Excellence".

These reports are very thin on theoretical analysis and theoretical "perceptions". Whilst reports (cf. Beeby, 1986b; Renwick, 1986) note changes in society there is little or no attempt to come to terms with complex descriptions and explanations of such changes or, indeed, the role of schools in society more generally. Lacking theoretical analysis, the various reports' "solutions" seem little more than sporadic lurches in response to shifting winds and changes in society. They are neither continuous nor cumulative in following a coherent, thoughtful direction. In the 1980s new policies on work experience and computer education were good examples. The former appeared in response to calls to do something for unemployed young; the latter appeared in response to calls for educating for the year 2001. No one asked whether these policies might simply be smokescreens for the redeployment of capital or the restructuring of the New Zealand economy and the welfare state.

In that same period the kind of research supported by the Department clearly indicated positivistic tendencies (Adams, 1985): it was clearly designed at improving the system and not at challenging its basic assumptions and strategies. Longstanding policy aims, such as the promotion of "equality of opportunity," were never investigated critically until the Lauder, et al. research of 1984. Illich's claims about the ways in which schools manipulated the young were "poo-hooed" by the Department of Education (DE, 1974). Yet eventually, and somewhat ironically, Beeby himself was to refer to equality of opportunity as a "myth" (Beeby, 1986a)!

As has been noted above, in a widely disseminated article (*This Side of Paradigm* [Renwick, 1986]) – Renwick tries to give to the notion of educational research a set of characteristics that separate educational research from other activities, including what he refers to as research *in* education. Educational research should be concerned with "learning and teaching in the institutional or organisational settings", where "the essential function... is to help learners and teachers by providing evidence that will assist them, and others, in the evaluation of their educational aims and the usefulness of various means of achieving them." What should be noted here is the tendency to direct attention away from larger structures and processes, toward individual teachers and learners; the givenness of the context of teacher and learner; the implicit priority ascribed thereby to psychological research into teaching and learning *processes*; the unlikelihood of economic and political factors entering the discussion of educational aims and means; and, finally (though Renwick is less clear on this issue) a separation of ends and means for teachers and learners.

Beeby, the first director of NZCER, wrote (1935, pp. 9-10): "Nor will much time or money be spent on the standardisation of tests beyond that of a simple intelligence test the results of which will be needed in a wide variety of researches". He was referring to the Otis Test which, along with the Stanford Binet test were the only international psychometric tests available in New Zealand. A third New Zealand test (TOSCA) was later to be developed by NZCER as it entered the testing industry and market. Progressive movements in education had been a strange mixture of child-centred romantics and tough-minded and postivistically inclined scientific empiricists (McKenzie, 1988, p. 76). Beeby and NZCER seemed to resist this second strain, though research into testing played some part in the activities of NZCER during the 1940s (Moss, 1988, p. 61). But the Universities were also involved in testing – foe example, Victoria was standardising an oral reading test, and Auckland, along with staff at Victoria and Canterbury, was standardising *The Stanford Binet Test of Intelligence.*

Yet NZCER seemed reluctant to involve itself in testing in the first thirty years of its existence. This was to change, and for three main reasons: First there were changes in membership of NZCER's Council (Moss, 1988, p. 65). Second, from 1954-55 onwards, Annual Reports of NZCER increasingly expressed concerns about its financial situation and becoming dependent upon Government funding. Finally there were dramatically increasing demands by schools for this kind of material from the late 1950s onwards. Now testing is part of the core business of public education.

This general framework did little to remedy the plight of the Maori, arguably the most researched international indigenous community. Little had been done to close widening gaps between the educational achievement of Maori and pakeha. But this research was in the main done by pakeha researchers and involved Western and positivistic methodologies. A major report in 1960 by Don Hunn warned New Zealand of these problems and by the 1980s enough Maori academics and researchers were surfacing to set different research agendas and to define research issues differently. If Maori were seen earlier as *the* problem, the 1980s and 1990s saw a move away from simplistic victim blaming to a belief in education (including educational research) *by* Maori, *for* Maori, and *in* Maori. While good research was being done, supporting recommendations that challenged the institutionalised and bureaucratic structures in which Maori were underachieving, little happened. This in spite of a report in 1986 by the Treaty of Waitangi Tribunal that the education system had failed Maori. In some cases such research was attacked methodologically and buried (for an example see Marshall & Peters, 1995).

At least two positive trends in this second period must be noted. First, as noted, there was an expansion of Departments of Education within the universities to include scholars and researchers from wider theoretical backgrounds, which produced research that was more critical of systems and institutions. Second, since the 1960s, counselling (as opposed to vocational guidance) was introduced into schools and educational programmes for training counsellors into universities. Counselling is of course a contested theoretical domain and no one theory is dominant in counselling practice (Besley, 2001).

Post-1988: The March of Performativity

The structural changes which have taken place in New Zealand since the mid 1980s, and in education since 1988, are usually described as *neoliberal*, sometimes by the slightly wider concept of *new right*. New right ideology is made up of two major elements: a neoliberal element, which is committed to the free market and to the substitution of market-like arrangements for the state, including the application of business management structures to all institutions, including education; and, a neo-conservative element, which is committed to fundamentalist and conservative moral values. These elements are united by the belief that state intervention to promote egalitarian social goals has been responsible for the present economic decline, and has represented a violation of individual rights and initiative. From this combined view, the new right believes that equality and freedom are incompatible and that freedom construed in individual and negative terms (i.e., freedom from intervention) is indispensable for economic vitality and well-being. Such views privilege the market as an institution above all others, and promote market values over other values (see further Peters, Marshall & Massey, 1994).

Since 1998 we can notice moves in education to a *Ministry* of education and the off-loading of resource and support activities, including curriculum writing, to contracted organisations and individuals. Universities, which had previously operated under separate Acts of parliament, were brought under the control of the Ministry of Education and were placed in *competition* with each other and with tertiary providers who began to offer degrees under the New Zealand Qualifications Authority. For example, there has been a fourfold increase in the numbers of providers of qualifications in pre-service education of teachers. In 1999 there were moves by the Government and the Ministries of Education, Science and Technology to align education and research toward the "knowledge economy" and the "knowledge society" (see the special issue of *Access, 19*(2), 2000).

The underlying assumptions of these new education priotities can be gauged by considering changes in the research folio in education – in particular what kinds of research have been supported and funded. In what follows we will consider research and theory in education by examining the four institutions who support research in education, including university research: NZCER; Ministry of Research Science and Technology, including the Marsden Fund; the Ministry of Education; and Research in Tertiary Institutions. Their statements of intent about research and about which research programmes will receive support from Ministries and Government agencies are extremely revealing, reinforcing the charge of performativity.

New Zealand Council for Educational Research (NZCER)

NZCER enjoyed a very good relationship with the first Minister of Education of the 4th Labour government (1984-1990), Russell Marshall, gathering research on equity and equality for Marshall's *Curriculum Review*, especially in the areas of Maori and Pacific Island, Women, Special Education Services (including both disability and giftedness). There was a strong culture of evaluation at NZCER (later to become a celebrated notion of neo-liberal policy). At the end of the 1980s NZCER was also producing some research projects in history, philosophy, sociology and critical policy analysis, and they spent a great deal of effort in building links with several Pacific Nations, particularly the Solomon Islands and Tonga. In addition to the testing business discussed above they also had a strong record of producing and publishing teacher resource materials, which contributed to NZCER's financial independence.

Prime Minister David Lange, dissatisfied with the liberal tone of Marshall's 1987 *Curriculum Review*, took over the portfolio of Minister of Education in 1989. Lange initiated a series of changes which cut funding to NZCER and altered the Act under which NZCER operated. In Lyotard's terminology the formerly independent NZCER was, like public education, becoming subsumed under the demands of efficiency and performativity, like the Universities.

First, the government commissioned an external review of NZCER in line with the general reforms of educational administration. The terms of reference mentioned organisational structure; funding; relationships to the Minstry of Education and the Education Review Office; and relationships to The Ministry of Research, Science and Education (MoRST) and to other research institutions and activities, including Universities.

But this review somewhat surprisingly, was favourable to NZCER, insisting that NZCER be consistently funded, and offering only relatively minor suggestions for change. Lange's concerns revolved around the organisation being efficient and well co-ordinated with the new government agencies, ensuring that educational research in New Zealand would be carried out as efficiently as possible and in a coordinated manner (Lange, *NZCER Newsletter*, 1989).

On January 26 1990, Lange made a number of changes to the relationship of NZCER and the government, including:

a. a set of changes to the NZCER Act (1972), to remedy the purported disestablishment of some educational administrative bodies and to establish several new agencies;
b. a review of staffing and publication policies, in a call for efficiency and better use of resources, which entailed limiting the number of research themes; and,
c. a reduction in the core grant over three years (*NZCER Newsletter*, 1991).

The research activity of NZCER shows a marked change post-1990 and it is clear that the breadth and depth of NZCER's research has been hampered by the implementation of these neoliberal policies and the reduction of government funding.

Ministry of Science, Research and Technology (MoRST)

MoRST, through the Foundation of Research, Science and Technology (FoRST), began to finance Public Good Science from 1991. Crown Research Institutes, Universities, and other Tertiary Institutions must pay into this fund and then compete for contestable research grants. FoRST argued that New Zealand needed to position itself to develop a sustainable, competitive advantage in the new global economy. This required a culture of fostering innovations that could be commercialised and used; a change "from negotiating portfolios of research with providers to negotiating portfolios of research based upon the achievement of a balanced set of outcomes designed to achieve social and environmental benefits as well as economic outcomes". FoRST states clearly that investments in research must develop partnerships that increase investment, that are value added, that respond to emerging sectors and opportunities, and that base investments on research strategies developed with stakeholders rather than "individual" disinterested or "pure" research providers.

It is quite clear that FoRST, as "an intelligent investor" in research, expects research to move toward "new strategic outcome-based portfolios". They believe that social science research will both increase wealth and close social gaps. But their approach is immersed in the language and associated practices of performativity, and cannot succeed. It will not be the instigators or providers of research who will define the gaps to be closed, or the type of research methodology, but the stakeholders, presumably the government. It is not at all clear that the *recipients* of such gap-closing research will be conceived as stakeholders.

Marsden Fund

This is a new source of funding for Public Good Research administered by The Royal Society of New Zealand for the Ministry of Research, Science and Technology. It is not subject to quite the same social and economic criteria as the Public Good Science Fund, as it is directed at basic research and is designed to be investigator-driven. The latter point is important in light of the statement quoted above that FoRST was not to be an allocator of funds. The social sciences are one of eight designated areas and some interesting grants have been made in that area, which do not obviously fall into research directed at performativity. Certainly some of the contracted researchers would not see their research in these ways.

Educational Research in the Ministry of Education

After1998 we can note the formation of a new sub-division of Demographic and Statistical Analysis, within the Research and Statistics Division, massive increases in funding within the Ministry for "research", and a marked shift in the direction of that research, which was to be prioritised into areas before funds would be allocated by the Minister of Education.

In 1982-84 there was a strong emphasis on research in the area of curriculum. By 1988-1990 research projects in the area of curriculum had more than doubled – no doubt preparing for the new review of Curriculum (MoE, 1993) – and the investment in such research had risen almost eight-fold. Evaluation research changed from evaluating practices of education to identifying performance indicators for resource allocation. Separate studies on management also increased, again stressing demands for efficiency, i.e., performativity.

Other research changes included increases in research activity and funding for early childhood and special needs. Early childhood has benefited from a long term evaluative project between 1991 and 1997, along with a number of other studies. Special needs research has increased considerably post 1994 (no doubt in preparation for mainstreaming). Research in Maori Education has also gradually increased as has research in the area of Pacific Island education. The level of qualitative and quantitative studies has increased, with better use of sociology, while other theoretical disciplines such as philosophy and history have been substantially ignored. Research into literacy and technology increased after 1994, with the advent of the Technology Curriculum document in 1995.

Research in Tertiary Institutions

Whilst the Universities are contributing to Public Good Science they still offer traditional research support to staff for research projects, i.e., for instigator research. But external research contracts have become an important aspect of Schools (and Departments) of Education's business, in both number and value. Many academics are in a position to buy their teaching time "out" in order to engage, almost full time, in research. Much of that research is directed toward performative (and positivistic) ends. Other tertiary institutions are obtaining research and consultancy contracts in areas where their expertise is pertinent – e.g., Colleges of Education in curriculum matters, and in advising Pacific Islands nations on pre-Service education of teachers.

The problem with this approach is that it compromises the availability to students of teachers whose teaching is based upon "top" research, as some academics are now almost exclusively involved in external research projects. This of course undercuts the Universities' traditional claim that their teaching is based upon research. Once the "true" costs of research are known it could even be possible to hive off research entirely from teaching and, more disastrously, to locate research in separate "Crown Institutes of Research". Teaching might then be conducted in the downgraded and much cheaper "universities" by those much less involved with research.

Conclusion

Over the course of the narrative provided here, we have tried to show that a positivistic element in educational research, which has always existed, has more recently been harnessed and intensified as education, its institutions and curricula, and its theory and research, have been subsumed under Lyotard's notion of performativity. Apparently neutral and even potentially salutary criteria such as efficiency, practical usefulness, and service to constituencies have been interpreted and applied in ways that have driven the content and methods of research into particular tracks and have silenced or suppressed important perspectives on educational policies, practices, and institutions.

References

Adams, R.S. (1985). Educational Research in New Zealand. In J. Nisket (Ed.), (1985), *World yearbook of education 1985: Research policy and practice.* London/New York: Kogan, Page and Nicholls.

Beeby, C. (1935). *Educational research in New Zealand* (NZCER Educational Research Series, No.1). Wellington: NZCER.

Beeby, C. (1986). The place of myth in educational change. *New Zealand Listener,* 8 November.

Besley, T. (2001). *Self, identity, adolescence and the professionalism of school counselling in New Zealand: Some Foucauldean perspectives,* Ph.D Thesis, University of Auckland.

Butcher, A.G. (1930). *Education in New Zealand: An historical survey of educational progress amongst the Europeans and the Maoris since 1878.* Dunedin: Coulls Somerville.

Department of Education (DE). (1974). *Teaching and learning* (Vol. 2). Educational Development Conference, Wellington: Government Printer.

Hearnshaw, L.S. (1965). *Psychology in New Zealand.* Quoted in R. St George (Ed.), (1979), *The beginning of psychology in New Zealand: A collection of historical documents and recollections* (Delta Research Monograph No. 2). Palmerston North: Massey University.

Lauder, H., Hughes, D., & Taberner, S. (1984). Education, class and inequality (University of Canterbury Monograph). Reprinted in *Delta, 36,* 30-37, 1985.

McCulloch, G.J. (1986). *Education in the forming of New Zealand Society* (Monograph No. 1). Palmerston North: NZCER.

McKenzie, D. (1988). Little and lightly: The New Zealand Department of Education and Mental Testing 1920-1930. In Olssen (Ed.), *Mental testing in New Zealand. Critical and oppositional perspectives* (pp.76-89). Dunedin, N.Z., University of Otago Press.

Marshall, J. D. (1987). *Positivism or pragmatism: Philosophy of education in New Zealand* (Monograph No. 2). Palmerston North: NZCER.

Marshall, J.D., & Peters, M.A. (1995). The governance of educational research. *The Australian Educational Researcher, 22,* 107-120.

Ministry of Education (MoE). (1987). *Administering for excellence* (known as the Picot Report), Wellington: Department of Education.

Ministry of Education (MoE). (1993). *The New Zealand curriculum framework.* Wellington: Print Media.

Ministry of Education (MoE). (1995). *Technology in the New Zealand curriculum.* Wellington: Print Media.

Moss, L. (1988). The role of the NZCER in mental testing. In Olssen (Ed.), *Mental testing in New Zealand. Critical and oppositional perspectives* (pp. 60-75). Dunedin, N.Z., University of Otago Press.

Peters, M.A, Marshall, J.D, & Massey, L. (1994). Recent educational reforms in Aotearoa. In E. Coxon, K. Jenkins, J. Marshall, & L. Massey (Eds.), *The politics of learning and teaching in Aotearoa/New Zealand*. Palmerston North: Dunmore Press.

Peters, M.A., Marshall, J.D., & Fitzsimons, P. (1999). Poststructuralism and curriculum theory: Neo-liberalism, the information economy and cultural authority. *Journal of Curriculum Theorising, 15*, 111-130.

Renwick, W.L. (1986). This side of paradigm. In *Moving targets: Six essays on educational policy*. Wellington: NZCER.

Simon, J. (2000). Historical perspectives on education policy in New Zealand. In J.D. Marshall, E. Coxon, K. Jenkins, & A. Jones (Eds.), *Politics, policy, pedagogy: Education in Aotearoa/New Zealand*. Palmerston North: Dunmore Press.

II. EDUCATIONAL RESEARCH AS A DISCURSIVE PRACTICE
(Section Editor Thomas Popkewitz)

JOURNALS AND THE MAKING OF EXPERTS AND EDUCATIONAL KNOWLEDGE
Exploring a Portuguese Pedagogical Journal (1921-1932)

Luís Miguel Carvalho

This article addresses the role of pedagogical journals as infrastructures for the circulation and legitimisation of educational knowledge. My focus here is on the international educational models referenced in a Portuguese pedagogical journal, the *Revista Escolar*, published at a time of differentiation and legitimisation of educational experts and their "specialised" knowledge in Portugal (see Nóvoa, 1998).

My starting point is the notion that journals - through affiliations, preferences and affinities that their texts establish with others - constitute important vehicles for the regulation of valuable knowledge and for the social affirmation of experts (see Schriewer & Keiner, 1992, Schriewer, 1998). In this paper, I give particular attention to the selective mobilisation of foreign educational models (countries, authors, books, and educational organisations), within a framework of analysis committed to the articulation of the processes of diffusion and reception of educational knowledge (Schriewer, 2000; Nóvoa, 2000, see also Carvalho, 2000). Thus, I will therefore favour the reasoning that leads, using the terminology of Tom Popkewitz (2000), to the *multiple and multidirectional ties* of ideas (see also Nóvoa, Carvalho, Correia, Ó., & Madeira, 2002).

I will start the paper by bringing together the new institutionalist perspective on "world culture" (Boli & Thomas, 1999) and the notion of "discourse structuration" (Wagner & Wittrock, 1990). My interest here is to emphasise the overlapping nature of educational knowledge circulation, which combines transnational and national scripts, as well as institutional and strategic layers of social life. Drawing on the previous discussion, in the second and main section of the article I develop an analysis of the Portuguese will emphasise the representation of the pedagogical journal as a space for the conveyance of education modernisation models (and for a modality of thinking the national through the mobilisation of foreign pedagogical experiences). I will also take into account the shaping of power relations between, on one hand, university professors and school inspectors (the organisers of the journal and the more "prolific" authors of the main articles of the *Revista Escolar*), and on the other hand, primary school teachers (the target population of the journal).

Circulation of Models within Overlapping Contexts

According the new-institutionalists, the word-wide isomorphic spread of mass schooling – both as an organisational form and as an ideology – is understood as a theorised change, supported by expert knowledge producing agencies:

> *Long before the development of the Unesco and worldwide conferences as explicit organisational carriers of world models of education, international definitions of educational reality and norm setting were well underway. (...) These standards operate in non-hierarchical but nonetheless influential lateral fashion, providing the bases for structural conformity and organisational isomorphism.* (Ramirez & Ventresca, 1992, pp. 52-53)

Within their framework, a nodal point of the argument is the notion of a (educational) transnational "level of culture and organisation formation that operates as a constitutive and directive environment" for collective and individual actors (Boli & Thomas, 1999, p. 3). This perspective does not imply, however, either the idea of a (over) determination of national policies or cultures by the "world culture", or the "mechanical recitation of highly specified scripts" (op. cit., p. 18). Invoking Ann Swidler (1986), Boli Thomas (1999, p. 18) recognise that actors "actively draw on, select from, and modify" those scripts. Moreover, they add that such enactment, in a local or specific context, is also a component of the elaboration, modification and transformation of the transnational frames.

Consequently, analysis of educational models that circulate in the pedagogical press must be aware that such presence of external references also depends on the national cultural realm and the national agencies involved in the structuration of educational knowledge. The affairs of the reception context largely participate in the determination of what can (locally) be "imported" (see Bourdieu, 2002 [1990] Espagne, 1999). The notion of "discourse structuration", suggested by Wittrock and Wagner (1990), in their analysis of the "State-social science(s)" relationships and developments, is particularly interesting for the consideration of the "import" of educational models:

> *The emergence and evolution of social sciences have critically depended on their ability to find an epistemic grounding on important intellectual traditions; to find ways to institutionalise and reproduce their particular forms of discourse in knowledge-producing institutions; to establish some kind of linkage to politi-*

> cal-administrative institutions; and to be able to draw on some kind of discursive affinity with socially significant broad policy traditions (...). (op. cit., p. 117)

The formation of educational knowledge and experts must then be analysed by taking into consideration the ability of their actors – those who act towards the differentiation of a field of educational knowledge – to "achieve a minimum of intellectual, institutional, political-administrative, and societal legitimacy" (op. cit., p.117). Popkewitz' analysis of the rising of educational psychology in the US, in the early 20th century, clearly shows the achievement of societal and political-administrative legitimacy. Psychology became the first science in the pedagogical discourse, owing to the technologies of assessment of attitudes and skills needed for social integration of individuals – instruments able to function on a micro and macro scale – complemented by other "pedagogical" technologies that accommodated the imaginary of progress engendered from the effort of autonomous and self-disciplined individuals. In short, psychology became the councillor and framework of school reforms, receiving political-administrative institutional legitimacy, but also unfurled an agenda and a production corresponding to the dominant discourses on society, capturing the 'societal' legitimacy (see Popkewitz, 1991). The accounts of Schriewer Keiner (1992) and Schriewer (1998) concerning the remarkably different destinies of educational science in France and Germany, are also powerful illustrations of the relationships between the legitimisation processes and the configuration and content of disciplines. Those differences – in Germany, a concentric communicational space, the intradisciplinary coherence, the presence of a tradition of thought on education, and in France, a disperse communicational space, the pluraldisciplinary overture, the centrality of contemporary theorisation – are understandable *vis-à-vis* diverse intellectual affiliations (philosophy versus human and social sciences) and contrasting (time and setting) trajectories in the university field.

A look at the (selective) circulation of educational models in the Portuguese period attempts, therefore, to bring together the reason for the presence of (certain) discourses and transnational organisation with the characteristics of the discourses and national agencies implied in the educational sector. In addition to the two great axes of legitimisation and differentiation of a disciplinary scientific terrain proposed by Wagner and Wittrock (the internal, including intellectual traditions and organisations of production of knowledge, and the external, including political discourses about society and administrative political organisations), one can propose a third: that which includes the rules of the *worldwide culture of education* (i.e., the generation of models of thinking and acting in education) and the transnational organisations that produce and diffuse them (i.e., the making and burgeoning of infrastructures, networks of knowledge and specialists).

The relations established between those that, on a national level, make themselves specialists and local agencies, constitute social conditions of production and legitimisation of the theorising on education and of the differentiation of a field of specialists who are politically more autonomous and symbolically more valuable. Thus, the (selected) references that circulate in the educational journals have to be seen as part of and the result of global-regional power relations (see Popkewitz, 2000). The references to educational models (nations, authors, organisations, books, and so on) in the journals have to be seen as part (both "effect" and "cause") of a wider and multidirectional social process of production of authorised and authoritative "texts-experts".

The Promises of the Journal: Modernising Education" and "Cultivating Teachers"

Revista Escolar was an important Portuguese pedagogical journal, with a life cycle of almost fifteen years. Between 1921 and 1925, under the management of three school inspectors, the agenda of the journal had mainly addressed themes related to educational policy – the expansion of primary education and primary teachers' careers and status. Between 1925 and 1928, under the orientation of a university professor and New Education advocate (Faria de Vasconcelos), the journal extended its attention to the rest of the modalities of school education and accentuated the scientific and pedagogical hallmark. Between 1928 and 1931, this facet persisted under the stewardship of another teacher trainer and university professor. Finally, in the last period and under the guidance of one of its founders, the journal divided itself between the ideas of New Education, through articles and foreign news, and the diffusion of school legislation (see Nóvoa, 1993).

Despite the outlined differences, the journal's guiding ideas – as stated in the Editorial themes marking the start of the first three phases described above - remained constant. Indeed, the editorials recurrently represent the journal as a space for the modernisation of Portuguese school education through the reception and diffusion of (foreign) specialised pedagogical knowledge: the Revista intends to *"bring readers up to date with the advance of the school in the cultured world, and bring the scientific issue to the fore"* (1921), to keep them *"informed of the shifts in the huge movement of pedagogical ideas and experiences that are circulating around the world"* (1925), and to be *"a modern pedagogical journal, which is not a poor relation in comparison with our foreign counterparts"* (1928). Parallelly, the Editorials repeatedly advocate the journal commitment in shaping the field of pedagogical knowledge and its agents: the Revista Escolar aims to *"bring about a more perfect preparation of the teaching body"* (1921), to *"provide an environment of general pedagogical culture common to the teaching body of the different modalities of national education"* (1925), and to *"bring to light"* a Portuguese *"educational school of thought (...), represented by a notable elite of young minds, and occasional elderly individuals with youthful souls"* (1928).

Even whilst penned by various hands, the purposes of the Revista Escolar unite a set of logics about specialised pedagogical knowledge and its specialists. I discuss these common ties below: one deals with the innovative experience of countries considered modern, and another the regulation of relations between an elite and the practising mass – the teachers.

Keeping rack with Progress

A brief examination of the editorials shows the recurring presence of the representation of the journal as a place for the reception and diffusion of pedagogical modernisation models, but also the preference for thinking of what is national through the mobilisation of foreign pedagogical experiences. These experiences were located in a "cultivated, moving, modern and positive" world. This mobilisation of the foreign was also one of the criteria that defined the authority of the journal and the specialist-discourses that it put into circulation: *we will attempt to be a modern pedagogical journal, which is not a poor relation in comparison with our foreign counterparts*, reads one of the cited editorials.

In the pages of the journal, the "positive" world legitimised the autochthonous claims relating to reform of ideas and practices. The pedagogical modernisation models appear in the *Revista Escolar* in various forms. They appear as references in the main articles of the journal – those with the right to appear in the summary of the journal, with an identified author and an autonomous title. In addition, they appear in translations of foreign texts, in critiques, and in the in the news section.

The pages of the *Revista Escolar* sought to be in accordance with movements considered to be in the forefront of "pedagogical innovation," which would install the writers and its readers into a world of pedagogical merit and comparison between nations. Obviously the journals were not the only mechanism for this circulation and comparison (other channels functioned, such as translations of works or funded study visits abroad, or visits and conferences from foreigner thinkers). However – and this is my point here – the journal stands for a way of thinking the reality that obliged the reading of the national in a relation of dependence with a "greater other". Thus, the journal presents itself as a "spokesman" of the pedagogical innovation as well as a mediator between the foreign progress and the (desired) national renewal. But, in so doing, it also constituted a space of selection, a central component of the social conditions of the circulation of ideas (see Bourdieu, 2002 [1990]).

Observation of the processes of circulation of the educational models cannot be dissociated from the *circumstances of the context of reception*, which largely involved the determination of what can be *imported*, or, possibly, *reactivated* (Espagne, 1999, p. 23). As such, the presence of the "cultured and modern world" should, in part, be attributed to a Portuguese intellectual-political environment, which from the middle of the 19th century onwards showed itself receptive to the adoption of outside models – calling for the *Europisation* of the nation – and advocating the transfer of certain foreign pedagogical models as the solution for "national regeneration."

So what countries were looked at and talked about in the *Revista Escolar*? In *ranking* the most cited countries (see 1), the Eurocentric character of referencing is evident (76% of all references), and the centrality of the powerful European and World States is unquestionable.

Table 1. *Countries Referenced in the Articles (1921-1932)*

Country	f.	%	Cumulated %
France	117	14	14
Germany	94	11	25
United States	77	9	34
England	67	8	42
Belgium	64	8	50
Switzerland	61	7	57
Spain	57	7	64
Italy	42	5	69
Others [48]	253	31	100

The frequent presence of references to Belgium and Switzerland is probably best explained by the existence, in both countries, of poles of production and diffusion of discourses about scientific approaches to education related to the New Education movement. This mark is clearly visible when observing the organisations cited therein. Regarding this indicator, the relevance of the *Institut des Sciences de l'Éducation – Jean Jacques Rousseau* (1912) stands out, the relevance of which increases if we also consider references made to other organisations – some created under its aegis, as well as others whose creation was connected with some of its members. The journals illustrate the well-known centrality of this organisation in the international scientific and professional network that emerged at the end of the 19th century (see Hofstetter & Schneuwly, 1999).

Another space for selection – as well as for the journal procession and affiliation with New Education – is the reference to authors. In *the Revista Escolar*, in tandem with the greater frequency of references to Portuguese and French authors, there is a greater concentration of references to Belgian and Swiss authors (see 2 and 3).

Table 2. *Authors by Nationality and "sum of the references to authors by natioality / number of authors referenced by nationality" Ratio (1921-1932)*

Nationality	Number of authors referenced (a)	%	Number of references /(a)
Portugal	181	30	2.7
France	144	23	3.1
Germany	76	12	3.4
Switzerland	25	4	**12.1**
Belgium	13	2	**19.0**
Total	613	100	3.8

Table 3. *CAuthorsReferenced in More Then 20 Articles (1921-1932)*

Author	Number of articles
Decroly	56
Montessori	37
Rousseau	35
Ferrière	30
Pestalozzi	30
Claparède	29
Froebel	20
Faria de Vasconcelos	20

Here (and again), it is not the country or the model society that counts. What carries weight are the names (the model authors), either contemporary, such as Decroly, Montessori, Ferrière, Claparède, Vasconcelos, or the "classics", such as Rousseau, Froebel, and Pestalozzi. Concomitantly, what carries weight is the international educational community – the New Education (and their authors).

The "Cream-Mass" Relationship

The prominent presence of Decroly and Montessori, authors who established themselves by introducing bridges between "scientific knowledge" and "practices", is somewhat borne out with the regard to the books most frequently referenced in the Revista Escolar, either about teaching methods or related to the teaching of reading. The same trend can be inferred from the journal, marked by the predominance of articles whose main themes include teaching methods, the teaching of reading, or "active school" (see Table 4).

Table 4. *Articles by Keywords (freq. more then 20) (1921-1932)*

Descriptors: keywords	Number of articles	%
Teaching methods	109	20
Active School	42	8
Reading (Teaching of)	39	7
New Education	32	6
Education and Social Development	31	6

The salience of these authors and themes makes us move to a closer analysis of the type of educational knowledge put into circulation in the journal. It was a knowledge that proposed to mediate scientific production and pedagogical practice. Thus, the predominance of methodological reason runs parallel with the purposes of guiding teachers to those declarative and practical repertoires. Having arrived at this point, we have to turn our attention to the relationship between the character of the journal and the authors of its articles.

The *Revista Escolar* was not an infrastructure of an already established national scientific field. Rather it was an infrastructure of a field still in formation, heterogeneous and porous. Geared chiefly towards primary teachers – its largest body of subscribers – and inspectors, the journal's authors were predominantly inspectors, teacher trainers, and/or university professors (see Table 5).

Table 5. *Authors of Main Articles, by Occupation (1921-1932)*

Occupation	Number of articles	%
Inspector	135	42
University professor and/or teachertrainer	84	26
Primary teacher	66	21
Others	36	11
Total of classified authors	321	100

Table 6. *Number of Articles by Author (identified by occupation), Between 1921 and 1932 (authors with 10 or more main articles published*

Occupation	Year	21	22	23	24	25	26	27	28	29	30	31	32	T
School Inspector		8	3	7	5	5	2							30
School Inspector		1	6	2	1		1	1						11
School Inspector		3	1	2	2		2							10
School Inspector			3	1	5							1	1	11
School Inspector		3	1	3			1	2					1	11
School Inspector		2	2	3	1	2	2	2	1	1	4	2	2	24
University professor					1	1		6	1	4	6		1	20
University professor					1	7	1	1	3	1	4	1		19
Teacher Trainer			1		1				1	1		1	5	10

However, throughout the lifespan of the journal (see Table 6), one can detect a progressive and gradual change in the makeup of the collaborators that contributed the main articles (that is, a shift in those who wrote the longest articles, occupying the first pages of the journal, and those who only had the right to a summary with a register of the title and author). The reduction in the number of inspectors and primary teachers penning writing articles, particularily from 1926 onwards increases proportionately the contributions from university professors and teacher trainers as contributors.

What united the inspectors and the teacher trainers? In addition to proximity in ideology, at least educationally, was their "social place" as teachers.

It is important to remember the role that teacher training schools, and the development of applied sciences and methodological reason played in mediating – or acting as a bridge between (and to) the sciences and pedagogical practices during this era (see Nóvoa, 1998). The effect of this mediation, by those who presented themselves as specialists in the application of the "mother sciences" to the educational universe, was to enable the "scientification" of the practices and the professionalising of the educational actors.

We return briefly to the editorials of the *Revista Escolar*. In affirming itself as a *journal of the inspection and teaching body* and in advocating for the creation of a *general cultural and common pedagogical environment for the teaching body*, the journal makes a distinction between the elite (who wrote in the Journal) and the mass (readership) of the community. This means that the journals, in addition to being the bearers of ideas signalling a particular pedagogical orientation, also defined their own place, and that of their texts' authors and the readers,-- simultaneously creating a particular community through linking a pedagogical body of knowledge and professional educators.

The journal attributed a *position* for itself; it was responsible for putting a calculated knowledge into circulation and generating a common cultural basis for the teaching body, but it also had to regulate and filter this imparting of ideas. This selection could occur in the name of an issue of a scientific nature, the virtuousness of the contributors, the commitment to the reform of mentalities and practices, the quality and rigour of the thinking, criticism, and the information diffused. We are not interested in discussing it here, but rather stressing the right of the journal to authorise, and as such, to determine the discourses and which writers are praiseworthy or valid.

The journal was therefore a space for the establishment of the hierarchy of knowledge and people; it exercised an order on both through an arbitrary register of assessment. The texts published are a mixture of technical work and political work, insofar as their senses and the value attributed to them are not independent from a set of conditions and strategies that make them legible and valuable. The acceptance of these experts would depend upon their capacity to produce a discourse for themselves and more important perhaps, the ability to transform these discourses again for possible consumption by laypersons. Because these new experts established a legitimacy for themselves, they could now create a discourse through which the *interessement and enrolment* (Callon, 1986) of teachers could be achieved. For these reasons the journal had a dual purpose and emerges as a *boundary object* (Leigh Star & Griesemer, 1999), around which cooperation and communication between different social worlds is fostered.

Hence, the models present in the pedagogical journals were "objects-products" of *multidirectional ties of ideas* (Popkewitz, 2000), and were equally "objects-products" of a rising community of experts and the power relations through which it was constructed.

References

Boli, J., & Thomas, G. (1999). Introduction *and* INGOs and the organisation of world culture. In J. Boli & G. Thomas (Eds.), *Constructing world culture* (pp. 1-10; 13-48). Stanford: Stanford University Press.

Bourdieu, P. (2002 [1990]). Les conditions sociales de la circulation internationale des idées. *Actes de la Recherche en Sciences Sociales, 145,* 3-8.

Callon, M. (1986). Some elements of a sociology of translation. In J. Law (Ed.), *Power, action and belief* (pp. 196-233). London: Routledge & Kegan Paul.

Carvalho, L. M. (2000). *Nós Através da Escrita: revistas, especialistas e conhecimento pedagógico (1920-1936)*. Lisboa: Educa.
Carvalho, L. M., & Cordeiro, J. (2002). *Brasil – Portugal nos circuitos do discurso pedagógico espacializado*. Lisboa: Educa.
Espagne, M. (1999). *Les transferts culturels franco-allemands*. Paris: Presses Universitaires de France.
Hofstetter, R., & Schneuwly, B. (1999). L'avènement d'un nouveau champ disciplinaire: ressorts de l'universitarisation des sciences de l'éducation à Genève, 1890-1930. In R. Hofstetter & B. Schneuwly (Eds.), *Le pari des sciences de l'education* (pp. 79-116). Bruxelles: De Boeck Université.
Leigh Star, S., & Griesemer, J. (1999 [1989]). Institutional ecology, "translation", and boundary objects. In M. Biagiolli (Ed.), *The science studies reader* (pp. 505-524). New York: Routledge.
Nóvoa, A. (dir.) (1993). *Imprensa de educação e ensino – Repertório analítico (séculos XIX-XX)*. Lisboa: IIE.
Nóvoa, A.(1998). *Histoire & comparaison*. Lisboa: Educa.
Nóvoa, A. (2000). Tempos da escola no espaço Portugal-Brasil-Moçambique. In A. Nóvoa & J. Schriewer (Eds.), *A difusão mundial da escola* (pp. 121-142). Lisboa: Educa.
Nóvoa, A., Carvalho, L. M., Correia, A., Madeira, A., & Ó, J. (2002). Flows of educational knowledge: The time-space of Portuguese-speaking countries. In M. Caruso & H.-E. Tenorth (Eds.), *Internationalisation: Comparing educational systems and semantics* (pp. 211-247). Frankfurt am Main: Peter Lang.
Popkewitz, T. (1991). *A political sociology of educational reform*. New York: Teachers College Press.
Popkewitz, T. (2000). Globalisation/regionalisation, knowledge and the restructuring of education. In T. S. Popkewitz (Ed.), *Educational knowledge* (pp. 3-27). Albany: State University of New York.
Ramirez, F. & Ventresca, M. (1992). Building the institution of mass schooling. In B. Fuller & R. Rubinson (Eds.), *The political construction of education* (pp. 47-59). New York: Praeger.
Schriewer, J. (1998). Études pluridisciplinaires et réflexions philosophiques: la structuration du discours pédagogique en France et en Allemagne. *Paedagogica Historica*, Supplementary Series, Vol. 3, pp. 57-84.
Schriewer, J. (2000). World-system and interrelationship-networks. In T. S. Popkewitz (Ed.), *Educational knowledge* (pp. 305-342). Albany: State University of New York.
Schriewer, J., & Keiner, E. (1992). Communication patterns and intellectual traditions in educational sciences: France and Germany. *Comparative Education Review*, 36 (1), 25-51.
Swidler, A. 1986. Culture in action. *American Sociological Review*, 51, 273-286.
Wittrock, B., & Wagner, P. (1990.) Social science and state developments. In S. Brooks & A.-G. Gagnon (Eds.), *Social scientists, policy, and the state* (pp. 113-137). New York: Praeger.

FROM SCHOOLS OF THINKING TO GENRES OF WRITING. NEW ROLES FOR PHILOSOPHY OF EDUCATION

Bas Levering

The discipline of education at universities in the Netherlands is a subdivision of the faculty social sciences. "Education" here means "upbringing" in the broadest sense and is not limited to what is supposed to take place in schools. The strongest sub-discipline in education is special education. Next to so-called fundamental research which is linked to developmental psychological research, much research is carried out to develop support programmes for parents who, supposedly, do not succeed in their educational tasks on their own. Teacher education is not taught at universities but in special institutes covering elementary and secondary education. Research on school reform at universities went through a considerable reduction of staff and research during recent years.

We need this information to be able to sketch a clear picture of the position of philosophy of education among the Dutch educational sciences. Philosophy of education is not a sub-discipline of philosophy but is part of the discipline of education as a social science. To understand its position we need to know the history of the German *Geisteswissenschaften*. The *Geisteswissenschaften* or human sciences are distinguished from the natural sciences on ontological and methodological grounds. The distinction, introduced by the German philosopher Wilhelm Dilthey (1833-1911), is connected to the distinction *Erklären und Verstehen* (Explanation and understanding). In terms of research the distinction is connected to the distinction between quantitative and qualitative research. Philosophy of education, from the beginnings of the last century is the cradle of qualitative research in the Netherlands, was originally not a sub-discipline of its own. But education as subject matter – in the broad sense – raised genuine philosophical questions, not only ontological and methodological questions, but also important anthropological and ethical questions.

At this point we need to introduce the term pedagogy, because whereas philosophy of education is not seen as a discipline on its own among the other disciplines of education, pedagogy is seen as an autonomous discipline among the other social sciences like psychology and sociology. The relative autonomy of pedagogy was supposed to stem from the idea of the pedagogical relation as a relation *sui generis*. However, it was thought to be impossible to reduce the pedagogical relationship to something like a special form of influencing-as psychology and sociology tend to do. The pedagogical relationship, the relation between parent and child, the relation between teacher and student, is two-sided from the start (Spiecker, 1984). Such a view on the pedagogical relation has considerable consequences for the relation between pedagogy and pedagogical practice.

The *geisteswissenschaftliche* pedagogy dominated the scene till the beginning of the nineteen sixties. At this time the so-called empirical turn took place starting in curriculum studies. The empirical-analytic approach slowly became the dominant research style in the educational sciences and remains so at the present time. In the late nineteen sixties critical pedagogy tried to set foot in the universities. In the Netherlands critical pedagogy never became a mainstream approach in educational research, but there has been some critical pedagogical thinking among philosophers of education over the last few decades. In the general introduction of students in the educational sciences since the early seventies however, those three main schools of thinking in the educational sciences are presented as if they were equivalent. On the meta-theoretical level there are good arguments to do so.

Focusing on the main objective of the three distinguished schools of thinking a real trilemma emerges, because empirical-analytical research is heading for reliable and indubitable knowledge, while human science oriented research aims at helpfulness, and critical pedagogy, in its turn, concentrates on justice. By speaking of a trilemma we mean to say that we are confronted here with three possible goals of educational research, each which can be defended on its own grounds. But if one chooses one of the research styles, one implicitly decides not to choose the other two. So, if the choice is for reliable and indubitable knowledge, it can easily be defended for the layman. If one asks the man in the street, – what scientific research should do, – to produce reliable and indubitable knowledge, would be understandable answer. This answer can even hold against the argument that such kind of scientific knowledge has little to bring for educational practice, for instance, because reliable and indubitable knowledge is the one and only goal of scientific research. In the case of education, a thoroughly value laden subject matter, one could argue that the idea of value-free research, which goes together with the empirical-analytical point of view, is a rather peculiar point of view. But on the other hand, one could also argue that scientific research should go for the facts and that values ask for a practical or political choice, even if one knows that the fact-value distinction is not at all a clear distinction.

In the general introduction of students in the educational sciences those three main schools of thinking in the educational sciences are still presented as indicated above. The question is if this makes sense after more than twenty years of postmodernism. We can indeed take Lyotard's *The Post-modern Condition* – first edition in French of 1979 – as the starting point of postmodernism in philosophy in the late twentieth century. In his still convincing analysis, the grand narratives of the Enlightenment suffer from a chronic disease named mouldability-optimism. But those three main schools of thinking in the educational sciences have a striking resemblance with Lyotard's grand narratives. So if it is true that if the three main schools of thinking in educational research indeed represent the grand narratives of truth, helpfulness and justice, the question emerges to what extent those research traditions have taken into account the critique of postmodernism in the last twenty years.

Main Schools of Thinking in Educational Research and Twenty Years of Postmodernism

To ask for an analysis of the way the empirical-analytical approach has taken into account the criticism of postmodernism is posing a strange question because the empirical analytical approach has been one of postmodernism's main objects of critique. In the nineteen sixties Habermas criticised the empirical-analytical approach for its focus on control, but it seems that the world was far more a total institution when Lyotard analysed its post-modern condition in 1979. And now, more than twenty years after Lyotard's analysis, the situation has deteriorated even more. We have to realize that Lyotard was completely right in his pessimism, unless he could not yet foresee the tremendous influence of information and communication technology on the development of total control. Empirical analytic research is more dominant than ever in Dutch social science research. From an epistemological point of view this school of research has not made any step forward since the sixties, but the knowledge factory flourishes as never before. Empirical analytic research is favoured by a peculiar publication policy in Dutch universities as Paul Smeyers and I showed some years ago but there is more to say about the reason why people believe in the defective knowledge produced by it (2000). First, it is indeed the ideology of performativity itself shaped as a form of simple circular reasoning saying: "If a medicine does not work, more of that medicine is needed". Second, for a long time we thought that the outcomes of empirical analytic research did not work because the reported effects were restricted to laboratory situations. But we now know – mainly thanks to analyses of Bruno Latour – that the success of science is due to the fact that reality itself is converted in a lab, not in the sense of varying the conditions, but indeed in the sense of complete control. It is not question anymore if we want to live in a techno world or not, as there is no other place to go. Third, fakery and corruption rule empirical analytic research knowledge production. In a book entitled *De onwelkome boodschap* (The unwelcome message) Tromp and Köbben present a considerable number of research project showing that the taskmaster forbids the researcher to publish the results, because the results tell what the taskmaster did not want to hear. In the year 2001 the Dutch under-minister of education decided to invest 100 million Euro in a huge pre-school project of which she knew that research showed that it was defective.

What did the life-world approach do with the critique of postmodernism? To answer that question we focus on the phenomenology of the so-called Utrecht School. In the nineteen fifties the Utrecht School consisted of an influential group of sociologists, psychologists, criminologists and educational scientists who concentrated on the perseverance of the humane world and criticised the process of the world becoming more technical. One of the proponents, Van den Berg, qualified phenomenology in 1953 as a method bound to its time. Phenomenology was indeed connected to an orientation of an integrated social community while the post-modern condition is characterized by fragmentation. Nowadays many governmental and political programmes speak of the promotion of social cohesion. Phenomenology is connected to an orientation of a life-world of children that does not exist anymore. Phenomenology is connected to pedagogical values that are under attack today. The old ideal of autonomy seemed to be more attainable in the fifties of the 20th century than in the beginning of the 21st century. Phenomenology was always conscious of the fact that the knowledge produced did not exceed the here and now. In the turn to hermeneutics the post-modern insight that "it is all interpretation" was fully taken into account. In the turn to hermeneutics, phenomenology turned into a post-modern approach. But qualitative research, a successful Dutch product of exportation till the mid-eighties, disappeared from universities as a consequence of research policy favouring empirical-analytical research.

The analysis of the way critical theory has taken into account the criticism of postmodernism leads to the conclusion that thinking in terms of mouldability is a main characteristic of the three main schools of thinking in educational research. For empirical-analytical thinking, with its thinking in terms of control, this is evident. For historical-hermeneutical thinking with its practical ambitions, it is perfectly comprehensible. But for critical thinking, with its emancipatorical ambitions, it is really paradoxical. Masschelein 2001) shows that from the first moment on, critical theory was typified as utopian pessimism, a pessimism that is linked to the old doctrine of original sin and the so-called prohibition to make images of God or to make images of the good. After the Second World War radical negative utopism becomes the characteristic par excellence of critical theory (with Habermas as a significant exception). For critical theory the time of revolution has gone and the mission is to rescue the individual in a totally managed world. Here critical theory really comes close to postmodernism. The realisation of happiness for everyone, one of the original ambitions of critical theory, is the opposite of real freedom. Masschelein concludes that critical theory is assuming the need for an ideal unwillingly utopian and, given its pedagogical practice, unwillingly technological. This instrumental view on education is not an exclusive feature of American critical theory, but could already be found in Adorno and Horkheimer a long time ago. For Masschelein, the big challenge for today's critical theory is to develop a concept of critique that is not bound to positive utopism and a concept of pedagogical action that is not instrumental. Again the mission of critical theory can hardly be distinguished from the mission of postmodernism, if it can be formulated. The concept of utopia should be freed from the order of representation and should be connected to the order of affect. When critical theory succeeds in keeping alive the longing for a radically different world it opposes the last ten years of capitalist triumphantalism.

From Grand To Small Narratives: About Pedagogical Truth

We should keep in mind that Lyotard's declaration of the end of the Enlightenment's grand narratives did not bring about an end to performativity in educational research. Nevertheless, we can understand Lyotard's declaration of the end of the grand narratives as a plea for small narratives. Lyotard's plea for plurality asks for all kinds of qualitative research that can effectively unsettle the erroneous belief in general laws. However, Latour's analysis shows the tremendous difficulty of this task. Research does not simply register the general laws that rule the world: research actually changes the world into a world ruled by general laws. But a social science that is really interested in plurality should explore all kinds of qualitative research methods. As said previously, in the Netherlands, qualitative research is still losing ground. It seems that the arguments defending the deeper insights of qualitative research have lost power in the discussions about research policies. From a certain perspective however, it can easily be shown that narrative research is in some respects superior to traditional forms of research. The main schools of thinking in educational research ran aground- as far as the research of some specific central questions is concerned. As we will show narrative research is capable to reopen these questions. With a rather loose reference to Jerome Bruner (1990) we will take a closer look at five of these central questions.

In the first place there is the question about human development. In the social sciences in general we are still confronted with dilemmas like nature-culture and nature-nurture. After centuries of research the social sciences did not come up with real answers to these dilemma's and it does not look like that definitive answers will be formulated in the near future. In many cases the scientific debate seems to have darkened the complexity of social reality. Looking for simple explanations result in creating an image that is too simple. In the stories that people tell about there own lives they generally do not feel bothered by such academic questions about the origins of human development, but when we take a closer look at those stories we will see that they offer a differentiated view on those phenomena. Stories are about persons who are affected by circumstances and who act on their own grounds, who take responsibility and who run away from it, who look like their parents as two peas in a pod and who differ from them like strangers, who fall into the water and who win the lottery, etcetera, etcetera. In the drama of the ordinary narrative scientific questions about human development have become open questions again. Thanks to the dramatic aspects of stories, seemingly settled answers to those questions can be discussed again. This is the way deficiency in grand scientific theories come into sight. It is said that reality is more complex than established theory, but above all, life is stronger than doctrine. Sometimes people seem to be able to live strictly according to theory, but at other moments it seems that they do not care a rap.

The second question is the question about the relation between thinking and acting. In science, and philosophy, all kinds of models of human behaviour are to be found. In one model human acting is seen as initiated by impulses from the unconscious, in another model free choice determines what people actually do. In a third model human behaviour is seen as completely determined by external stimuli. In narratives however there is no preoccupation with any model of the relation between thinking and acting, both are presented next to each other. In stories we learn about what people do and what they think. In stories we hear what people say and so we discover that they present every now and then, an unsound picture of what is going on. In stories we learn how doubt is combined with behaviour that looks as determined as can be. Etcetera, etcetera. Stories do not depart from an established relation between thinking and acting, but offer examples of possible relations. On the one hand, the author presents the relation between thinking and doing as a riddle, on the other hand in his story the author offers to the reader a view on a possible world. The thrill of a story is of high pedagogical value.

The third question is the question of the relation between facts and norms. Many social scientists consider the question of facts and norms to be so difficult that they do not like to speak about it. They like to hold the view that there is an unbridgeable gap between facts and norms, so a science heading for facts best leave the question of facts and norms as it is. In stories however, facts and norms – just like thinking and doing – go very well together. In stories a proponent can live a virtuous life, but there is another possibility that he or she does not care about norms at all. In stories people appear on the stage who are constantly confronted with their own norms and people who do not care. Etcetera, etcetera. In narratives the general normative and ethical problems are always particular ones. That is why since time immemorial stories are told to teach a moral lesson. In some stories the moral is even summarized at the end as a sort of general principle. But in every story facts and norms are presented as interwoven.

The fourth question, which is related to the previous one, is the question about the separation of the normal and the deviant. Indeed, science prefers not to speak about norms. On close inspection however science tacitly qualifies the majority as normal and the minority as deviant. Stories can show how the ordinary and the exceptional can exist next to each other. Most of the time stories tell about the peculiar integration of the normal and the deviant. Stories can bring up in an easy way the mad next to the bad, the dull next to the thrilling, and the morbid next to the terrifying. Narratives are capable of showing the ordinary of the exceptional. But narratives can show how special the ordinary is as well. Most of he time, scientific reports tell about the ordinary of the ordinary. It is not easy to tell what is most important; to present the special of the ordinary, or the ordinary of the deviant, but the pedagogical importance of both is evident.

The fifth and last question is the question of truth and untruth. Actually in science this is the question of highest priority. It is remarkable that for a narrative this very question has the lowest priority. For the narrative, as a source of insight in what education is, and how it should be, it is of minor importance whether a story is true or untrue in the scientific sense. For the worth of such an insight, it is not relevant if the story is based on a fairy-tale, an anecdote, shocking biased news or reliable and valid scientific facts. It looks like that all previous questions come together in this fifth question. A pedagogical truth differs from a scientific truth. Pedagogical truth has to be lifelike in the first place, but that is not enough. Pedagogical truth is really something other than scientific truth. That is why we often speak of veracity instead of truth. Veracity has something to do with credibility. Pedagogical truth is about what is worthwhile. It may sound high-flown, but a pedagogical truth has something to do with the meaning of life. A pedagogical truth is an insight in a practical-normative sense. A pedagogical truth does not only refer to a lifelike reality, it shows the way.

The statement that scientific truth is of minor importance for pedagogical truth can create confusion. It does not mean that in education we could say whatever we want. If we want to defend narratives a as source of pedagogical knowledge we do not want to work according to a rule that is said to be heard among tabloid journalists. From a pedagogical point of view the credo "Never let the facts spoil a good story" is a sin. The question is that to be of pedagogical worth, it is often really of minor importance if all small facts are correctly reported, or if indeed it all really happened. On these grounds novels and other kinds of fiction can be of great help to discover what is pedagogically worthwhile.

Pedagogical truth is not about facts in the first place, but more about possibilities. The imaginary and the fantastic show the possible or the limits of the possible. So it is not easy to determine if a statement is pedagogically true or untrue. Because the truth of a pedagogical insight depends, in part, upon the cogency of the story and so from the assent of the listener, in the end the pedagogical truth has something to do with facts. When the impossible really becomes impossible, or the imaginary really gets inconceivable, every story will lose its cogency.

Genres of Academic Writing

Paul Feyerabend was right when he prophesied in 1975 that church science, as an institution, would lose its central position in the near future. He holds the view that science is only one ideology among many and should be separated from the state just as religion is separated from the state. It is not that scientific knowledge is worthless, scientific knowledge is of high economic value, but science, as an institution no longer dictates how its products are used. Like the position of political administrations, the position of science as an institution is indeed reduced to one of the players on the worldwide economic battleground. We do not live in a knowledge society, our societies are not post-industrial as Daniel Bell foresaw in 1967, and capital is still ruling the world. The question emerges: What is left for philosophers? To answer that question there is a need to rephrase the relation between theory and praxis. To rephrase the relationship between theory and praxis we need to concentrate on what we, as philosophers actually do: read and write. So let us try to distinguish between the different forms of academic writing and focus on their place in academic communication. Here is a brief overview.

As the first genre of writing we present the *study* oriented to the search for the undivided truth. A closed form of reasoning characterizes the study as genre of writing. The supposition is that if one of the many steps in the argumentation is found to be untrue, if one of the building stones turns out to be too weak, the whole argumentation tumbles down. The communication language of the study is brimming with militaristic metaphors. One attacks or defends theses. As soon as one can no longer hold a position one has to leave it. (Dutch language has only one word for thesis and position). In certain views on studies, one is even expected to attack one's own theses. Unexpectedly the philosophical study resembles the (empirical analytical) study. Argumentation runs according to the rules of formal logic.

As the second genre of writing we present the *essay*. In an essay we literally try out an idea or thought. The writer of an essay is not bothered too much by possible counter-arguments. It is even permitted to strengthen a position by hiding the weak points. It is the question even if position is the right word in the case of an essay. In any case, one sole counter-argument is by far insufficient to show the imperfection of the essayistic "truth". If a certain idea or thought is of worth, it will become clear as a matter of course. The pitcher goes so often to the well that it comes home broken at last. If you really want to say something against an essay you should write another essay. An essay is not oriented on undivided truth, but on credibility and cogency.

The difference between the study and the essay may need further elaboration from an epistemological point of view. The difference does not stem from the idea of representation or mirroring on the one hand, and other kinds of metaphors for pictures on the other hand. The difference between the study and the essay has to be found indeed in the different forms of reasoning: logocistic on the one hand and non-logocistic on the other.

As an example of a good short essay I would like to refer to "The death of the family" by the German sociologist Alexander Schuller (2001) that was published in a Dutch newspaper (originally published in the *Frankfurter Allgemeine Zeitung*). Most people believe that the generation gap that ruled family life has vanished since the seventies of the last century, and today's parents and children seem to go on very well together. Schuller defends the opposite. He states that the family does not exist anymore. He states that parents now leave their pedagogical tasks to institutions. Schuller claims that parents and children do not really speak to each other nowadays, that parents and children have their own subcultures and that children cannot find a role model in the family anymore. Parents look at their kids as if they are representatives of an occupying power. The peculiar thing is that both these pictures of the post-modern family, Schuller's and the generally accepted one, are true.

Another example. The Australian cultural anthropologist Derek Freeman went to Samoa in the early nineteen eighties and discovered that Margaret Mead had been completely wrong in sketching the picture of the happy family under the sun. In his book *Margaret Mead and Samoa* he claims to have falsified Mead's theory. But now, twenty years later, scholars seem to have forgotten about Freeman (1983) and his research, as Margaret Mead's essay is still alive. When we look at the way children come of age, we can never forget to look at the cultural context.

As far as the relationship between theory and praxis is concerned, the study and the essay seem to belong to different worlds. The study belongs to the world of application, while the essay belongs to the world of challenge. The study suits the old modern idea of mouldability, while the essay fits in a modest post-modern form of self-interpretation. Is it not strange that in post-modern times philosophers keep on writing studies oriented on the outdated idea of the one and undivided truth? Is it not strange that we organize our philosophical discussions in an outdated style by trying to find that weak spot to turn the whole construction down? Yes, it is strange, but academic communication can be organized in another way. We could try to make the building of our fellow philosophers stronger. We could try to add supporting observations. If the original idea or thought is not strong enough the building cannot carry the additional "truths" and will tumble down anyway.

Maybe it is not too post-modern to recommend a just feeling for the distinct genres using the possibilities of the different forms of communication. Is it not strange that book *reviews* nowadays turn out to be the starting point of discussions? Philosophers and scientists evaluate each other's writings. The review has to meet certain characteristics. Ideally a reviewer presents an accurate summary followed by internal critique (critique in terms of the questions posed by the authors), alongside, but clearly distinguished from, external critique (critique beyond the questions asked by the authors), resulting in a balanced judgement. The review is a one-way affair, but in the course of academic communication the roles of reviewer and reviewed will go from one to another constantly. Today I judge, tomorrow I am judged. Apart from cases with blatant faults one should not react on reviews. Every genre of academic writing has its own rules. Saying that a book review could be something other than the starting point of a discussion is not to say that we should not organize academic discussions. It seems that there is too little discussion, debate or even polemic in our journals.

References

Bruner, J. (1990). *Acts of meaning*. Cambridge: Harvard University Press.
Feyerabend, P. (1978). *Science in a free society*. London: NLB.
Freeman, D. (1983). *Margaret Mead and Samoa. The making and unmaking of an anthropological myth*. Cambridge: Harvard University Press.
Habermas, J. (1971). *Knowledge and human interests* (J.J. Shapiro, Trans.) Boston: Beacon Press.
Latour, B., & Woolgar, S. (1986). *Laboratory life: The construction of scientific facts* (2nd ed.). Princeton: Princeton University Press.
Levering, B. (2003). *Poems as sources of qualitative data*. Invited address at the Fourth Annual Advances in Qualitative Methods, May 2003. Banff, Alberta, Canada.
Lyotard, J.-F. (1979). *The postmodern condition: A report on knowledge* (G. Bennington & B. Massumi, Trans.), Manchester: Manchester University Press.
Masschelein, (2001). Kritische theorie in kritische pedagogiek. In P. Smeyers & B. Levering (Eds.), *Grondslagen van de wetenschappelijke pedagogiek. Modern en postmodern* (pp. 93-111). Amsterdam: Boom.
Schuller, A. (2001). De dood van het gezin. *NRC-Handelsblad*. September 8.

Spiecker, B. (1984). The pedagogical relationship. *Oxford Educational Review, 10,* 203-206.

Smeyers, P., & Levering, B. (2000). Educational research: Lessons and content. Lessons in publication policies from the Low Countries. *British Journal of Educational Studies, 48,* 70-81.

Tromp, H., & Köbben, J.F. (1999). *De onwelkome boodschap, of Hoe de vrijheid van de wetenschap bedreigd wordt.* Amsterdam: Jan Mets.

Van den Berg, J.H. (1953). Verantwoording. In J.H. van den Berg & J. Linschoten, (Eds.), *Persoon en wereld. Bijdragen tot de phaenomenologische psychologie* (pp. 1-10). Utrecht: Bijleveld.

THE DISCIPLINARY TERRAINS OF SOUL AND SELF-GOVERNMENT IN THE FIRST MAP OF THE EDUCATIONAL SCIENCES (1879-1911)

Jorge Ramos do Ó

> *"The aim of all education, we must never forget, is to shape the child for independence, making him able to govern himself"*
> Élie Pécaut, 1887

In this paper I intend to show that the historical sedimentation of a coherent discourse, both regarding the scientific status of pedagogy and regarding the aims of the modern educational act, must be understood in the general framework of the moral and the expansion of the policy of self-government. I argue that a pedagogic discourse was formed at the end of the 19th century embracing the core of ethical material, assimilating it to the axiom of illuminist-humanist power which tells us that the civic behavior of the citizen must arise from the commitments and decisions of the private sphere of his consciousness.

The analysis focuses on a relatively short historical period. I will discuss the so-called Compayré Moment, giving it the name coined by Nanine Charbonnel (1988), and which is demarcated by the publication, in 1879, by Gabriel Compayré, of the *Histoire critique des doctrines de l'éducation en France* and the articles on "Education" and "Pédagogie" that Durkheim published in 1911 in the *Nouveau dictionnaire de pédagogie*, under the stewardship of Ferdinand Buisson. I will discuss the texts from an entire generation of Francophone pedagogues who predominantly reflected on the epistemological status of the Sciences of Education and who systematized an encyclopedic knowledge based on an education and teaching with modern characteristics.

I aim to show that government of the soul or disciplinary training of the will of the pupil was at the core of reform proposals defended by this group of pedagogues.

My idea is to continue a theoretical reflection begun by Michel Foucault in his final writings. He defined a field of analysis therein, which allowed permanent crossing of the domains of ethics and politics. The term *governmentality* and the expression *technologies of the self*, interoperating with each other and clarifying each other, are what best define the inflexion operated in his last historiographical projects, looking to understand the basis on which modern practices of *subjectivation* have been built in modernity (Foucault, 1978, 1988). This analytical perspective has many ramifications in current social research. I am particularly inspired by the critical works of Nikolas Rose, in the fields of power-knowledge that characterize the social affirmation and consolidation of the psychological science, and the way that Thomas Popkewitz questions educational theory and pedagogical research with his works on the self and the other (Rose, 1996; Popkewitz, 1998). Analyzing the discursive devices, through which the actors are represented, classified and standardized, these researchers enable us to understand the schooling of the masses either as a human technology or as a moral technology. They show us how the dynamics of promotion of subjectivity intertwine profoundly with the goals of government of the populations.

Rationalization of Conduct in the Context of the Definition of the Education Sciences

I begin my reflection with two questions asked by Gabriel Compayré in 1885: is there a science of education or not, and is its object different to the rest of the social sciences that were establishing themselves at the time? The author of *Cours de pédagogie théorique et pratique*, immediately came up with an answer: "nobody disputes the viability of an educational science today." Thus, Compayré made a distinction between pedagogy – which would be the theory of education – and education, which constitutes the practice of pedagogy. "There is indeed a science of education, a practical and applied science, whose principles, laws and vitality are documented by a large number of publications." From the methodological conceptual perspective, pedagogy aspired to make itself legitimate solely as an *applied psychology*. The science of education took as its rules the maxims that derived from the laws of mental organization, (i.e. the work developed by the psychological science). This is the fundamental reason underpinning this marriage "psychology is the source of all applied sciences that are related to the moral faculties of man; pedagogy contains all the parts of the soul and must use always psychology" (Compayré, 1885, pp. 10-13).

Moreover, we see how an apparently innocent sentence, because it is centered only on the aspect of the epistemological framework of a discipline, allows one clearly to understand the forms of specific social regulation. From the beginning, pedagogy, or the science of education, took on the ambition to act on the spirit and the body of children and the young. It arose, historically, as another version of *bio-power*. Its method would consist only in observing the facts of the physical and moral life of man. Its biggest problem was making each subject visible and able to be manipulated. This task was only imagined possible if undertaken through systematic dissection of the spirituality of the educated subject: the general laws and respective inductive reflection of pedagogy would focus on obtaining the rational construction of intimate facts, in order to establish fully the map of the human soul.

From the very start, speaking about the object of the new science was to speak about the possibility of a laic moral. From Compayré I will move on to another author, Henri Marion, bearing in mind the article "Pédagogie" that he wrote in the first version of the influential *Dictionnaire de pédagogie et d'instruction primaire*. Marion began by reproducing Littré's classic definition, according to which pedagogy is the moral education of children, and all his considerations derive from this standpoint. The entirely ethical substance obliged him to discuss the position of discipline in the general spectrum of the sciences. Marion had no doubts that this prevented it from being classified in the exact sciences, which based their reasoning on sequences of pure and complex notions. Pedagogy was not similar to the physical and natural sciences, because it could never purport to attain laws of absolute necessity and infallibility. However, this ambiguity, or rather, this positional uncertainty did not pose a problem for Marion. It was instead a reality that pedagogy shared "with the whole family of the moral sciences, whatever they may be" (1887a, p. 2238). The pedagogical discipline should be categorized as a third sector of the scientific field – that of knowledge that helps to free man through the path of reason. Its chief objective is to show that all human life can be rationalized, and thus, *make the creation of a state of hyperconscience in each educated subject*.

The effort linked to the initial debate around the sciences of education assumed the possibility of, through them, constituting a morality independent from any religious or metaphysical fact. "The question", Ferdinand Buisson pointed out, "is knowing whether it is possible to create a disposition in the child's soul through a purely laic moral education, i.e. a moral that solely acquires its strength, prestige and authority through the moral idea itself; this is the conviction upon which the French Republic is grounded" (1911, pp. 1348-1349). The principles of the catechism of progressive science were now viewed as an effective device of social regulation. Henri Marion, in the program of his *Cours d'Instruction Morale pour les Écoles Normales Primaires*, made exhaustive lists of individual duties at the start of the huge Moral Practice Section. Also, when he wanted to define the space of this terrain, he only allowed for what he called the "main forms of self-respect: individual virtues (moderation, prudence, courage, respect for the truth and the given word, personal dignity, etc.) (Marrion, 1882, p. 1768). Just one step separated that point from the affirmation, as Compayré stated (1885, p. 92), that education of the conscience is interconnected with education of all the faculties of the soul. The action should fortify the psychological reflection aimed at ensuring that the individual has the capacity for self-governing. There seemed to be no doubt that the formation of a moral spirit was, fundamentally, "a *technique*, the technique of human action in society" (Buisson, 1911, p. 1350).

The reason-responsibility conceptual pair is inscribed as the essence of this logic of development of a scientific reasoning of practical vocations (Nóvoa, 2002). At the basis of the moral conscience, we would find the first element. Reason was viewed as "the spirit itself, considered in its own constitution, its innate requirements, its universal and eternal needs" (Marion, 1887c, p. 2529). It responded as such to the need to find a common basis for all men, and at the same time, to define thinking and civilization as *natural* elements. Here the idea was established that the ethical commandments were realities, but realities that supposed a *clarified acceptance* of the citizens. Education was hence justified as the operation able to take children and the young and incorporate the social rules through the path of intelligence and rational knowledge. It was as if a commandment, in order to exist and grow in the spirits, had first to be known. For the pedagogues at the end of the 19th century, responsibility thus supposed "a moral education that had enlightened the conscience and developed the idea of good and duty", a task of constant *mentalisation* of the obligatory laws. They established a direct association with the most important political concept of modernity, the concept of *freedom*. Responsibility supposed it entirely. The pedagogical discourse thus affirmed that the human condition was to submit oneself voluntarily to the commandments of law. "Responsibility", pointed out Compayré, "can define the character of an intelligent and free self, who, in knowing what he does and being able to act in way other than what is usual, must face the consequences of his own acts" (Compayré, 1882d, pp. 1855-1856). The pedagogical reflections aimed to associate, if not unify, what common sense would have led one to understand as corresponding to contradictory realities or paradoxical hypotheses.

The sociologist Durkheim also consecrated many pages of a doctrinal nature, justifying the fusion of opposites, starting invariably from the absolute value of scientific reason and the conscience of the moral. He insisted on the principle that any educational project, to present itself as modern, would have to translate *personal autonomy* into *mastering of the self*. Durkheim intended to justify the thesis that only *subjectivation* of the rules of the moral would provide a secure basis for a healthy social life. He therefore had to unify the great binary oppositions that any educational relation contains. Freedom and authority, constraint and consent, devotion and sacrifice, and reason and conscience were for him terrains that could not be separated under any circumstances. His long article "Éducation" closes with a paragraph that summarizes the whole power-knowledge program and the promotion of the regimes of self-government that the 20th century school would effectively make universal. I reproduce it in its entirety:

> *We have sometime opposed freedom and authority as if these two factors of education contradicted and restricted each other. But this is a false opposition. In fact these two terms are far from being opposite, intertwining with each other. Freedom is the offspring of well-understood authority. To be free is not to do what one wants, it is to be the master of oneself, to act through reason and to do one's duty. It is in fact exactly in bestowing the child with self-discipline that the authority of the teacher should be used. The teacher's authority is nothing more than an aspect of authority of duty and of reason. The child has to be trained to recognize progressively the authority in the educator's word; this is the condition that leads to a later discovery of authority in his own conscience and his own personal judgment.* (Durkheim, 1911a, p. 536).

The Faculties of the Soul and Psychological Individualization of the Pupil

The notion of a modern educational relation establishes a causal connection between particularized knowledge of trends, habits, desires or emotions of pupils and the molding of their moral sensibilities. It was the attempt to make this socializing technology of a disciplinary character viable that was the genesis of the *discovery of the pupil* and his differentiated treatment from the last quarter of the 19th century onwards. If the individual personality had become the central element of the intellectual culture of the time, from politics to economics, even to art, it was also necessary that the educator begin to account for the germ of individuality that was within each child. Instead of treating the school population in a uniform and invariable form, the modern teacher should vary his methodologies "according to the individual temperaments and the evolution of each intelligence", noted Durkheim in his other article "Pédagogie" (1911b, p. 1541).

It was child psychology that would respond to the need to ascertain the three faculties of the laic soul – "sensibility", "will" and "intelligence" – because it was obliged to acknowledge the diversity of individual characters. Henri Marion provides again an appropriate definition of the discipline: "psychology means science of the soul: the field of psychology changes according to the way one understands the soul and according to whether one accepts that there can be a scientific knowledge of it" (Marion, 1882, p. 1761).

The first faculty was the one given most importance and was even viewed as the common basis for all phenomena of the moral. It would be through *intelligence* that the educator should begin.

The faculty of intelligence was given priority as it was viewed as the common basis for all phenomena of the moral and it is this faculty that the educator should focus on first. The more the powers of intelligence are developed the more enlightened the perception of consciousness of duty becomes. In a well-organized intelligence, all the other segments of the soul would also have a defined position. The objective was to show that the intellectual work of the memory would strengthen individual identity: "each new fact of conscience is a new element of the idea of the self" (Compayré, 1882b, p. 1555). Therefore the part of intelligence that would have as its object the child personality, would be worked on through school education through the strengthening of psychological reflection. This was the only way, indeed, able to ensure possession and government of the self. Therefore, the part of intelligence that would have as its object the child's personality, would be worked on through the strengthening of psychological reflection, which was viewed as the only way to ensure government of the self. The psycopedagogical discourse claimed it possible to introduce a naturalist teaching methodology. All the logic on which school work was structured – the constant repetition of processes allied to a progression in learning through levels of growing complexity and abstraction – arose with the reproduction of the rules observable in nature itself, aiming also to enable the pupil to "find" himself. As such, it was demonstrated that reason would be inscribed in the world of natural things. Compayré explained: "pedagogical action in the field of the faculties of the soul should come as close as possible to the order of nature; in this way an evolution is favored that leads from the concrete to the abstract, from instinctive life to reflective life; in this way the faculties of the soul gain their own activity, a dynamism and an energy that will allow them to increasingly develop by themselves throughout the life; therefore, school education can be succeeded in all ages by a personal education, by a self-education" (Compayré, 1882a, p. 986).

The faculty of *sensibility* would be dealt with through identical processes to rational progression. It was explained, for example, that one could not demand that a student love his country without first informing him of its existence and its historical importance for life in society. But, in contrast to the previous faculty, here the problem was not only in developing and enlarging it. For highly noble feelings to take root it was supposed that opposing faculties be simultaneously regulated, monitored, moderated and contained, or even prohibited. While it was easy to celebrate the creative force of the imagination, patent in many cultural creations that school promoted, it was also imperative to stamp out the dangers, errors and pernicious illusions that were often hidden within the child. It was important that the child understood that reason should prevail over the heart, that it was the unrestrained fantasies of the heart that could divert one from the path of truth. The world of impulse therefore became, in these terms, defined as purely fictional, while that of reason was identified entirely with the principle of reality. Hence, throughout the school cycle, as the years passed, first in the spirit of the child and then in the young adolescent, there would be a natural process of the passage of the lesser modalities from (i) "self-love", presented as selfish, to another kind of inclination defined as (ii) "altruistic" – and illustrated with cases of patriotism and sacrifice for one's neighbor or even for humanity. The process ended with the eruption of a (iii) "purely abstract love" for the values of truth, beauty and good. The major question of popular education would therefore be the gradual and consolidated *substitution of the sensation with the idea.* "The development of sensibility", proclaimed Compayré, "is intimately linked to the progress of intelligence" (1885, p. 183). There was no virtue other than that which tended towards a love of virtue itself. The fancy of the ardent imagination of children and the young would be contained through forms of positive knowledge, judicious reflection and healthy examples.

The task to instill the moral became delicate rather than difficult when applied to the third faculty – the *will*. The school attempted, in another approximation to nature that will overcome desire. Desire was identified as a solicitation exterior to the subject, while will was assumed to be the result of free resolution. But even so, will could be structured against child spontaneity, given that this was where the distinctive and independent mark of each child resided, which had to be preserved. Elie Pécaut tackled this delicate problem head on. He had no hesitation in stating that "obedience is the first and indispensable condition of all education". He even translated the educational relation into "spiritual constraint, moral domination, absolute empire – noble and sacred in its aims – of the science on ignorance, or, to sum up, of strength over weakness". Moreover, this clear conscience about the orthopaedics of souls did not impede Pécaut from also dealing with the question of autonomy and free will. Pécaut carefully described the two educational paradigms present at the time. The first, which he labelled theocratic, was based on the principle that all human nature was evil, and therefore a person could not be left to his own vices. Every combined effort, from instruction to education, from the moral to opinion, from custom to the reiterated use of force, had proved historically insufficient before the gigantic task of "reducing to absolute impotence the spontaneity of man – which is an error and a corruption – and thus *deprive man of self-government,* giving him up to unfailing hands, under the dignified stewardship of faith, and the power of those whose earthly authority comes from a divine origin" (Pécaut, 1887, pp. 2121-2123; my italics). The authoritarian spirit, grounded on ancient tradition, had looked for support for the civilizing task *outside the child*, and in so doing, was to be absolutely condemned. The error had been in not wanting to face the fact that nothing could save man apart from man himself. The second model – inspired by Rousseau and spawning from the Enlightenment and Progress – believing in the original goodness of human nature, attempted, on the contrary, to stimulate and strengthen all the instincts of independence and rights inherent to the realization of the person. This was the great promise. In fact, Pécaut considered that the most important cog in the civilizing task of humanization of the child was to count on the child itself. The crux was to achieve a consented and docile obedience that did not collide with the personal energy of each subject. Truth, justice, goodness, duty and sacrifice would be taught as corresponding to a law inscribed in the very conscience of the child.

The Disciplinary Device Designed by Modern Pedagogy

In taking on board the idealization of the child and the educational relation, disciplinary practices would undergo a complete mutation. The refusal of repressive modalities in the school context would be, however, the last measure tending to impose *as natural the civilising idea that an outside stimulus would correspond to a voluntary movement within*. Modern standardization arose, in fact, on the great idea of spontaneous discipline. Modern pedagogues came to agreement on this point: "the system that best suits a child is that in which he learns self control" (Buisson, 1882a, pp.716). This principle can be translated into various maxims. First, and from the intellectual perspective, the pupil would be led to value study and reflect on himself. This led to constant appeals for personal, free and voluntary work. Second, with regard to the moral aspect, the old system, completely alien to the pupil, of material reward-corporal punishment, would be exchanged for strategies of direct responsibility: the pupils would comply with the several school cycles, hearing that experiences of good and evil and pain and joy would always be natural consequences of his individual acts. Each pupil would be taught that the only reward he could obtain would be the satisfaction of his most elevated inclinations. In truth, modern pedagogy would suggest that school guarantees that each individual would be able to win over himself upon completion of his studies.

It should also be noted that the authoritarian model was identified by these pedagogues as essentially linked to the regulatory formulas inspired directly from military discipline and criminal type logic. The punitive and compensatory prerogatives that the schoolmaster used, since Classic Antiquity, were applied largely to sanction or punish lack of knowledge. These only focused on *instruction* and not *education* of the pupil. In its absurd materiality, violence applied to the child began to be looked on by this progressive generation as artificial and without any value on conduct. The liberal dynamics of government of the self demanded, in the educational field, a much more complex set of practices that acted on the group of behavioral dispositions and not only on fear. But the determination to end corporal punishment and humiliation did not mean a restriction or economizing of means. On the contrary, it was a process of amplification and diversification, leading *discipline* as far as possible, i.e. exactly to the point when it was no longer necessary. Compayré confessed so clearly: "its aim, in any case, is to become needless" (1885, p. 457).

Discipline could not live without a careful and complete staging of the open spaces. The statement is extremely subtle and loaded with historical substance: "There is no other way to accustom the spirit to freedom than to imprison it in continuous and enforced sensations" (Compayré, 1885, p. 97). In these terms the new disciplinary apparatus aimed to create objective structures of behavior, but through a practical positioning that attended above all to the involuntary situation and the multi-directional movements in the various places where the action took place. This was the point on which the essential of the discourse of educational innovation became centered at the end of the 19th century. In the article "Education", that he wrote for his *Dictionary,* (1882b, pp. 805-811), Buisson fully embraced this framework of *psi* origin. For Buisson, the faculties of the soul and the very freedom of the child were developed by the most powerful instrument that education had at its disposal, the *habitus*. Virtues and vices would be positions running through any spirit: will was, however, the exclusive offspring of habit. Buisson and his contemporaries argued that the effect of regularity, repetition and discipline, through pedagogical strategies such as duly staggered timetables in weekly cycles, would shape, over time, the whole *framework of existence*. The learning of the curricular content would run in parallel with the task of acquisition of moral values, whose everyday repetition would turn into voluntary energy. Conforming to duty would make one feel like a "perpetual and pleasing imprisonment" (Buisson, 1882b, p. 809). At the end of schooling, the habit of doing good would have become second nature. It would be identified with subjectivity itself (Carrau, 1880, p. 948).

It is no exaggeration to say that the *discovery* of the child in last the century derived directly from this project of power. Gaillard, also in the *Dictionnaire de pédagogie*, endeavored to show the advantages of a differentiated study of individual characters. It was not by chance that his article was titled "School Discipline". After stating that the psychological science had proved that it was impossible for two soul mates to exist, Gaillard made knowledge depend on individual diversity of a panoptic vigilance of the pupil – in the classroom, in the playground, along the route that the child took home and why not inside the home – thus proving that, one by one and separately, *all the pupils could be governed*. His portrait should be read as a remote expression of the methods that would bring about the modern disciplinary practices, which leads to systematic and in-depth observation to remove the need to act directly on the bodies or the consciences.

> *Pupils cannot all be treated in the same way. Some of them oppose our efforts with an indifference that seems insurmountable; others react with a exasperating indolence; for many it is a question of breaking their pride; some are crude and apathetic, and it is therefore necessary to stimulate them at all times in order to arouse their attention; the shy ones require encouragement, the active and impetuous ones should be calmed down all the time. Some are led on by their colleagues and don't have any initiative, while others command and turn into little despots... The scope of the individual characters that teachers face is extremely wide, as is extremely high the number of proper procedures that they must employ to guide and try to modify their pupils. The personal characteristics will be better known if the pupils are observed, not only in the classroom, but also in the playgrounds and other spaces, given that, when free from all constraints, they show their true selves; The teacher will know them better as well through contacts made with their families. The teacher will accept the children as they truly are and will make a bigger effort to turn them into what they should be. All school discipline must train the pupils to win over themselves.* (Gaillard, 1882, p. 719)

Conclusion

We know that the discourses around the moral problem and the corresponding creation of disciplinary technologies have accelerated significantly and become ever more complex in modernity. Pedagogy also wanted to translate this political program, while claiming for itself the status of positive science. The discursive formation drawn up from the last quarter of the 19th century gave us without doubt the idea that freedom would be the great accelerator of authority and discipline. The psychopedagogical considerations concerning the internal structure of the soul and the play of contrasts that would demarcate the child-youth passions, were nothing more than the transfer, to the educational field, of the interests and investments of governmentalized subjectivation. Indeed, for this group of first pedagogues it was already very clear that each singularity was becoming viewed as a point of passage directed towards principles and forces of power. A permanent striving would characterize modernity – to govern without governing through the amplification of power to its furthest limits (i.e., the choices of autonomous subjects in their decisions).

References

Buisson, F. (1882a). Discipline. In F. Buisson (Ed.). *Dictionnaire de pédagogie et d'instruction primaire* (pp. 715-717). Paris: Hachette.

Buisson, F.(1882b). Éducation. In F. Buisson (Ed.). *Dictionnaire de pédagogie et d'instruction primaire* (pp. 805-811). Paris: Hachette.

Buisson, F. (1911). Morale. In F. Buisson (Ed.). *Nouveau dictionnaire de pédagogie et d'instruction primaire* (pp. 1348-1352). Paris: Hachette.

Carrau, L. (1880). Habitude. In F. Buisson (Ed.). *Dictionnaire de pédagogie et d'instruction primaire* (pp. 947-948). Paris: Hachette.

Charbonnel, N. (1988). Pour une critique de la raison éducative. Bern: Peter Lang.

Compayré, G. (1880). Facultés de l'âme. In F. Buisson (Ed.), *Dictionnaire de pédagogie et d'instruction primaire* (pp. 752-754). Paris: Hachette.

Compayré, G. (1882a). Facultés de l'âme. In F. Buisson (Ed.). *Dictionnaire de pédagogie et d'instruction primaire* (pp. 983-986). Paris: Hachette.

Compayré, G. (1882b). Raison. In F. Buisson (Ed.). *Dictionnaire de pédagogie et d'instruction primaire* (pp. 1554-1555). Paris: Hachette.

Compayré, G. (1882d). Responsabilité. In F. Buisson (Ed.). *Dictionnaire de pédagogie et d'instruction primaire* (pp. 1855-1856). Paris: Hachette.

Compayré, G. (1885). *Cours de pédagogie théorique et pratique*. Paris: Paul Delaplane.

Durkheim, E. (1911a). Éducation. In F. Buisson (Ed.). *Nouveau dictionnaire de pédagogie et d'instruction primaire* (pp. 529-536). Paris: Hachette.

Durkheim, E. (1911b). Pédagogie In F. Buisson (Ed.). *Nouveau dictionnaire de pédagogie et d'instruction primaire* (pp. 1538-1543), Paris: Hachette.

Foucault, M. (1978). La gouvernementalité. In *Dits et écrits (1976-1979)*, (Vol. 3, pp. 635-657). Paris: Gallimard.

Foucault, M. (1988). Les techniques de soi. In *Dits et écrits (1980-1988)*, (Vol. 4, pp. 783-813). Paris: Gallimard.

Gaillard, J. (1882). Discipline scolaire. In F. Buisson (Ed.). *Dictionnaire de pédagogie et d'instruction primaire* (pp. 716-721). Paris: Librairie Hachette.

Marion, Henri (1882). Psychologie. In F. Buisson (Ed.). *Dictionnaire de pédagogie et d'instruction primaire* (pp. 1760-1769). Paris: Hachette.

Marion, H. (1887a). Pédagogie. In F. Buisson (Ed.). *Dictionnaire de pédagogie et d'instruction primaire* (pp. 2238-2240). Paris: Hachette.

Marion, H. (1887b). Psychologie. In F. Buisson (Ed.). *Dictionnaire de pédagogie et d'instruction primaire* (pp. 2482-2486). Paris: Hachette.

Marion, H. (1887c). Raison. In F. Buisson (Ed.). *Dictionnaire de pédagogie et d'instruction primaire* (pp. 2528-2530). Paris: Librairie Hachette.

Nóvoa, A. (2002). La raison et la responsabilité: Une science du 'gouvernement des âmes'. In R. Hofstetter & B. Schneuwly (Ed.), Science(s) de l'éducation 19e-20e siècle champ professionnel et champ disciplinaire (pp. 243-263). Bern: Peter Lang.

Pécaut, E. (1887). Obéissance. In F. Buisson (Ed.). *Dictionnaire de pédagogie et d'instruction primaire* (pp. 2121-2127). Paris: Hachette.

Popkewitz, T. S. (1998). *Struggling for the soul: The politics of schooling and the construction of the teacher.* New York: Teachers College Press.

Rose, N. (1996). *Inventing our selves: Psychology, power and personhood.* Cambridge: Cambridge University Press.

EDUCATIONAL RESEARCH AND CONSTITUTING THE AMERICAN SCHOOL AT THE TURN OF THE 20TH CENTURY[1]

Thomas S. Popkewitz

Cosmopolitanism is a word in vogue in contemporary scholarship. It brings past European Enlightenment's commitment to reason and science into today's landscape of a new globalism. The cosmopolitan is an individual who values universal human rights and freedom that transcends provincialism and local traditions. The images and narratives of a cosmopolitanism also move historically through the progressive pedagogies of the school. Schooling is to produce the child who acts as a global citizen who participates through the use of reason and science. The educational sciences have played a practical role in that production of the child. The notions of the cosmopolitan individual, however, were never universal. They were bound to the making of "home" and belonging of the nation that had global pretension and local exclusions.

"Cosmopolitanism" provides a way to think historically about *the evaluation and criteria of educational sciences,* this book's focus. My argument follows this line of thought. Pedagogy is an assemblage of cultural practices that fabricates principles of action and participation in the name of universal cosmopolitan values.[2] The site of intervention is the interior of the child (*the soul*) – to change how a child thinks, "sees," feels, and acts in everyday life. The sciences of pedagogy are the inscription devices. That is, they function as intellectual tools that map the interior of the self, rendering the characteristics of the individual visible and amenable to government (Foucault, 1979). The inscriptions of cosmopolitan reason in theories of the child, family, and the classroom normalize and divide the capabilities of "reason" and the "civilized" from those that stand outside of reason, the "uncivilized." To evaluate and examine the criteria of educational research is to examine the cultural practices that order reason and the reasonable person through the expertise of science.

---

[1] I appreciate the comments on earlier drafts by Lynn Fendler, Barry Franklin, David Hamilton, Jodi Hall, Ruth Gustafson, Kenneth Hultqvist, Elizabeth McEneaney, Angelo van Gorp, Dar Weyenberg, and my graduate seminar on National Imaginaries.

[2] I use fabrication to deploy its double quality in talking about pedagogy: it embodies *fictions* about who the child is and should be; and makes particular human kinds through its theories and actions of teaching and evaluation.

This essay focuses on contours in the formation U.S. schooling and social science at the turn of the 20th century. The first section places the practices of science as linking two registers of modern governing: the social administration of "reason" and the freedom and liberty of the individual. I then look at different scientific practices that calculate the "reason" of the child's acts and participation. I argue that the sciences of education are one response to the instabilities and pragmatics embedded in the conditions of democracy, capitalism and the Republic-as-nation. The sciences of the child, family, and schooling stabilize or tame change through generating principles that govern reflection and action.

Registers of Social Administration and Freedom: Fabricating the Citizen

Cosmopolitanism inscribes the double notion of freedom (liberty) and social administration (discipline). This individuality was a radical break from previous notions of a world fixed by placement by birth, of humans as subject to fate or the gods, and of a world in which the future was fixed. Liberty and freedom involved proper planning to provide direction not only to the evolution and progress of the institutions of society but also to the development of the modern citizen (Wagner, 1994).

The joining of the registers of administration and freedom embodied new alignments in the governing of the individual. Enlightenment notions of liberty were placed in the care of the state that not only protected territorial boundaries of the nation but was to care for its populations. That care was no only to protect from risk, such as the spread of disease, old age, or unemployment. The state was to "make" the citizen whose liberty and freedom were ruled by the principles of a cosmopolitan "reason." Reason was to discipline the free individual through ordering the dispositions and capacities to act in the uncertain futures.

In the United States, 18th century Enlightenment thought was brought into the political realm to "make" the citizen of the nation and nation-ness. There was no consciousness among the colonists of "being" an American nor of a nation-ness at the beginning of the 18th century.[3] "To the democratic idea of popular sovereignty (an emergent ideal of the later Enlightenment) was added the emotional force of nationalism, and the combination consumed and perverted the rationalistic, individualistic, cosmopolitan ideas of the Enlightenment" (Schlereth, 1977, p. 135).

---

[3] *American and Americanism* as terms used in the literature reviewed, although it is important to recognize that it is referring to a particular geographical and cultural space in North America.

The cosmopolitanism of the nation emphasized the primacy of reason, the reliability of human understanding, the value of individual freedom, trust in method, faith in education, belief in progress, and a corresponding disregard for tradition, constituted authority and received dogma (Ferguson, 1997). Thomas Jefferson, in the early 19th century, spoke of a global harmony guided by the binding principles of a universal citizen who resided in multiple republican nations around the world. For John Dewey a century later, the cosmopolitanism was formed through the shaping of the individual in a community through a universal problem-solving.

The Enlightenment cosmopolitanism was transmogrified into a particular American Exceptionalism that made its Republic and democracy into a civil religion.[4] The United States was called The New World, a phrase that overlapped religious conceptions of a Garden of Eden with the imaginary of the new nation that escaped the evils embodied in the Old World traditions and its disfigurements (Ross, 1991). The American was the incarnation of that universal "reason" that projected the Enlightenment ideas of humanity and progress as the embodiment of the nation.[5] The history of the modern American nation was projected as a history of particular sets of values, morality and identities of the cosmopolitan individual spoken about in transhistorical ways – inalienable rights, human rights.

The soul was the site of change (Popkewitz, 1991). Revelation and redemption no longer gave attention to the afterlife. Salvation was ordered through a calculated reason to achieve personal development, self-reflection, and the inner, self-guided moral growth of the individual. The administration of reason generated principles through which options are made available, problems defined, and solutions considered as acceptable and effective. The educational purpose was "forming mental habits that the adult student will need" to confirm the future greatness of the nation through the "cultivation of the power of discriminating observation; by strengthening the logical faculty of following an argument from point to point; and by improving the process of comparison, that is, the judgment" (National Education Association, 1892/1969, p. 169).

Reason was to be inscribed in the individual to enable freedom. But that freedom is not an ideal adorning the individual but a calculated project of the administration of the self. Nicholas Murray Butler, who formed the first

---

[4] All nations produce notions of their exceptionality, often tied to a religious destiny, to give them some privileged position in the world system.

[5] rogress was not an invention of the Enlightenment. What is peculiar to the 18th century onward is its epistemological use as the secular and planned ordering of the past/present/future which I discuss later.

major U.S. teacher education institution, saw education as making the child in an image of a cosmopolitan citizen. "Freedom of the will is not . . . a metaphysical notion, nor is it obtained from nature or seen in nature. It is a development in the life of the human *soul. Freedom and rationality* are two names for the same thing, and their highest development is the end of human life" (Butler, 1895, p. 79-80; italics added).

The reason of science, however, was never without the sublime – Weber's notion science as a disenchantment with the world was never so. Science merged with religious and romantic images of nature. An inevitable, natural evolution of the social order and individuality were revisioned as a nature that could be guided and ordered artificially. G. Stanley Hall (1905/1969) viewed the new disciplines of psychology and child study, for example, as replacing moral philosophy in the challenge put forth by the materialism of Darwin.[6] He spoke of the *soul* in describing psychology and its relation to pedagogy. For Hall, psychology was to reconcile faith and reason, Christian belief and "Enlightenment" empiricism.

The administering of *the self* as the site of educational struggles is, in one sense, not a new historical project. Durkheim (1938/1978) described the Reformation and the Counter-Reformation as individuating and disciplining consciousness with the values of religion. In this process, popular piety and Christian folk belief were suppressed and transformed. The governing in the modern school and its sciences is the fabricating of the cosmopolitan's freedom, but the kinds of liberty to make the subject free involve particular inscriptions to map the paths that govern that freedom. The criteria and evaluation of educational research embody historically interrogating that normalizing project and its mutations over time.

Educational Sciences as Taming Change

At first, science was a vague and seemingly romantic notion of rationality to order progress; by the end of the 19th century science became an exercise in systematic planning.[7] The American Social Science Association, the first such association formed after the American Civil War (1865), saw its general obligation as reforming welfare policies. But as journalists and philanthropists, among others, they had no special training in the field of social

---

[6] hile we associate Social Darwinism as an offshoot of Darwinism, it was not. The notions of evolution and a universal natural order in fact predated the scientific Darwinism and in fact made it possible to order and revision scientific thought.

[7] I use the 19th century to mark where the social science develop formalized theories and methods, and receive institutional homes in the governing patterns related to the modern welfare state.

science. By the end of the century, science and scientists had a more vocational and calculated cultural trajectory to harness progress in the social realm. The battles of science against poverty and the evil effects of modernizations, and gender were intertwined in the moral crusades of the city.

Progressivism of the late 19th century America was a political and cultural movement that brought a new professional expertise into the realm of public and personal problem-solving. Science was to provide the methods to secure the future through ordering reason and the dispositions and sensitivities of the family and the child who was to become the future citizen. The calculating of reason was the mechanism to secure that future citizen through schooling. Charles Eliot, a president of Harvard (and the chair of a major 19th century school reform report), considered an education that demanded strict obedience to authority and the passive reception of imposed opinions to be inconsistent with the development of reasoning power and independent thought. After the emergence of studies of child development and other sciences related to the pedagogical practices of the school, Charles Eliot argued for a new form of scientific expertise in organizing teaching. There is a need for educators to consider, Eliot said, the "bodily changes in childhood and youth, and undertakes to mark off the years between birth and maturity into distinct, sharply defined periods, bearing separate names like childhood and adolescence, and to prescribe appropriate pedagogical treatment for each period" is important to the formation of the curriculum and thus needs to be paid attention to because of its "the idea of individual differences and a scientific educational theory" (Eliot, 1892-3, p. 342-3).

The curriculum related democracy to the theories of the child and the family in the name of an American Exceptionalism. America's Exceptionalism is brought to the fore as Dewey argues that the "The old culture is doomed for us because it was built upon an alliance of political and spiritual powers, an equilibrium of governing and leisure classes, which no longer exists" (1916/1929, p. 501-2). Dewey saw science as making democracy possible. The science was called pragmatism. It was a way of ordering thought that is to be progressive by responding to the contingencies of life and freedom that is not "monolithic, related to one single and universal system of truths or fixed and closed orthodoxy, as there is no dead monotonous uniformity of practice and aim" (p. 198).

Opening of the Interior of the Child:
Making the Future Through Rewriting the Past/Present

In this and the next section, I discuss the criteria of research in the new educational sciences through two overlapping cultural practices. There was a taming and stabilizing of the future through calculating reason that ordered action. And the social and educational sciences inscribed theories of the actor and agency that focused on the administration of social interactions, "communities," and interior of the child and family.

In medieval thought, the future was not something that could be regulated nor had a temporary sequence. Time and the future was owned by God and if there was any question about the two, it centered around whether one went to heaven or not. But this notion changed through multiple cultural practices as the future, past, and present were linked not only in historical narratives but in the designing of the interior of the child.

Perhaps the most striking place in the invention of the future as part of a calculated relation of past and present is with the making of modern history in the 19th century. Classical thought functioned as fantasy of origins. Everything in the present had its place-as in a set table. History told of man's finitude as defined as an indefinite time. There was no interiority to the self. The Enlightenment, with strong debate, viewed the past as inferior to the present, believed in progress that could be ordered by "man."

The ordering of time which made modern history possible overlapped with a range of cultural practices that enabled ways to calculate reason in an interiorized self. By the end of the 19th century, changes in the practices of philosophy, art, and science ordered perception and attention through an ordering of time (Crary, 1999). The photography of Muybridge's time/motion studies in the imaging in photography, the paintings of Cézanne and other modernists, the tachiscopes and the new field of optics, as well as time-motion studies incorporated later into patterns of work produced by Frederick Taylor, embodied new technologies for administering the self and the making of "consciousness."

The formation of modern sociology and psychology can be understood with this new ability to order time and space. The new ways of calculating perception and attention overlapped with the time/space relations embodied in the invention of a history as a chronological ordering of plotted time (Steedman, 1995, p. 4). The assemblage of practices made it possible to fabricate an individual as an active temporally bound agent that could simultaneously be ordered into discrete and calculated elements for observation and planning of a future. The agential individual was an object of science in the name of administering freedom.

The invocation of the future in the construction of the agential child appears forcefully in discussions of the school formation in 19th century America. Schooling was to ensure the future of the Republic and the happiness of its people through "making" the child. Horace Mann, the first Secretary of a State's of Massachusetts' Board of Education and a leader of the public school movement in the 19th century, viewed education as bringing progress to the future of society. The duty of education, Mann argues, is to guarantee the future through educating the child (Mann, 1867). The citizen, he continued, is one who can deal with the uncertainties of future in a capable (disciplined) way.

Schooling was to unwrite a past in order to produce a progressive future. Writing after tremendous dislocations and challenges to the nationhood during the first decades of the 19th century, Mann argued that education is not only for "wealth, possessions, whatever makes up the external part – the *body*, if we may so speak – of human welfare," but with "a general amelioration of habits, and those purer pleasures which flow from a cultivation of the higher sentiments, which constitute the *spirit* of human welfare, and enhance a thousand-fold the worth of all temporal possessions, – these have been comparatively neglected" (Mann, 1867, p. 7, italics in original).

The future was tied to the notion of progress that was regulated through the inscriptions of "reason" and the "reasonable person." Securing the future is a central motif in the new sociology and psychology that appear at the later part of the 19th century. The writings of Albion Small (1896), one of the founders of American sociology, argued the need to relate science and teaching to ensure the future of society. The sciences of the child and the family would not only provide a cognitive knowledge, but also discipline the capabilities, values, dispositions, and sensitivities through which individuals conducted their lives. Small (1896) saw pedagogy as "the science of assisting youth to organize their contacts with reality" that was not only concerned with thought but for "for both thought and action" (p. 178). For Small and later for his colleague, John Dewey, the social significance of the curriculum was in its promise of social progress. "Sociology knows no means for the amelioration or reform of society more radical than those of which teachers hold the leverage. The teacher . . . will read his success only in the record of men and women who go from the school eager to explore wider and deeper these social relations, and zealous to do their part in making a better future" (Small, 1896, p. 184).

The imaginary of the New World is embodied in the new social disciplines. The sciences would fulfill the promise of the future by reconfiguring the relation of the past and present in the principles that ordered the life of the city, the immigrant, and the child and family. The Social Darwinism found in Dewey's writing, for example, was revised from an evolutionary natural theory into a social theory for thinking about how science and social policy could intervene in making a citizen whose participation contributed to social betterment through individual development. Dewey argues that the United States hesitation in entering World War I against Germany was to recognize the maturity of the New World. That maturity involves a pragmatic thinking about the nation and "the national mind." The nation, he argues has not yet found a "national mind, a will as to what to be . . . It is not easy to make up the mind, for the mind is made up only as the world takes on form. We have hesitated in making up our mind just because we would make it up not arbitrarily but in the light of the confronting situation. And that situation is dark, not light." Dewey continues that "This is itself proof that a New World is at last a fact, and not a geographical designation. We no longer can be spoken to in the language of the Old World and respond . . . This is the fact of a New World. The Declaration of Independence is no longer a merely dynastic and political declaration" (Dewey, 1917/1929, p. 445).

The imagined destiny of the national Exceptionalism is narrated by the pragmatism that makes the individual as the agent of democracy through the everyday working of life. One can read Dewey's arguments about reason (methods of science) as the inscription of a particular cosmopolitan individual who acts through principles of a universal problem-solving. Dewey's pragmatism, suggests that The New World Exceptionalism "denotes faith in individuality, in uniquely distinctive qualities in each normal human being; faith in corresponding unique modes of activity that create new ends, with willing acceptance of the modification of the established order entailed by the release of individualized capacities" (Dewey, 1922/1929, p. 489). The individual is to recognize that "The idea of a universe which is not all closed and settled, which is still in some respects the indeterminate and in the making, which is adventurous and which implicates all who share in it, whether by acting or believing, in its own perils . . ." (Dewey, 1927/1929, p. 439).

The pragmatic image and narrative of the nation are brought directly to the problem of the new immigrants to the United States at the turn of the 20th century. For some of the early social scientists and social reformers, the Old World cultures had to be destroyed through re-socializing the immigrant family and child. But for other social scientists, the city and the immigrant groups produced the ideal of the future. The matrix of the city redefined "the old world traditions" that were no longer valid but, in what we can think of as a tradition of pragmatism (Lindner, 1990/1996, pp. 112-113). The narratives of freedom and democracy were not universal and as Morrison (1990) argues in 19th century literature, inscribed a language that "powerfully evoke and enforce hidden signs of racial superiority, cultural hegemony, and dismissive "Othering" of people and language (p. x).

My argument about the criteria and evaluation of the educational sciences has been to this point that the theories and methods of science function as cultural practices that inscribe principles about who the child is, should be, and who is not that child. My point is historical rather than about the good or evil of science, nor with its bias or subjective elements. My concern is with its duality: its modes of thought and methods of inquiry are produced in an assemblage of cultural practices that continually need to be scrutinized and historicized.

Civilizing the Family and the Child

Science as the taming of the future overlapped with other cultural practices that were to *civilize* the child and family. Parents prior to the 18th century did not have moral and spiritual function to order a child development and thus the future. Parents were more influenced by what they felt themselves than by thoughts on what they and their actions meant to "develop" children through a childhood. There was no architecture in the household to separate children from adults. But in the 19th century, children were "discovered" as having a life distinct from parents. Parents begin to have formal obligations in the development and civilization of the child.

The school was formed in an image of the family- culturally and legally – as a civilizing process. It removed the child from adult society, and interned them in a childhood distinct from adulthood. Childhood was a process to make the child as cosmopolitan citizen whose *home* and belonging related to a collective image that tied the individual to a nation-ness.[8]

That nation-ness was made in images of a cosmopolitanism that gave the nation and its citizen a privileged position in relation to other nations. Discourses of philosophy and science focused on reason as civilizing principle of an eternal right and justice, and as the natural laws of history. But the civilizing of the child was a self-consciousness of the West, and of national consciousness. The universality of the norms of civilization played down the national differences of people by emphasizing what is common or what should be common to all human beings.

The civilizing of the child and family was a strong theme in the community sociology that emerged in Chicago at the turn of the 20th century. Sociology was to civilize the child in order to guarantee the future of the Republic. Frank Lester Ward, an early sociologist, viewed education the processes to bring forth civilization. Ward (1883) argued that sociology is to identify the fundamental laws of human action to give direction to freedom and thus to enable the education of the child.

The invention of the notion of the *primary group* was to place the child in a network of relations in this civilizing process. The child and family

---

[8] My use of "civilizing" is historical and non-normative, giving attention to the formation of particular habits, dispositions, and sensitivities produced in a field of cultural practices.

were to be socialized in a pattern of action that produced a sense of belonging and home with the larger values and norms of an American identity. Charles Horton Cooley, another sociologist at Chicago, saw the family as *a primary group* where a child learns of civilization through face-to face interaction. The communication systems of the family would establish the family on Christian principles that stressed a moral imperative to life, and self-sacrifice for the good of the group. Parents, under the guidance of the new social theories of health, would develop altruistic instincts that expressed self obligation and self-responsibility in their children.

The *civilizing* of the child and the family connected narratives and images of a collective moral order of the nation to the characteristics and capabilities of the individual. The family as "a primary group" was a moral technology in which God's work was to be done in this civilizing. It now became possible to think of the *self* as part of a collective moral order of the nation. Images of the Protestant moral and ethical life were overlaid with science to humanize and personalize individual discipline. The discourse of the primary group universalized and naturalized people of different ethnicity, religion, race, and language.

The civilizing process of education was a corrective for deviancy. The use of direct and coercive methods in socialization related to a lesser form of civilization – "the savage and used by stagnant people" (Ward, 1883, p. 159-160, italics in original). Ward argued that the *uncivilized* need to be neutralized or it will lower all of society. Education needs an "absolute universality," "to raise the *uncivilized* classes up toward its level" (p. 595).

Again, the disciplining of the present to citizen and thus make the free citizen also carried its opposite – the barbarian who was not civilized and thus would destroy the cosmopolitanism of the nation if not fought against through education.

Some Concluding Notes: Research as a Cultural Field of Practices

This essay outlined a diagnosis of the modes of thinking that ordered the objects of reflection and action in the turn of the last century school research. Its historical narrative weaved philosophical, cultural and pedagogical strands into a single plane that problematized the ways of working and thinking played out in the educational sciences. My assumption is that the evaluation and criteria of research are embodied and constituted in this field of cultural practices. Without such historical scrutiny, there are epistemological obstacles, to use loosely Gaston Bachelard's (1984) famous term, for understanding that very phenomena of educational research.

The notion of cosmopolitanism provided a strategy to organize the inquiry in the knowledge of educational sciences. Cosmopolitanism was viewed as an assemblage of practices and not a set of universal ideals. It gave focus to the administration of reason in the name of freedom, the fabrication of the agential actor, and the production of a system of reason whose principles were to tame the contingency and uncertainty embodied in the new projects of liberty.

The sciences of education functioned as inscription devices or intellectual tools to map reason so as to render the child administrable for freedom. The theories and methods of the educational sciences brought a particular normativity into the practical relations of face-to-face interactions of the child, family and classroom. Individual thoughts, acts and participation were ordered through the distinctions and differentiations of research.

Pragmatism was one inscription device, a major innovation of the invention of 19th century to bring the Enlightenment principles of reason as a governing practice in everyday life. The sociological theories of the primary group were another inscription device. The intellectual tools of the sciences linked individuality to a collective "home" and belonging related to an American Exceptionalism.

The evaluation and criteria of educational sciences were not only about the learning and teaching of children, nor of describing, narrating or interpreting the life of schooling. "Cosmopolitan reason" was the will to empower, to borrow from Cruikshank (1999), which inscribed a relation between the freedom and will of the individual, and the political liberty and will of the nation. The educational sciences were normalizing practices in which the discipline of a cosmopolitan reason was the cornerstone of liberty, but also the limit and object of government.

References

Bachelard, G. (1984). *The new scientific spirit*. Boston: Beacon Press.
Butler, N. (1895). Presidential address: What knowledge is of most worth? *Journal of Proceedings and Addresses, Session of the Year 1895* (pp. 69-80). St. Paul, MN: National Educational Association.
Crary, J. (1999). *Suspensions of perception: Attention, spectacle, and modern culture*. Cambridge, MA: Massachusetts Institute of Technology Press.
Cruikshank, B. (1999). *The will to empower: Democratic citizens and other subjects*. Ithaca, NY: Cornell University Press.
Dewey, J. (1917/1929). The emergence of a new world. In J. Ratner (Ed.), *Characters and events: Popular essays in social and political philosophy* (pp. 443-446). New York: Holt.

Dewey, J. (1916/1929). American education and culture. In J. Ratner (Ed.), *Characters and events: Popular essays in social and political philosophy* (pp. 498-503). New York: Holt.

Dewey, J. (1922/1929) Individuality, equality, and superiority. J. Ratner (Ed.), *Character and events; Popular essays in social and political philosophy* (Vol. 2, pp. 486-492). New York: Henry Holt.

Dewey, J. (1928). Progressive education and the science of education. *Progressive Education, 5*, 197-204.

Dewey, J. (1927/1929). Philosophy and the social order. In J. Ratner (Ed.), *Characters and events: Popular essays in social and political philosophy* (pp. 435-42). New York: Holt.

Durkheim, E. (1938/1977). *The evolution of educational thought: Lectures on the formation and development of secondary education in France* (P. Collins, Trans.). London: Routledge, Kegan & Paul.

Eliot, C. (1892-93). Wherein popular education has failed. *The Forum, 14*, 411-428.

Ferguson, R. (1997). *The American Enlightenment, 1750-1820*. Cambridge: Harvard University Press.

Foucault, M. (1979). Governmentality. *Ideology and Consciousness, 6*, 5-22.

Hall, G. (1905/1969). *Adolescence: Its psychology and its relation to physiology, anthropology, sex, crime, religion, and education* (Vol. 1). New York: Arno Press and *The New York Times*.

Lindner, R. (1990/1996). *The reportage of urban culture: Robert Park and the Chicago school*. (A. Morris with J. Gaines & M. Chalmers, Trans.). Cambridge, UK: Cambridge University Press.

Mann, H. (1867). *Life and works of Horace Mann* (Vol. 2). George C. Rand & Avery.

Morrison, T. (1992). *Playing in the dark: Whiteness and the literary imagination.* Cambridge, MA: Harvard University Press.

National Education Association. (1892/1969). *Report of the Committee on Secondary School Studies*. Washington, DC: US Government Printing Office.

Popkewitz, T. S. (1991). *A political sociology of educational reform: Power/Knowledge in teaching, teacher education, and research*. New York: Teachers College Press.

Ross, D. (1991). *The origins of American social science*. New York: Cambridge University Press.

Schlereth, T. J. (1977). *The cosmopolitan idea in enlightenment thought: Its form and function in the ideas of Franklin, Hume, and Voltaire, 1694-1790*. South Bend, IN: University of Notre Dame Press.

Steedman, C. (1995). *Strange dislocations; Childhood and the idea of human interiority, 1780-1930*. Cambridge, MA: Harvard University Press.

Small, A. W. (1896). Demands of sociology on pedagogy. *Journal of Proceedings and Addresses of the Thirty-Fifth Annual Meeting of the National Education Association,* (pp. 174-84).

Wagner, P. (1994). *The sociology of modernity*. New York: Routledge.

Ward, L. F. (1883). *Dynamic sociology or applied social science as based upon statistical sociology and the less complex sciences*. New York: D. Appleton.

RESEARCH AND REVELATION: WHAT REALLY WORKS?

Richard Smith

Increasingly teaching is seen as a technology which needs to be evidence-based. Educational researchers therefore should be busy establishing a determinate body of knowledge: "an agreed knowledge-base for teachers", "evidence of what works in what circumstances" (Hargreaves, 1996, p. 2). Thus educational research is increasingly cast in the empirical mould. The papers for any Education research conference, such as those for the annual meeting of the British Educational Research Association (BERA), for example, amply confirm this. Programmes of postgraduate research training meanwhile are redesigned to incorporate mandatory elements of statistics and quantitative methods, but not philosophical approaches. Meanwhile, the UK government steadily increases pressure for academic educationalists to research "what works": to focus their research, automatically seen as a matter of empirical investigation, on what will be useful in the school. Empirical social science thus becomes the only variety of social science worthy of respect. It is vital that this theory be challenged. For *theory* it is, much though its proponents dislike hearing it called that, just as they dislike (I find) being asked just what empirical evidence the theory itself is based on. And it is vital that those of us whose research is not wholly empirical demonstrate that there are other kinds of research and other values.

Most of this paper consists of examples of the empiricist approach to educational research, together with my attempts to draw out the underlying assumptions and conflations. I try to articulate just what is wrong with the idea that educational or any other research should essentially aim to discover "what works", since this is the weapon above all that is currently being used to beat all other forms of research, or thought, into submission. Lastly I make some brief remarks about some strategies which educational research that resists these pressures might helpfully take.

Doctoring the Children

The UK's Teacher Training Agency (TTA) has a Web-site (http://www.canteach.gov.uk/) which tells us that it is "active in supporting the Government in its drive to promote teaching as a research and evidence-based profession". Throughout the site "research" is carefully conjoined with "evidence"; "evidence" quickly becomes conflated with "information" and "data". There is a link to a TTA Conference speech by Malcolm Wicks MP, Parliamentary Under Secretary for Lifelong Learning. Wicks compares education to medicine: "We demand information about the best treatment or drugs...we expect doctors treating us to offer advice informed by research". So too Wicks thinks that a growing body of agreed knowledge in education will tell us much. He gives an example:

> *We are increasingly able to demonstrate that life chances, including health, are related to educational attainment and thereby to schooling. Evidence from my own department's research centre on the Wider Benefits of Learning shows that when other factors such as family background are taken into account, attaining at least level 1 in numeracy skills:*
> *Reduces the probability of having a long-term health problem by*
> *– as much as 9%;*
> *– Increases earnings by 10%.*

The picture of educational research here is naïve : you correlate this with that, and behold, you have a significant finding. Thus it was that correlating outbreaks of malaria with wind-direction and nearby marshes led to the conclusion (enshrined in the French for malaria, *le paludisme*, ie marshfever) that the causal factor was gas emanating from the marshes and reaching towns down-wind. Might it not be that, say, not living in poverty increases the child's chances of attaining at least level 1 in numeracy skills, avoiding illness and earning more? This does not occur to Wicks (or rather, to be fair, to whoever wrote his speech), who is happy to draw the conclusion that if teachers don't find and use the relevant research evidence then they can be accused of making their pupils ill. He believes that the correlation he reports supplies

> *justification enough to suggest that pupils deserve an education informed by valid and reliable evidence about effective teaching. Teachers have a professional duty to ensure that evidence informs their practice. Not to do so, amounts to reducing pupils' life chances.*

There is furthermore a heavy and unpleasant hint that to fail to attend to relevant evidence might leave you open to being sued for professional negligence ("Prior to the recent spate of legal actions relating to dyslexia, it was almost unheard of for anyone to challenge teaching methods in court").

Mythologising Research

Christopher Ball (Chancellor of Derby University, UK, chairman of the Global University Alliance and founder of the National Campaign for Learning) writes in *The Guardian* (20.2. 2001) of what he calls the seven myths of research:

> *... One irony of the 20th century was that, having won the second world war by applying strategic research (radar, Enigma, the A-bomb), the allies decided to win the peace by investing in pure research (the second myth). They lost the peace to Japan and Germany. Good research satisfies the twin tests of rigour and relevance. Rigour relies on professional integrity. Market forces are the best way to ensure relevance.*
>
> *The third myth [of research] claims that academic research is essential to the national interest. Is it? Good research benefits everybody, not just the nation of origin. Penicillin, the jet engine or the microchip are universally available. Good ideas spread like wildfire. In research freeloading works.*
>
> *Not all subjects yield good or useful research in equal measure (the fourth myth). Compare the amazing achievements of 20th-century science, technology and medicine - in genetics, electronics or disease, say - with the impact of social science. For all the research effort and expenditure, we know little more today than we did a century ago about how best to raise children or cope with crime. What we do know - the importance of motherhood and investment in people, or the failure of prisons and communism, for example - is derived from human experience.*

Ball tells us (*ibid.*) that academics "research every subject under the sun, except for research itself". And if they did research – enquire into – research, how would Ball have them do it? The research would have to be *rigorous*, of course ("Good research satisfies the twin tests of rigour and relevance"). Now this is a word that should immediately raise suspicion. It is often used rhetorically (compare "effective") to persuade us that the speaker or writer is a tough-minded individual whose criteria are unlikely to be easily met, and if anyone has to ask what those criteria are, then clearly he or she is a hopeless cases. Ball of course does not give us much insight into his criteria, telling us only that rigour relies on "professional integrity". This however is a further mystery. There is a hint of circularity: good research is rigorous, and rigour is what satisfies the relevant professional canons of research. At the same time there is again the scent of moralizing bombast – everyone should know what professional integrity is. Who would dare to confess their ignorance? An opportunistic researcher who fabricates his research findings presumably lacks professional integrity. But such a person could rigorously expose the logical fallacies in an argument (undistributed middles, asserted consequents, etc.), expressing his points in formal logic for the sake of extra rigour. As for the claim that "market forces are the best way to ensure relevance", one can but wonder at the naivety: as if research never risked being subject to the whims of fashion and funding agencies. There is an equivocation here in the idea of "relevance": between popularity and importance.

Ball mentions Radar, Enigma, the A-bomb, penicillin, the jet engine and the microchip. Bad ideas spread like wildfire too – thalidomide, CFCs, the A-bomb; the jet engine can be entered in both categories. But the central assumption here is that social science must operate like "hard" science and justify itself in the same way. What has social science ever done for us? It is tempting to take one of Ball's examples, such as the failure of prisons, and reply that social science has indeed given us many insights. The example might be given of the well-known Stanford prison experiment, which revealed how readily prison guards (here student volunteers playing the role) become brutalized. Ball however dismisses such knowledge as the result of experience, not of social science, the implication being that it is simple commonsense. It does not seem to occur to him that commonsense itself is informed by social science (rather slowly, to judge by the number of politicians and others whose first and last response to all manner of offences is to urge that the offenders be locked up). And so social science, unable to display a hovercraft or a Cruise missile as a result of its efforts, is relegated to the status of myth.

The Importance of Strategy

The tendency towards diktat and centralised control of research becomes stronger all the time. There is a new organisation, the UK's National Educational Research Forum (NERF), which has the remit of developing a strategy for educational research, guiding the co-oordination of its support and conduct, and promoting its application to the world of practice. It hopes to stimulate "high quality research relevant to the issues of practitioners, policy-makers, and learners of all ages", and provide "advice and guidance on priorities for basic and applied research". Its terms of reference can be found on the Web (http://www.nerf-uk.org/).

Before turning to detail here it is worth noting that the ambition to discover the right strategy or methodology for research, especially for scientific research, goes back a long way. Francis Bacon, for example, was eager to establish a scientific *method* (characterised principally, of course, by the induction of general principles from particular facts). The great advantage of having proper scientific techniques was that once properly formulated they required little special talent but could be used by anybody: the business could proceed "as if by machinery" (Bacon, in the *New Organon*). Indeed, insight and creative thinking were positively discouraged. "My way of discovering sciences goes far to level men's wits, and leaves little to individual excellence; because it performs everything by the surest rules and demonstrations" (*ibid.*, LXI). The modern obsession with research *methodology*, in education or elsewhere in the social sciences, looks particularly interesting in this light. Just as teaching is to be teacher-proof, so research is to be researcher-proof. There is less interest in having people of "individual excellence" conduct it than in ensuring that it can be carried out in the absence of any great intelligence or "wits" at all. This appears to confer power on those who authorise the methodology rather than those who carry out research, which should perhaps not surprise us.

NERF published a document titled *Research and Development for Education* in the autumn of 2000. A typical excerpt reads as follows:

> *Incentives for investigators to pursue excellence in the design and conduct of research need to be explicit. Quality criteria based on fitness for purpose, originality, rigour, transparency and accessibility need to be developed. Such quality standards are essential for the development of a knowledge base for education.* (p. 7)

This, however, betrays a shortage of wits on the part of those with the ambition to determine methodology. First, there is presumably a conflation of "incentives" with "quality criteria", unless NERF believes that researchers engage in their task purely for the sake of monetary or other reward, and would do better research if these rewards were advertised more openly. Quality criteria are not incentives, and if they are of the sort set out here they look more like powerful disincentives. Second, it is interesting to apply these criteria to any interesting and influential piece of educational writing, from Plato's *Republic* to Jean-François Lyotard's *The Postmodern Condition: A Report on Knowledge*. Were these fit for their purpose, and were they transparent? It is a fair guess that whatever the Conseil des Universities of the Government of Quebec were expecting it was not *The Postmodern Condition*. Something wholly fit for its purpose would be to an extent predictable and, to that extent, unnecessary. The idea of fitness for purpose reveals the rampant instrumentalism here. Lyotard himself (1984, p. xxv) makes a gentle criticism along these lines:

> *It remains to be said that the author of the report [ie The Postmodern Condition] is a philosopher, not an expert. The latter knows what he knows and what he does not know: the former does not. One concludes, the other questions...*

"Transparency": would not a piece of writing that was wholly transparent achieve that by including no language, no ideas that were not completely familiar, nor used in any but their most familiar sense? So too "accessibility" (accessible to whom?); perhaps philosophy should *challenge* the reader, thwart the progress of his day-to-day ways of thinking, even baffle him from time to time. Lyotard's writing does this frequently, and reminds us in the process just how mired we are in the habits of technical reason. It seems quite clear what the Forum's basic assumptions are: good research is research that constitutes a convenient "knowledge base" for practitioners to access in order to discover "what works".

Responses were made to *Research and Development for Education* which at first sight offer some reassurance. The Forum has published a summary of these responses on its Web-site (above).

> *Much of the research community felt that the proposals are centralised, government-driven and a threat to academic freedom and diversity...There was a widespread concern that the emphasis was on short-term policy evaluation at the expense of blue skies research... not all research can or should have an impact and ...this should not be a main driver.* (p. 1)

There is "enormous reservation about the Forum", especially its potential for restricting academic freedom. There are remarks on the dangers of trying to emulate research in medicine too closely; there is even the thought, offered as a major concession it seems, that educational research should not be confined to randomised control trials. It is said that there is already widespread agreement on quality criteria within research organisations and funding bodies. For this reason the Forum's chief *raison d'être* appears, to some, unsound and its existence redundant.

But reassurance is premature. A certain kind of language and a particular range of ideas are beginning to make themselves at home here, and it would be careless to take them for granted. How easy it is to approve of "widening participation to ensure a greater range of stakeholders can contribute to these processes", and how easy it is not to notice that once the practitioner is called a "stakeholder" her right to demand accessibility in the research she encounters is all but established. Then perhaps no educational research should be published that is not interesting to and readily understandable by the classroom teacher. If any particular set of proposals relating to quality criteria are unacceptable, all the more reason, it seems, to develop a better set: never mind whether it really makes sense to look for general criteria, over the whole diverse range of research. Glib phrases such as "efficacy of research outputs" create a climate in which writing and thinking that espouse values other than efficacy begin to seem exotic to the point of constituting an effete and offensive luxury, the product of ivory towers at their most pointless and elephantine.[1]

The Truth-Teller's Tale

One particular form this empiricism currently takes is the insistence that what matters – perhaps all that matters – is "what works". There is a need for ways of understanding the limitations of "what works" as a chief criterion for educational research and a need to make these limitations vivid and memorable. It is important to show, to put it in a deliberately effect-seeking way, that *"what works" doesn't always work*. Consider first how visions of good education and of the good life more broadly are always at stake here. If it could be shown that administering severe electric shocks improved children's reading scores, there would be no bland proclaiming that electric shocks work. If monotonous, repetitive drilling, "teaching to the test", improves pupils' test scores then clearly such teaching works – but only if the point of the teaching is simply and only to increase the test scores. All kinds of assumptions are built into the equation between improvements in such scores and the raising of educational standards. Our notion of good education has been replaced by talk of "what works", to the point that it is easily forgotten that the two may be at odds. You cannot judge what works without a full sense of what you are trying to achieve: of your ends or purposes, and how they are related to contiguous ends and purposes. That is familiar enough to philosophers, but the truth of it needs to be more widely known.

What, too, if effective solutions and answers are manifestly flawed? A recent short book on Francis Bacon, John Henry's (2002) *Knowledge is Power*, has the telling subtitle: *How Magic, the Government and an Apocalyptic Vision inspired Francis Bacon to create Modern Science.* Today's science, Henry argues, has its origins in natural magic, in systematic efforts to find the sympathies and antipathies between things. Natural magic in turn rejected speculative philosophy in favour of experimentation. The true ends of knowledge, Bacon wrote, are "not the pleasure of curiosity, nor the raising of the spirit": they lie in restoring man to the sovereignty and power he had before the fall of Adam. In other words their aim is simply to find "what works". By this criterion the Paracelsian treatment of battlefield wounds – applying ointment not to the injury but to the weapon that caused the injury – satisfied the demands of experimental science. It worked extraordinarily well, since it meant that the injury itself was largely ignored and consequently not infected by the salves (sand, ground-up egg-shells and so on) prescribed by the standard treatments of the time.[2]

---

[1] This section expands on some of my Editorial in *Journal of Philosophy of Education* 35.2, 2001.
[2] This paragraph is based on part of my *Booknotes*, *Journal of Philosophy of Education* 36.2, 2002.

A literary example helps to refresh our sense of what is wrong with the criterion of "what works".[3] In Kipling's short story *Marlake Witches* (set at the beginning of the nineteenth century) a consumptive 16 year-old girl is persuaded by the local "witchmaster" or purveyor of white magic and country-lore, Jerry Gamm, to adopt a charm to cure her cough:

> *You know the names of the Twelve Apostles, dearie? You say them names, one by one, before you open window, rain or storm, wet or shine, five times a day fasting. But mind you, twixt every name you draw in your breath through your nose, right down to your pretty liddle toes, as long and as deep as you can, and let it out slow through your pretty liddle mouth. There's virtue in those names spoke that way...* (Kipling, 1928, p. 99)

It is not clear whether Gamm himself believes in the "charm" or whether he is concealing his medical knowledge beneath the veneer of magic designed to appeal to country-folk. Of course it hardly matters, if all that should concern us is whether these things work.

By narrowing all question of value down to "what works" the empiricist imagines that he achieves an unquestionable connection with reality. "Look", he cries, pointing to the latest educational initiative and the test scores that have resulted. "You can see – actually see it working!" There is an interesting tendency for empiricism however to replace one kind of experiencing by another: if the important thing is to register what is real, perhaps it is just as good to register it *as* real. Thinking like this underlies the popularity of "stress management skills" where it might rather be supposed that the sensible thing was to address the source of the stress – the abusive partner, the bulling line manager. If you can manage your stress and feel ok, then things are (for you, *experienced* as) ok. Here is a variant on the theme of "you can't change the world but you can change yourself" (cp Smith, 2001). This is a natural consequence of imagining that "it works" is the only, or a superior and overarching, value. The novelist Iain Banks satirises this brilliantly in *Complicity*, where one of the characters finds his first experience of smoking a cigarette a revelation (pp. 47-8):

---

[3] It was sugggested to me by Jim Mackenzie, who alludes to the story in an insightful article (Mackenzie, 2002). He notes that "Kipling was very conscious that the causal efficacy of an action is independent of the intentions and understanding with which it is performed". It hardly needs saying that intentions and understanding need to be right if what works is to go on working.

This was better than religion, or this was what people always meant by religion! The whole points was that this worked! People said Believe in God or Be Good or Do Well At School or Buy This or Vote for Me or whatever, but nothing actually worked the way substances worked, nothing fucking well delivered like they did. They were truth. Everything else was falsehood. ... I became a semi-junkie that day...Truth and revelation. What is actually going on? What is literally the case? What really works?

There you are, the Journo Catechism, the truth-teller's tale, written in any damn scrip or script you care to choose to denominate, elect to go for or designate, WHAT FUCKING WORKS?

I rest my case.

Value and Meaning

The lines of argument advanced in this chapter are broadly philosophical. Philosophers have a strategic difficulty. They interest themselves in questions of value, and like to remind the world, as I have done in the previous section, that values are bound up in what to many appear to be matters of pure fact. There is little point in rehearsing the evident truth of that position. But philosophical approaches have been marginalized by those who find philosophy's focus easy to caricature. David Reynolds, doyen of the school effectiveness movement, writes in an article rather chillingly entitled "The school effectiveness mission has only just begun" (*Times Educational Supplement*, February 20,1998):

> *The centrality of school effectiveness and improvement has not been achieved without heavy opposition, especially from education researchers within higher education. Status in British educational research has customarily been given to the most "use-less" research, not to the useful. Many have wanted to prolong our uniquely British love affair with the goals debate, rather than focus on means, as school effectiveness research tries to.*

It is worth noting in passing the ignorance and insularity of one who imagines that what Reynolds calls the "goals debate" is uniquely British.

> *Our progress has been due to our agreement as to what the goals of education were, to our problem orientation and to the interaction between people who were focused on effectiveness, and those*

concentrating on improvement, across a number of countries. Precisely because we did not waste time on philosophical discussion or on values debates, we made rapid progress within these limits. (ibid.)

Philosophers, then, are time-wasters, idly debating values and goals while standards go to ruin or, alternatively, the school effectiveness researchers forge ahead and improve our schools.

It has to be said that in several respects philosophy of education, as it has developed over the last half-century in the English-speaking countries, has been vulnerable to some of these charges. First, analytical philosophy of education, in seeing itself as heir to Hume's critique of religious faith and Ayer's attack on moral and aesthetic talk as mere persuasion, was always uncomfortable with norms and values. There was a positivism in this tradition which brought with it a widespread scepticism about norms, notoriously dismissed as "nonsense" by the verifiability principle. This often had the effect of limiting the scope which philosophy of education took for itself. In the case of the "is-ought gap" or "naturalistic fallacy", for example, the effect was to reduce the rich field of ethics to a matter of making "value judgements".

Secondly, analytical philosophy of education was far too inclined, in some of its modes, to see itself sallying forth equipped with multi-purpose techniques to do battle with fallacies lurking in relativism or the sociology of knowledge. It is not so much that this latent instrumentalism compromised it in its struggle against technical reason, as that it rested complacently on this conception of its role and saw no reason to develop any other conception. A new theorising of theory itself has been required, not as legitimation for principles and actions but as a form of deeper reflection on the nature and implications of the enterprise of education. Conceived like this, the role of theory begins to look more like interpretation than explanation. Wittgenstein of course described the role of philosophy itself in similar terms, and this was developed by Peter Winch in *The Idea of a Social Science*. Winch writes (p. 17) that:

Many of the more important theoretical issues which have been raised in these [ie social] studies belong to philosophy rather than to science and are, therefore, to be settled by a priori conceptual analysis rather than by empirical research.

Although talk of *a priori* conceptual analysis has an outmoded ring to it there is both an insight and a strategy here worth developing. The insight is that, first, many of the most important issues in need of research in education require interpretative investigation rather than explanation, investigation in terms of meaning rather than of cause. Empiricists here often achieve such successes as they do precisely by assimilating all research to the search for causes. Yet it is *meaning* which often calls out for elucidation. Consider for instance David Reynold's well-known ambition to turn schools into Totally Reliable Organisations, in which risk and error are as intolerable as they would be in a nuclear power station or in air-traffic control. This seems a prime candidate for the sort of approach that Richard Pring calls for in his recent book *Philosophy of Educational Research*: clarification of the nature of that into which research is being conducted, with proper attention to the meaning and significance of educational practices – the careful drawing of distinctions concerning such matters as learning, teaching, personal and social development, or culture. "Failure to recognize these distinctions has led in the past to overblown theories of learning which simply do not apply in practice and are now leading us to an oversimplified science of teaching" (Pring, 2000, p. 158).[4]

Secondly, philosophy of education has done itself considerable damage by the claim to be an autonomous discipline. It purchased this separate statehood at the cost of marginality. As Winch urges, philosophy should be conceived as merging into social science at one end of its spectrum; I would urge that it be seen as merging into literature at the other. All are kinds of writing, and must foreground and problematise their own uses of language. At this end of the spectrum it can engage ambitiously in explorations of what education might be or might become, doing the kind of thing that Plato, Rousseau and Dewey were engaged in on a grand scale. For is it not true that many of the key texts that have shaped modern conceptions of education are literary or hybrid in form (e.g., *The Republic*, *Emile*)? They are almost explicitly utopian, rather than claiming any great basis in empirical fact. And utopianism gives us a unique way of addressing the future, of education as well as of any other feature of our world. In an interesting discussion of Thomas More's *Utopia* as early social science, Wendell Bell writes (1997, p. 10):

> *More did not limit himself to previous experience. Like futurists today, he went beyond it by conceiving the possible and not yet existent social forms consistent with his understanding of the potentialities contained in then-current knowledge. He was doing protosocial science, to be sure, but he was doing more than most*

---

[4] I have drawn here on some of our joint introduction, in: Nigel Blake, Paul Smeyers, Richard Smith and Paul Standish, (Eds.), *Blackwell Guide to the Philosophy of Education* (Blackwell, 2002).

contemporary social scientists do, both in creating a possible alternative society and in clearly incorporating value judgement into his analysis.

In thus "conceiving the possible" philosophers of education would return to their proper place in addressing values; in aligning themselves with one end of social science, the end at which social scientists concern themselves with meaning rather than with cause, perhaps they can make more clear their important and distinctive role in educational research.[5]

References

Banks, I. (1990). *Complicity.* London: Abacus Books.
Bell, W. (1997). *Foundations of future studies: Human science for a new era.* Somerset, NJ: Transaction.
Blake N., Smeyers, P., Smith, R., & Standish, P. (Eds.). (2002). *Blackwell guide to the philosophy of education.* Oxord: Blackwell.
Hargreaves, D. (1996). *Teaching as a research-based profession.* London: Teacher Training Agency.
Henry, J. (2002). *Knowledge is power: How magic, the government and an apocalyptic vision inspired Francis Bacon to create modern science.* Cambridge: Icon Books.
Kipling, R. (1928). *Rewards and fairies.* London: Macmillan.
Lyotard. J.-F. (1984). *The postmodern condition: A report on knowledge* (G. Bennington & B. Massumi, Transl.). Manchester: Manchester University Press.
Mackenzie, J. (2002). Stalky & Co.: the adversarial curriculum. *Journal of Philosophy of Education, 36,* 4.
Pring, R. (2000) *Philosophy of educational research.* London: Continuum.
Winch, P. (1958). *The idea of a social science.* London: Routledge and Kegan Paul.

---

[5] This chapter is based on my paper, Education, truth and revelation: what really works? given at the European Conference on Educational Research, September 2002, in Lisbon. That in turn was based on an earlier paper, Education as a social science, Vlaanderen Fund for Scientific Research: Philosophy and History of the Discipline of Education - Evaluation and Evolution of the Criteria for Educational Research, Leuven, Belgium, October 2001. I am grateful to all those who made helpful comments on those papers.

IDEAS IN THEIR HISTORICAL CONTEXT:
THE CASE OF GERMAN
"Geisteswissenschaftliche Pädagogik" as a National Grammar

Daniel Tröhler

On March 14, 1915, a young philosopher of education, Eduard Spranger, wrote a letter to Georg Kerschensteiner, the well-known reform educator who had been interested in Dewey's educational concepts in his laboratory school. In this letter Spranger quite accurately calls Kerschensteiner "Pestalozzi's true heir," and "that being so, I would like to see you disavow and distance yourself from the pragmatist Dewey. The economical and technical are not able to fill up the latitude foreseen in German education. The German idea of the state and the German idea of science are much richer than people over there [e.g., the Americans, DT] will ever understand" (cited in Englert, 1966, p. 30). In his response, Kerschensteiner hastens to reassure Spranger by emphasizing that even reading William James' some years before had left no impact on him. However, Kerschensteiner writes that he is indebted to Dewey for increased clarity, but only in those areas that he himself had been interested in for years: "I think I'm not a good student; I just learn what I'm driven to anyhow" (p. 34). A few days later, Spranger seems to be satisfied. In a second letter he considers some similarities between Dewey and Kerschensteiner on questions concerning "Lebenstotalität" (totality of real life), but pronounces Kerschensteiner to be well above Dewey's "kitchen and crafts utilitarianism" (p. 36).

This exchange reveals far more than the "normal" animosities between Germany and Western states during the First World War. It refers to "world views" that are diametrically opposed to each other. Kerschensteiner was not interested in Dewey's pragmatism, but in some of the concepts of industrial education embedded in a movement traditionally called progressive education, new education, *éducation nouvelle,* or *Reformpädagogik*. The key element of this international movement is well known: "It is a change, a revolution, not unlike that introduced by Copernicus when the astronomical centre shifted from the earth to the sun. In this case the child becomes the sun about which the appliances of education revolve; he is the centre about which they are organized" (Dewey, 1900/1976, p. 23). Thousands of statements emphasizing the child-centered view in education can be found in articles and books of the time from the United States, Sweden, England, Germany, France, Switzerland, or Italy, and it will not even be necessary to name the authors. Under these circumstances, historians of education were and are easily tempted to define the time around 1900 as the time of progressive education – at least in the Western world.

Ideas in Context

But where then does Spranger's harsh rejection of Dewey come from? In the following I sketch out the ideological background of the German tradition and compare it briefly with American Pragmatism. Rather than to define and specify the different arguments, my objective is to outline the crucial ideas. In contradiction to the traditional Platonic history of ideas, however, these ideas are not eternal: they are embedded in historical contexts. Following the methodological discussions of the Cambridge School on linguistic contextualism, I try to relativize the well-known gap between the traditional history of ideas and the social history of a discipline. Pocock, referring to meta-theoretic reflections stemming from the discussion on "the linguistic turn," sees history as an interaction between *langue* and *parole* (Pocock, 1987, p. 19 f.). In this view, history is a transmission of "acts of speech, whether oral, scribal or typographical." The acts of speech are determined by the contexts "in which these acts were performed." The *paroles* of any historical actor always depended on a specific *langue*: "For anything to be said or written or printed, there must be a language to say it in; the language determines what can be said in it, but is capable of being modified by what is said in it; there is a history formed by the interactions of *parole* and *langue*" (p. 20). The *langue* is the ideological context, and it has "the character of paradigms" (p. 21).

In other words, certain *paroles* in the form of slogans or arguments – like "child-centered" or the often-claimed importance of connecting life and school – may appear to be similar, and an epoch comes to be labeled "new education." But I maintain that this labeling misleads and hides the tremendous variety that is revealed when we examine *langues*. Quentin Skinner, a prominent member of the Cambridge School, concentrates on these *langues*, which he calls "ideologies." An example of his methodological approach to history will illuminate the manner in which I try to work. In his reading of Machiavelli, Skinner does not restrict himself to the question of what Machiavelli wants to say in "The Prince", but asks how and why it was possible in Renaissance times for someone to appear on the scene and assert that "[A] prince must learn how not to be virtuous" (Skinner, 1988a, p. 61). The interesting issue does not focus on the "pure" content of the statement, but on the historical context. The question is whether Machiavelli's cynical assertion was a common one *at the time* or whether it was singular, unique in character. In the first case we need to know why Machiavelli was confirming a prevailing public attitude; in the second, we must ask why he was challenging traditional morals. Without regarding the context in which a text was written we will never learn anything about a text.

While examining contexts rather than looking for "pure" ideas "leaves the traditional figure of the author in extremely poor health, we cannot regard him as a mere "precipitate" of his own context (Skinner, 1988b, p. 276f.). This method helps us, on the other side, to avoid believing in "'timeless' truths" to be found in different texts. Moreover, it helps us to understand the traditions within which we ourselves, as researchers, are positioned – knowledge that allows us in the end to "choose among," or rather balance, the different *langues* (Pocock) or ideologies (Skinner). "To discover from the history of thought that there are in fact no such timeless concepts, but only the various different concepts which have gone with various different societies, is to discover a general truth not merely about the past but about ourselves as well" (Skinner, 1988a, p. 67). To learn from the past means separating necessity from contingency, which is "the key to self-awareness itself" (op.cit.). This may well be considered the key to the quest for the criteria in educational research. In the following I attempt to do so in the case of Germany, or more precisely, of *geisteswissenchaftliche Pädagogik*.[1]

The *Parole* of Autonomy and *Bildung*

If we take a look at the dominant paradigm or ideology of education in Germany in the twentieth century, *geisteswissenschaftliche Pädagogik*, we immediately find a key slogan: autonomy. Autonomy was related to education as social practice, to education as academic discipline, and to institutions of education. The various understandings of autonomy were discussed widely in the definitive journal of education, *"Erziehung"* (1925 ff.), as well as in the codification of *geisteswissenschaftliche Pädagogik* in the five-volume *"Handbuch der Pädagogik"* (1928-1933). The first appearance of autonomy within *geisteswissenschaftliche Pädagogik* was a consequence of the debates on school law that were unleashed at the School Conference (*Reichsschulkonferenz*) of the Weimar Republic in 1920. One of the heroes of *geisteswissenschaftliche Pädagogik*, Herman Nohl, describes the debates as chaos, tumult, disunity, and inconsistency. The debates are interpreted as eclipsing *the* educational idea as "unity" (Nohl, 1926, p. 57f.), an idea that, in the words of another prominent exponent, Wilhelm Flitner, had been recognized ever since Pestalozzi, but never realized (Flitner, 1928, p. 356). Politics must be limited by the *inner* freedom of the educator (p. 369), which is the only basis that allows him do what he has to do: to be the child's advocate in defense against various societal claims (p. 361; Flitner, 1930, p. 253f.; Nohl, 1933, p. 17). Herman Nohl's later successor, Erich Weniger, mentions the different "powers of life" that call young people to follow them. These "powers

---

[1] I follow the arguments that I present in a broader way in an article in *Paedagogica Historica* (Tröhler 2004).

of life" are characterized as real devils; they are described as "wanting men with their skin and their hair". The job of the educator or teacher is therefore to save the "soul of youth" as well as "the human entity and wholeness" (Weniger, 1929/1952, p. 82). The different educational reform movements, Nohl analyzes, all lead towards "one ideal" of a "higher life," which is, in the German Protestant philosophical tradition, a life within *Geist* (Nohl, 1926, p. 59). This *Geist* leads to a new manhood, to a new Community, to a new folklore. Nohl excludes the sciences explicitly[2] and emphasizes nature, homeland, home, and Community in order to achieve the new *Volksgemeinschaft* – the basis and goal of the "unity of a new ideal of the German man" (p. 58). Flitner affirms that education must be oriented towards the *higher world of the whole*, the *true Volk*. Educators should always look exclusively to a higher instance for orientation: the true community (Flitner, 1928, p. 362). In Flitner's understanding, this orientation is "the true *Volk*, the invisible Church, the true Community," whose contents are legitimate if they have a place in the inward spiritual world of the *person*. It is in this that the autonomy of education lies when we examine the societal dependencies (op.cit.). Autonomy was thus the one core term; a second concept, used to describe the sublime process of education as well as the goal of education, was *Bildung*.

By the close of the Weimar Republic, the concept of *geisteswissenschaftliche Pädagogik* had matured to the extent that it could be codified effectively by Nohl and Pallat's "*Handbuch der Pädagogik*" and could take on "paradigmatic" character. The very first essay was dedicated to the "Theory of *Bildung*"; the second addressed "The History of *Bildung* and its Theory." Nohl himself wrote the concluding part of this history, entitled "The Educational Movement in Germany," which homogenized all variations in the progressive educational reform movement in Germany after 1900 and thus created the *premise* that allowed the "theory of *Bildung*" to appear to follow logically. In other words, the construction of history served as the basis of argumentation for the *Bildung* theory.

Nohl's programmatic essay on the "Theory of *Bildung*" contains all the elements of this *geisteswissenschaftliche* theory. Each cultural area, says Nohl in Platonic fashion, is led by "its own idea," and this idea is the *phaenomenon bene fundatum* that must constitute the starting point for the scientific theory (Nohl, 1933, p. 12f.). Nohl does not discuss why this is so. In the core of the "Theory" we find the "Autonomy of Education". Nohl asserts that the state, politics, economy, and the parties seek to exploit education as

---

[2] Another exponent of the autonomy of education writes that it is *not* primarily scientific knowledge of the empirical world that should fostered, but rather a world of ideas and values in order that the "subjective totality of the pupil" can evolve (Geissler 1929, p. 78 f.).

an executive organ carrying out their aims. In the face of the horrible struggle of these powers and worldviews, says Nohl, we must reinforce the autonomy of education that the "theory of *Bildung*" demonstrates (p. 15). The act of educating, or the pedagogical relation (*pädagogischer Bezug*), stands at the center of this autonomy, which has been possible in Germany only since Rousseau's discovery of childhood and its transmission by Pestalozzi. Its goal is the education of the whole man (p. 17). The educational community has as its goal the "awakening of a unified spiritual life," a "personal spirit [*Geist*]." In these polarizing times, we need the model of the educator-personality, Nohl continues, for the more scattered or incomplete that education is in a particular time, the more important it is for the pupil to see in the unified humanness of his educator a representation of the higher life (p. 22). Thus the goal of the autonomy of education is *Bildung*, which starts out from dualistic concepts and seeks personal totality. But, as Nohl sums up, this approach is possible only in a state that has a comprehensive *Volksbildung*. Nohl concludes from his discussion of *Volksbildung* that only in an educated *Volk* life does the individual also achieve this unified shaping and forming (p. 32).

The Context: Totalities

It is not difficult to recognize this "theory" as opposite to the process of modernization of the world, such as industrialization and democratization – it opposes the plurality of the modern world. Against this plural world two concepts of totality are being adhered to, the totality of what is called the "deepest roots in the tradition of the *Volk*" and the totality of the "highest inner spirituality in the personality" – which is both anti-political and anti-social. In *this* context, a "theory of *Bildung*" in an autonomous sphere of education was developed. This anti-political and anti-economical attitude towards education was mainstream and represents the dominant "discourse" of that time. We can cite, for example, one of the most famous writers of the day, Thomas Mann. In his book "Reflections of an Unpolitical Man", Mann is proud to stress that the German concept of education lacked the political element (Mann, 1918/1993, p. 103) as he rearticulates the long-established idea that the Germanic essence and the notion of *Bildung* is apolitical – and most of all antidemocratic. The true understanding of education puts social and political issues in their only proper place: inside the inner personality (p. 251). Education, says Mann, is the forming of human beings, and never will the German spirit view "human beings" exclusively or even foremost as "social human beings" (p. 263). Politicization of the German person has to take place in the context of *Volksstaat*, not democracy, for only so can the German people fulfill the tasks of "tasks of supremacy" (p. 264 f.). Wilhelm Flitner wrote in 1928 that it was not the task of educators to take sides, or in other words, it was not the job of educators to make people capable of engaging with democracy (Flitner, 1928/1989, p. 244).

Thomas Mann, writing on belief, offers a concise formulation of the way in which the empirical social dimension was marginalized in favor of the moral perfecting of both the religious individual and the nation as a religious vision: The "personal ethos" was the primary one, preceding the social ethos (Mann, 1918/1993, p. 518). Man was not a mere social being, for he was also – in a dualistic manner – a metaphysical one, the German person being a metaphysical being first of all (p. 274). For that reason, man was not merely individual, but more importantly "personhood" [*Persönlichkeit*] (p. 240), which meant an inward spiritual life that arose through effort and self-cultivation, or *Bildung*. Here Mann uses a concept that was also central in liberal Protestant theology regarding salvation from the deep *fin de siècle* crisis. The concept of *Persönlichkeit* was highly attractive to educators. In addition to inward personhood, however, the nation, or the "emergence of nationality from religious elements, the national idea as a religion," also took precedence over the political and social dimensions of man (Mann, 1918/1993, p. 518). Because the Absolute cannot be politicized, writes Mann, it is important to follow Kant and distinguish the spiritual, national life from the political sphere (p. 262) and to speak not of democracy, but of "*Volksstaat*," (p. 237; 263), or the ethnic nation, the community sharing an ethos.

In agreement with Mann, Sombart, one of the most influential early sociologists in Germany, writes that each individual person can perfect himself only in the framework of the typical characteristics of his folk (Sombart, 1915, p. 140). True individuality is not the individuality shown by persons who seek their own advantages, writes Sombart (p. 113). Western democracy is seen as a solipsistic "aggregate of individuals" and juxtaposed against the German concept of *Nation*, which is "a folk community composing a unity," the "deliberate organization of something transcending individuals," to which single individuals (p. 76), who are *Persönlichkeiten*, belong as parts. Sombart concludes that in addition to this orientation towards the concept of the whole, the fact that there should be a continuing, firm commitment to raise strong, unique, self-contained personalities, who are after all the most wonderful credit to the *Volk*, is self-understood (p. 126).

In this context, *Heimat* had become the crucial term and – besides the German language – the fundamental element of the curriculum of true education. Eduard Spranger, whom I mentioned at the outset, was a professor of education and philosophy in Leipzig and a prominent member of *geisteswissenschaftliche Pädagogik*. He saw in *Heimatkunde* (or the study of Heimat) the chance to overcome the increasing specialization of school subjects. The contents of *Heimat* reflect the organic in the world, the totality of life

(Spranger, 1923/1943, p. 22 f.). As it can not be dealt with using one science alone, says Spranger, it is the purest example of a total science (p. 33), a schooling in the concept of totality that we need in order to liberate ourselves from the mental-spiritual [*geistig*] fragmentation of the present (p. 43). Here again, this totality is seen in a double manner: in the unity of the *Volk* and in the mental-spiritual [*geistig*] unity within ourselves (p. 3).

The *Langue*: German Protestant Dualisms

The opposition to a pluralistic world is based on a dualistic way of thinking. This thought was very accurate and congruent to the German philosophy of *Geist*. This *Geist* was the decisive starting point of *geisteswissenschaftliche Pädagogik*, which the leading representatives indeed base on dualistic thinking, stemming from the philosophical discourse in Germany. The very few chairs of education within the universities in the 1920s were all held by philosophers of education, such as Eduard Spranger, Herman Nohl, Wilhelm Flitner, or Theodor Litt (Schwenk 1977) – the core members of *geisteswissenschaftliche Pädagogik*. Consequently, teacher training for primary school was excluded from the universities; future high school (*Gymnasium*) teachers studied education only as a "pure theoretical discipline" that was integrated in the philosophical faculties.

In Herman Nohl's frequently cited article, "Die Einheit der Pädagogischen Bewegung," these dualisms show up in concentrated form as:
– Empiry and *Geist*
– Plurality and Unity
– Outward and Inward

The juxtaposition is between plural, external reality versus the inward unity of the *Geist*, or mental-internal unity. Historians may argue, of course, that these sets of dualisms are not new but were discussed already in the context of eighteenth-century Enlightenment thinking. But that is precisely the point. The German philosophy of *Geist* did not challenge the problems of democracy (in the Weimar Republic) and industry by generating new questions or methods, but rather by regressing to a mode of thinking that was popular at a time when democracy and industry were not on the agenda. To recognize that this thinking was not limited to academicians, but has to be seen as a reflection of the general *discourse*. Thomas Mann wrote that the difference between *Geist* and politics encompasses the difference between
– Culture and civilization
– Soul and society
– Freedom and the right to vote
– Art and literature,

whereby Germanness *is* culture, soul, freedom, art, and *not* civilization, society, the right to vote, or literature (Mann, 1918/1993, p. 23; compare also p. 160 ff.; 240, 248). Mann thus viewed democracy as identical with materialism or capitalism (p. 233, 346), and he attacked all three, noting that politics in general was "un-German" or even "hostile to Germany" (p. 21 f.; 29; 256; 268), because the Germans, in their philosophy of life, were a "Folk of Life" (p. 76, 181 f.). The notion of Life, to Mann, was the most German, most Goethe-like, and in a religious sense, the very highest conservative notion, whereas democracy stood in contradiction to Christianity and betrayed the Cross (p. 419).

It is not surprising, therefore, to find Werner Sombart, a sociologist and national economist, describing the First World War as a war between the commercial and the heroic ethos (Sombart, 1915, p. 5) – the West having the soul of the petty shopkeeper, Germans having the soul of the warrior. What is remarkable is that even though Germany was the leading economic power in Europe at the time of the First World War, only the states to the West were reproached with materialism. This discrepancy between real economic prosperity and the prevailing ideology was not, however, due to a lack of knowledge about Germany's national economic potency. Instead, the contradiction was consciously nullified by another dualism: inward purity and outward corruption. This shows up clearly in the work of Rudolf Eucken, New Idealist philosopher of life (*Lebensphilosophie*) and winner of the Nobel Prize for Literature. Eucken acknowledges that Germany – like France, England, or America – had experienced tremendous economic growth in the nineteenth century. The crucial difference according to Eucken, however, was that this development did not corrupt the Germans' true "character": "Have we then fallen away from our own selves when we turned to the visible world, when we developed our forces on land and water, when we took the lead in industry and technology? Have we thus denied our true, inner nature?" Eucken asks, only to respond, "No and once again no!" (Eucken, 1914, p. 8). That true nature, that according to Eucken differentiates the Germans from the rest of the other nations, is an *inner spiritual life*, which was originally religious and through the course of history, states Eucken, came to characterize the whole of German life and supreme thought (p. 12 f.).

Upon this background we understand why the German mystics and Luther were the core heroes of the German thinking as a whole – not limited to theology. The writer Gustav Freytag declared Luther to have revealed the true inner German character to the Germans in a way that nobody before or after him had been able to do, knowing well the Augustine roots of Luther (Freytag, 1883/1927, p. 81). Freytag's text, originally written in 1883, was republished in a collection of articles under the title "The German Genius". Herman Nohl, lecturing on Fichte, said: "The whole movement [of the late eighteenth century in Germany, DT] aimed to a higher life, to nativeness, totality, life in a spiritual [*geistig*] world, and coherency with the invisible. It was a German movement, and this movement was connected with the Reformation" (Nohl, 1939/1970, p. 211). Life and education are inward orientated, aiming at totality, and this is German. "*Bildung*" is, as Wilhelm Flitner claimed in his 1933 "Systematische Pädagogik," "*innere Gestalt*" – inward form (Flitner, 1933/1983, p. 104).

Outlook

It was John Dewey who in 1915 analyzed, although not *explicitly*, this German *langue*. He asked why there is a philosophy such as the German philosophy that reflects so much on freedom and, on the other hand, a people such as the German people whose politics are so militaristic. He relates this paradoxical situation back to the influence of German Protestantism, e.g., to Luther and Kant (Dewey, 1915/1979, p. 146 ff.). Their doctrines, of the two empires (Luther) or the two worlds (Kant), have become the core convictions of the Germans, believing that true freedom exists in heaven (Luther) or in the pure (practical) reason (Kant) and are identified by Dewey as having expressed and enforced a long tradition of German thinking. The world of science and politics is labeled to be a world of obedience; the inner, moral world, completely separated from the outer world, is thought to be a world of (moral) freedom. It is superfluous to mention that it is the inner world that is the higher, true, and decisive world.

Thus, we see why Dewey's "child-centered" education should not be identified with the German version of *Reformpädagogik*. The *parole* is, or appears to be, the same, but the *langue* is not. Dewey is highly shaped by the Calvinistic heritage in America and republicanism, connecting religion, politics, and education. But Dewey never wishes to have the old times back, as he writes in 1927 in *The public and its problems*: Social changes are to be regarded as a challenge, not as experiences leading us back to the "real" and "true" essence of a *Volk*. Pragmatic thinking means that we ask how democracy can be fostered under real social conditions. How diametrically opposite this way of thinking, this *langue*, is from the German *langue*, we can witness in the journal *Die Erziehung*, where arguments in an article by H.A. Korff were officially supported in a note from the editors. Korff called modern education "education to civilization", and he himself promoted the "values of culture of our *Volk*" Korff [1929 p. 301]. He asks: "How it is possible, despite the new social conditions, to lead young people to the eternal values of the past in order to challenge the ridiculous bumptiousness of modernity" – modernity that he calls a "delusion of enlightenment" (p. 302) and a sort of "educational nihilism" (p. 308). Modernity was thought to be evil; redemption was to be found in the Protestant German past and in the inner sphere of manhood. It is not a surprise that the experience of the Weimar Republic and democracy had no chance to survive. The *paroles* of democracy were not "spoken out" in the *langue* of the democratic tradition of the Western world; "citizen" remained a foreign word in the *langue* of the subject-bourgeois. Heinrich Mann, Thomas Mann's brother, knew this when he wrote the novel *"Der Untertan"* [*The Subject*], and it was this novel that provoked his antagonized brother Thomas to write his "Reflections of an Unpolitical Man". Heinrich was an outsider; Thomas was in the mainstream. Thomas used the *langue*, or rather he was a prisoner of it, that supplied the *paroles* of the majority – academic, literary, political, or educational. This difference of *langues* led to rather comical – if they had not ended so tragically – attempts at translating Pragmatism into the German language. The reform educator Peter Petersen, who edited some articles by Dewey and Kilpatrick on the *"Projekt-Methode"* in 1935, wrote in his epilogue: "The word "democratization" would totally be misunderstood if it was thought in terms of European democracies. Translated into German it should be called *Volksgemeinschaft*, with the precise meaning that we give this word today" (Petersen 1935, p. 207).

Source Materials

Dewey, J. (1900). The school and society. In J. A. Boydston (Ed.), *John Dewey. The Middle Works* (Vol. 1, p. 1-109). Carbondale and Edwardsville: Southern Illinois University Press 1976.

Dewey, J. (1915). German philosophy and politics. In J. A. Boydston, (Ed.), *John Dewey. The Middle Works* (Vol. 8, p. 135-204). Carbondale and Edwardsville: Southern Illinois University Press 1979.

Dewey, J. (1927). *The public and its problems*. Athens, OH: Ohio University Press 1954.

Dewey, J. (1939). Freedom and culture. In J. A. Boydston (Ed.), *John Dewey. The Later Works* (Vol. 13, p. 63-188). Carbondale and Edwardsville: Southern Illinois University Press 1988.

Englert, L. (1966). *Georg Kerschensteiner – Eduard Spranger. Briefwechsel 1912-1931*. Wien: Oldenburg.

Eucken, R. (1914). *Die weltgeschichtliche Bedeutung des deutschen Geistes*. Stuttgart/Berlin.

Flitner, W. (1928). Zum Begriff der pädagogischen Autonomie. *Die Erziehung*, 3, 355-369.

Flitner, W. (1933). Systematische Pädagogik. In U. Herrmann (Ed.), *Flitner, Wilhelm: Gesammelte Schriften. Band 2: Systematische Pädagogik – Allgemeine Pädagogik* (pp. 9-122). Paderborn 1983.

Freytag, G. (1883). Dr. Luther – eine Schilderung. In H.M. Elster (Ed.), *Der deutsche Genius. Ein Sammelwerk aus deutscher Vergangenheit und Gegenwart für Haus und Schule* (pp. 81-89). Berlin 1927, [extract of the original].

Geissler, G. (1929). *Die Autonomie der Pädagogik*. Berlin.

Korff, A.H. (1929). Zivilisations-Pädagogik. *Die Erziehung, 4,* 301-309.
Mann, H. (1918). *Der Untertan.* Leipzig: Fischer.
Mann, T. (1918). *Betrachtungen eines Unpolitischen.* Frankfurt am Main: Fischer.
Nohl, H. (1926). Die Einheit der pädagogischen Bewegung. *Die Erziehung, 1,* 57-61.
Nohl, H. (1933). Die Theorie der Bildung. In H. Nohl & L. Pallat (Eds.), *Handbuch der Pädagogik: Band 1. Die Theorie und die Entwicklung des Bildungswesens* (pp. 3-80.). Langensalza: Beltz
Nohl, H. (1933). Die pädagogische Bewegung in Deutschland. In H. Nohl & L. Pallat (Eds.), *Handbuch der Pädagogik: Band 1. Die Theorie und die Entwicklung des Bildungswesens* (pp. 302-369). Langensalza: Beltz
Petersen, P. (1935). Nachwort. In P. Petersen (Ed.), *Dewey-Kilpatrick. Der Prejekt-Plan* (pp. 206-212). Weimar.
Sombart, W. (1915). *Händler und Helden. Patriotische Besinnungen.* München/Leipzig.
Spranger, E. (1923). *Der Bildungswert der Heimatkunde.* Leipzig 1943.

References

Pocock, J. G.A. (1987). The concept of a language and the métier d'historien: Some considerations on practice. In A. Pagden (Ed.), *The languages of political theory in early-modern Europe* (pp. 19-38). Cambridge: Cambridge University Press.
Schwenk, B. (1977). Pädagogik in den philosophischen Fakultäten. Zur Entstehungsgeschichte der "geisteswissenschaftlichen" Pädagogik in Deutschland. In H. Haller & D. Lenzen (Eds.), *Wissenschaft im Reformprozess. Aufklärung oder Alibi?* (pp. 103-131). Stuttgart: Klett.
Skinner, Q. (1988a). Meaning and understanding in the history of ideas. In J. Tully (Ed.), *Meaning and context: Quentin Skinner and his critics* (pp. 29-67). Cambridge: Polity Press.
Skinner, Q. (1988b). A reply to my critics. In J. Tully (Ed.), *Meaning and context: Quentin Skinner and his critics* (pp. 231-288). Cambridge: Polity Press.
Tröhler, D. (2004). The discourse of German *Geisteswissenschaftliche Pädagogik* – A contextual reconstruction. *Paedagogica Historica* (in print).

III. EDUCATIONAL RESEARCH: EPISTEMOLOGICAL ISSUES
(Section Editor Wouter van Haaften)

SELF-UNDERSTANDING AND SELF-DETERMINATION
An unfamiliar look at the philosophy of education

Jan Bransen

Introduction

I should like to start with a personal note. For the last twelve years or so I worked in the philosophy of mind and action, the last years with a lot of emphasis on the ways in which the questions I discuss originate from within the practical problems of daily life and are related to problems discussed in what is now generally known as moral psychology. It is from this background that I'm recently thrown into the deep waters of the philosophy of education by being appointed to the chair of philosophy of education at Nijmegen University.

With this in mind I seek to explore a possible view of philosophy of education that would allow me to address issues apparently central to the field in a way that requires and appeals to my competence as originally a philosopher of mind and action. Nothing in what I shall say should be understood as developing arguments to revise the philosophy of education. Not at all – as a novice I just have an interest in finding my own niche. The paper is in four parts. In section 1 I shall say something about a widespread view of the philosophy of education as a variety of applied philosophy, and about the order of relevance this view assumes between the philosophy of education and the more established branches of philosophy. In section 2 I shall elaborate a bit on the idea that education is a feature of human life that informs us about the fact that human nature is constitutively temporal and self-related. Then I shall make some very sketchy remarks about two current developments in contemporary philosophy of mind (concerning self-knowledge and personal identity) that seem to be heading in the wrong direction, and I shall suggest that work in the philosophy of education could contribute to inspiring and new moves in discussing these philosophical issues (section 3). In the concluding section 4 I shall raise the question of whether the suggested alternative order of relevance between the philosophy of education and "pure" philosophy can be defended against criticisms from people primarily and mainly interested in education.

Relevance Among Disciplines

According to a widespread view the philosophy of education is a species of applied philosophy, an enterprise characterised by the attempt to apply existing philosophical work to the study and understanding of educational practices. Of course philosophers working in the area, together with philosophers working in other branches of applied philosophy, are rightly quite unhappy with some of the unfortunate impressions it creates: as if philosophers of education are merely instrumentally and mechanically applying insights and results developed by more gifted "pure" philosophers, as if they sponge on the blood, sweat and tears of these original philosophers, as if their role is merely to serve educational scientists and practitioners, as if their status cannot be more than second-rate, as if their competence need not be more than that of a serving-hatch, as if they have taken the easy way out and show off by becoming one-eyed kings in the country of the blind. Even if we would succeed in arguing successfully against each and every of these nasty prejudices, and even if we would succeed in arguing successfully that the philosophy of education is rather a species of practical philosophy, and as such a branch of philosophy proper, it might still be that one connotation strongly associated with the idea of *applying* philosophy to a particular region of human action would survive. This would be the idea that there is an *order of relevance* among disciplines: if we would think of disciplines as related to one another in terms of relevance, the point of this order is that we would probably have to conclude that the more established branches of philosophy are relevant to the philosophy of education, rather than *vice versa*, and that, in turn, the philosophy of education is relevant to educational science and practice, rather than *vice versa*. Perhaps we could make a convincing case to partially revise this picture by arguing that the philosophy and the science of a specific region of reality are mutually dependent, beneficial *and* relevant to one another. But this revision would leave intact the assumption that I shall dispute in this paper: namely that there is a one-directional order of relevance that goes *from* the more central, established, "pure" branches of philosophy *to* the philosophy of education. This assumption is even implicit in a remark of Richard Peters, *the* exponent of an independent and autonomous philosophy of education, who observes that although "the philosophy of education should be a branch of philosophy proper… [this] is not to suggest that it is a distinct branch in the same sense that it could exist apart from established branches of philosophy such as epistemology, ethics, and philosophy of mind. Rather it *draws on* such established branches of philosophy" (Peters, 1973, p. 2; my emphasis).

Given this background the plan for the paper is simple: I shall argue that careful philosophical attention paid to the significance of educational practices to the organisation of human life, allows us to draw conclusions about two crucial features of human nature: its temporality and its self-relatedness. These features, or so I argue, are likely to remain unnoticed by philosophers of mind who fail to pay sufficient attention to the educational dimension of human life. Because of that, or so I argue, these philosophers are inclined to misunderstand certain philosophical problems central to the enterprise of human self-understanding, notably the metaphysical problem of personal identity and the epistemological problem of self-knowledge. Because of their misunderstanding of these problems, they fail to come up with the right kind of account of personal identity and self-knowledge, which is an account that emphasizes the role of educationally organised self-determination[1] in the enterprise of human self-understanding.

If I am right in all this – and I know this requires much more substantial, elaborate, and detailed argument than I can provide in this paper – it means that there is at least one area in which the order of relevance between the philosophy of education and the philosophy of mind goes in the opposite direction than what seems to be taken for granted in the widespread view of philosophy of education as a variety of applied philosophy.

Education[2], Temporality and Self-Relatedness

I have suggested in the previous section that we can learn something about human nature by concentrating on the importance of educational practices in daily life. The kind of thing I want to draw attention to is not so much a matter of empirical findings: I am not making a claim about certain facts that are true of most (or all) human beings as exemplars of human nature, but I will be making a claim about the concept of human nature, about how and what to think of exemplars of a kind that is in its manifestations so deeply characterised by educational practices.

I want to restrict my discussion to two features of human nature that should draw our attention when we think about the dominant presence of education in our lives. The first is the temporal character of human nature, the other its self-relatedness. Let me say a bit about each.

---

[1] As I have argued in Bransen (1996) it is important to take into account that "determination" is an intrinsically ambiguous notion, with both a contemplative and a constructive connotation, meaning both "to lay bare" (or "to discover") and "to lay down" (or "to decide on").

[2] I should like to emphasize that in speaking of "education" I do not mean to be speaking merely of what goes on in schools. I shall use the term "education" to denote any social situation in which some people accept their paternalistic responsibiulity to take care of those who are in the process of developing competences. Likewise I shall use the verb "to teach" not as merely referring to what teachers do, but as much more braodly referring to what anyone does who accepts a paternalistic responsibility to stimulate processes of developing competences. This is an ordinary use of the verb, as in cases in which parents teach their children how to ride a bicycle. In such circumstances I might be using the word "teacher" as referring to "those who teach" in this broad sense, thereby accepting that in some sense parents might be teachers.

Human nature is temporal in two, related ways: ontogenetically and historically. As an exemplar of mankind I instantiate human nature at any moment at which I am alive, but almost everything that was true of me when I was a baby is no longer true of me now, and almost everything that is true of me today was not true of me when I was a small boy, and won't probably be true of me when I'm an old man. This is the case not merely because of natural developments that will take place in whatever environment I happen to be in, but primarily, and this is what we can learn from the dominant presence of educational practices, because of the changes I go through by being educated: by being able *and moved* to learn from experience, from examples, from myself, and from my teachers. And this is not merely true of me, but of each of us. We all show what human nature is like by instantiating it in many different ways, and these ways are temporally related, and temporally to be distinguished.

The changes in how we instantiate human nature display a development, but not merely a natural development that is a matter of course, such as takes place between acorns and oaks, caterpillars and butterflies, cubs and lions. No. Children and adults are related through a series of developments that are not merely natural because they are watched over in a process called education. Education is something we *do*, intentionally, with an eye on the developments likely to happen, with an eye on the direction they should take, and with an awareness of the ways in which we could make a difference to the direction these developments will take. This is a complicated statement, but that the educational nature of our ontogenetic developments is significant and makes a difference, can be shown by stressing the striking character of our historical temporality. Here's an example to illustrate what I mean: acorns and oaks in ancient Greece were very similar to acorns and oaks today, and the ways in which acorns turn into oaks today is very similar to the ways in which acorns turned into oaks in Aristotle's time. But adults and children living today are very different from adults and children who lived in ancient Greece, and the ways in which children in ancient Greece developed into grown-up Greeks is very different from the ways in which contemporary children develop into the kind of adults who populate our world today.

We could come up with a variety of explanations for this obvious and intriguing historical character of human life, but it seems that an explanation in terms of education is most plausible – despite all the complicated difficulties involved in this concept, difficulties that require the dedicated attention of philosophers of education. If this is true, it has an interesting and important consequence for our understanding of human nature. That is, if we want to understand ourselves we should realize that what we are differs over time, and is at least in part a function of what we think we are, and of what we think we should be, and, strikingly, these latter two differ over time as well. Thus, if education is a dominant feature of the ways in which our lives unfold, this shows not merely that our human nature has a history, but also that history is itself a major feature of our nature! And this means that what we are is something that unfolds as a history in virtue of the empathic concern[3] of those who can read and write narratives with an eye to grasping their import.

I will elaborate on this theme in the next section where I shall use it to suggest that this insight from the philosophy of education could be used to develop a specific, promising contribution to a couple of contemporary discussions that seem to be heading down a blind alley. But let me first say something about the other feature of human nature that attracts the attention of those aware of the role of education in human life.

This feature, that I call "self-relatedness", is already implicitly prominent in what I just said about our temporality. In education, as I said, we attempt to make a difference to our ontogenetic developments in virtue of having an eye on the directions these developments should take, or, stated differently, in education we watch over the historical unfolding of our nature with an eye to grasping the import of this unfoldment. This means that in education we display a sensitivity to the fact that our humanity is not merely a fact but also always a commitment. The idea is that we cannot just *be* ourselves, but are always related to what we will become in virtue of our understanding of the import of the development that constitutes us.

This may sound quite obscure, but here is the kind of example that might help to make my point. An acorn will develop into an oak given the right circumstances. Of course the phrase "right circumstances" is a normative one, but in the absence of any agential responsibility, it is not a normative phrase *for* acorns and oaks. With respect to acorns and oaks we could determine the meaning of the phrase "right circumstances" simply by generalising over the characteristics of all actual circumstances in which particular acorns do develop into oaks. This is not simply true of, say, rabbit hutches. Of course a heap of board could develop into a rabbit hutch in the right circumstances. And obviously the phrase "right circumstances" is again a normative one.

---

[3] I don't mean *control*, but I do mean *empathic concern*, and if someone suspects that this observation displays anti-postmodernist overtones, I would feel invited to defend my case. We could elaborate on this issue, although it is not central to my argument. My scant thoughts in this area are that if moderns think of empathic concern as if it were control, and if postmoderns want to do away with empathic concern because they rightly doubt the possibility of control, then both are wrong. We cannot, and should not do away with empathic concern for the import of our human autobiographies, for it is this concern that makes the crucial difference between natural kinds that exist in an educational realm and those that do not.

However, in the absence of any intentional activity, heaps of board will *never* develop into rabbit hutches. With respect to heaps of board and rabbit hutches we could again attempt to determine the meaning of the phrase "right circumstances" simply by generalising over characteristics of all actual circumstances in which particular heaps of board do develop into rabbit hutches, but what we will discover then is that agents with an understanding of what it means to be a rabbit hutch are imperative to what could possibly be right circumstances for a heap of board to develop into a rabbit hutch. The normativity implicit in the phrase "right circumstances" is in such cases a function of the explicit normativity of the *idea* of a rabbit hutch. Without such an idea there would not be any rabbit hutches at all, and neither – and this is more important than might seem – would there be heaps of board that could *in whatever circumstances* turn into rabbit hutches.

Well, what about human beings? What about human nature, its temporality and its educational infrastructure? My inclination is to use the obvious absence of an educational dimension in the growth of natural kinds like oaks and the construction of things like rabbit hutches to emphasize and clarify the essential self-relatedness of human beings. We share with the oaks that we will develop anyway, that the phrase "right circumstances" might be given an empirical and natural meaning that is normatively idle on the assumption of the complete absence of agential responsiveness. But we share with the rabbit hutches that in any circumstances in which children do develop into adults responsible agents with an understanding of the idea of a human being are involved. This means that on any possible account of right circumstances responsible agents will be part of these circumstances, and this reveals that the assumption of the complete absence of agential responsiveness is in the case of human beings mistaken, which in turn means that the phrase "right circumstances" is in the case of being human necessarily a normatively significant phrase. That is why we make, and have to make, a distinction, in the case of human life, between development and education. And the distinction is twice a matter of self-relatedness.

Firstly, in education we are, as learners, responsible for the quality of the content of our mental states in the light of, among other things, the evidence we are confronted with concerning the truth of our beliefs and the desirability of our desires. In the literature this is mainly conceptualised as a matter of our minds' capacity to develop second order states, which is a matter of reflexive self-consciousness (Pettit, 1993; Frankfurt, 1971). Many philosophers nowadays work on a project called "naturalising the mind" which aims to show that our capacity to learn can be understood as a complication of our capacity to develop, and can be understood as naturally possible without education, i.e. without such explicitly normative notions as truth, rationality, and desirability (Dretske, 1995).

Whether or not this naturalisation of learning will be possible does not effect, however, the much stronger case for the prominence of normative self-relations in the other side of the educational coin: teaching.[4] For, secondly, in education we are, as teachers[5], responsible for the quality of the circumstances in which we could be confronted with evidence about, among other things, the truth of our beliefs and the desirability of our desires. This responsibility does require explicitly normative notions, such as truth, rationality, desirability, intelligibility, and also, and this is important for my argument, an explicitly normative notion of human nature. This normative notion of human nature is required, not merely because the whole enterprise of being responsible for the circumstances in which we could improve our *beliefs*, presupposes a normative notion of what it means to cope with reality as a minded creature. It is also required, more importantly, because the very idea of being responsible for the circumstances in which we could improve the quality of our *desires*, requires that we have to think about what makes our lives worthwhile as something that is, at least in part, not a matter of satisfying the desires we happen to have. The very idea of presupposing that there might be better desires than the ones we happen to have, and that we are – as (self-)educators – responsible for the circumstances in which we could develop these more worthwhile desires, requires that we should try to think of ourselves from without, as developments with an import that deserves our commitment.

There is more that should be said here, particularly about the way in which the normativity entailed in teaching presupposes that learning is normative in a way that might be much more difficult to naturalize than optimists assume, as well as about how to think clearly about what it means for a desire to be actual, to be more worthwhile, to be one's own, etc. I cannot do that here, but should like to conclude this section by emphasizing that its point was merely to show that the obvious educational infrastructure of our human lives highlights two intriguing features of human nature: that it develops in time, and that it is characterised by a normatively significant self-relatedness.

Personal Identity, Self-Knowledge, and Self-Determination

I have been quite brief and sketchy in the previous section, and I shall be blatantly so in this one. As said before, this paper is a first attempt to

---

[4] Note my remark about teaching in footnote 2.
[5] See footnote 2.

explore some of the ground where results from the philosophy of education might prove relevant and important for discussions going on in domains traditionally thought to be more central to "pure" philosophy.

The argument of the previous section suggests that the philosophy of education might be relevant to questions concerning human self-understanding, such as the metaphysical problem of personal identity and the epistemological problem of self-knowledge. What I should like to suggest here, is that discussions of these problems tend to set off on the wrong foot because of negligence of the fact that human nature develops in time, and is characterised by a normatively significant self-relatedness. Failing to take these important features of human nature into account is unlikely to happen once one is informed by the philosophy of education. That is why I should like to suggest that philosophers of mind would do well to pay attention to the educational infrastructure of human life. Such attention would strengthen an interpretation of self-understanding as primarily a matter of self-determination.

My suggestion is something of an empirical conjecture. That is, I notice the tremendous impact of Derek Parfit's picture of personal identity as a metaphysical question to do with re-identification (Parfit, 1984; Dancy, 1997) and the equally influential picture of self-knowledge as an epistemological question concerning privileged access and incorrigibility (Cassam, 1994; Wright, Smith, & Macdonald, 2000), and I suspect that these questions became framed the way they presently are due to a general failure to take the educational infrastructure of human life into account.

Let me illustrate what I mean very, very briefly with some comments on the question of personal identity. In the Parfitian tradition the problem of personal identity is the result of acknowledging that, strictly speaking, the concept of identity cannot apply to persons because (1) persons typically change over time, whereas (2) strict, or Leibnizian, identity over time requires that the object as individuated at t_1 shares *all* its properties with the object as individuated at t_2. Acknowledging this requires us to develop an alternative concept of identity for persons that is on the one hand strong enough to account for the commonsensical intuition that a person is and remains one and the same throughout all of her life, and on the other hand flexible enough to allow for developments over time that are characteristic of those parts of reality, such as persons, that have an intrinsically temporal nature.

Seen from an educational perspective it is obvious that the normative character of the temporal self-relatedness significant of personal existence should play a cardinal role in this alternative concept of personal identity. That is, as I argued in the previous section, the fact that we change over time is not just something that happens to us. It is a fact that of necessity requires and depends upon our dedicated attention, and that we will have to watch over with responsibility, with an eye to what we will become in virtue of our understanding of the import of the development that constitutes us.[6] This means that from an educational perspective our identity is, *even metaphysically speaking*, a normative fact.[7]

In the Parfitian tradition, however, this normative self-relatedness is strikingly absent. Of course, there is much, and even very detailed and technical, attention paid to the fact that we change over time, but these changes are investigated from without, so to speak, and conceptualised in terms of psychological continuity which Parfit proposes to analyse in terms of overlapping chains of strong connectedness. Introducing an educational perspective would, I suggest, support the development of some of the alternative accounts that are put forward in the literature, but, so far, do not receive the attention they deserve, such as Korsgaard (1989) and Schechtman (1996).

A very similar line of argument could be developed with respect to the problem of self-knowledge. The upshot of such an argument would be an awareness of the fact that a person's authoritativeness about the content of her own mental states is not an epistemological state of possessing privileged evidence, but an educational state of being responsible for the normative orientation of the development that constitutes the person. Introducing an educational perspective on the question of self-knowledge would withdraw the question from epistemological quarters and would present it as a question at home in moral psychology. Such a shift would support a similar, intriguing attempt undertaken in Moran (2001).

These scant remarks are, of course, absolutely unsufficient to convince anyone of the fact that the philosophy of education could contribute to

---

[6] A series of important problems is concealed in the deliberately ambiguous and multiple use of the plural personal pronoun "we". I talk about "*we* will have to watch over", and "what *we* will become", and also "*our* understanding", and "the development that constitutes *us*". But I do so without specifying (1) who among us is referred to in each of these phrases and (2) whether or not these multiple references are to proper, overlapping or even identical subsets of us. In common parlance it is taken for granted that the role of the teacher is occupied by another person than the role of the pupil. One of my implicit assumptions here is, however, that in speaking about "teacher" and "pupil" as *roles* I am not bound to accept that these roles are occupied by different people. I prefer the ambiguity for a number of reasons I cannot discuss here.

[7] Thinking of metaphysics as, at least with respect to certain regions of reality, inherently normative is, of course, not without problems. My argument for an educational perspective on personal identity is, however, not meant to solve all problems at once, but rather meant to draw attention to those problems that should be addressed in the first place.

the philosophy of mind. But I hope they are suggestive enough to raise an interest among philosophers of education to investigate issues in recent philosophy of mind *not* with an interest in learning from them *but* with an interest in contributing to them.

Is it Relevant to the Study of Education that the Philosophy of Education Is Relevant to Philosophy?

Two contingent facts about the way universities are organised raise a further problem I should like to address. The first fact is that philosophy departments are unlikely to create room for philosophy of education as a proper branch of what they consider to be their core business. The second fact is that the philosophy of education is traditionally located within departments of education. Because of these two facts one might wonder whether my attempt to develop a way to reverse the order of relevance between "pure" philosophy and philosophy of education could have any welcome consequences for academic policies. I might actually be making things worse, because if the philosophy of education is relevant to pure philosophy (rather than *vice versa*), policy makers in the department of education might wonder why they would continue to support their philosophers, whereas policy makers in the department of philosophy would continue to dislike revising their favoured picture of their core business. Because of the threat of such an unfortunate future scenario for philosophers of education elicited by my attempt, I should ask whether the fact that the philosophy of education is relevant to philosophy might itself be relevant to the study of education.

The question is not about the familiar reasons educational scientists and practitioners have to engage in the philosophy of education, nor about new reasons to counter possible negative effects produced by my attempt. The question is an optimistic one, about whether my proposal to look for ways to reverse the order of relevance between philosophy of education and "pure" philosophy would create any additional reasons for people interested in education to foster the philosophy of education.

I can think of two such reasons. One of them is more general, one more specific. The general reason starts from a picture of science as not primarily a practically oriented enterprise aimed at problem-solving, but as an undertaking fundamentally inspired by the wish to understand for the sake of understanding itself. This is a respectable and age-old picture of science that clearly is appreciated for its romantic charme, its overtones of independence, disengagement and contemplativeness, and its associations with such great, imaginative scientists as Pythagoras, Galileo, Newton, and Einstein. It is also, however, a picture that is not very popular in the present era, dominated as it is by technological appreciation of science and by a pragmatic instrumentalism. It is therefore also a picture unlikely to appeal to educational scientists who tend to be very practical and seriously in the grip of concrete usefulness. Nevertheless, this general reason emphasizes that the argument I've been developing shows that education is a crucial feature of human life, and therefore a central field of science conceived of as our most prestigeous and systematic attempt to understand ourselves. This reason might gain some force in evolutionary contexts in which it could be argued that the most impressive step forward on the evolutionary scale was made possible by the appearance of a biological species not merely capable of learning but capable of *reflective* learning, i.e. capable of teaching, or (self-)education.

The more specific reason is, I guess, also a more pragmatic reason addressing the educational scientists' desire to improve the quality of education through its systematic and scientific study. This reason concentrates on the fact that self-knowledge and personal identity are among the central aims of education. My attempt could be understood as an attempt to show we can gain a better understanding of these aims of education by emphasizing the import of their educational nature. This would imply that the proper study and practice of education could profit from my argument, albeit in an almost indirect way. That is, the philosophy of education supports, according to this argument, educational science and practice because it is relevant to the philosophy of personal identity and the philosophy of self-knowledge, and by thus being relevant, it improves our understanding of some important aims of education, namely personal identity and self-knowledge, particularly in their educational – i.e. normatively oriented developmental – form.

References

Bransen, J. (1996). Identification and the idea of an alternative of oneself. *European Journal of Philosophy*, *4*, 1-16.
Cassam, Q. (Ed.). (1994). *Self-knowledge.* Oxford: Oxford University Press.
Dancy, J. (Ed.). (1997). *Reading Parfit.* Oxford: Blackwell.
Dretske, F. (1995). *Naturalizing the mind.* Cambridge, MA: MIT Press.
Frankfurt, H. (1971). Freedom of the will and the concept of a person. *Journal of Philosophy*, *68*, 5-20.
Korsgaard, C. (1989). Personal identity and the unity of agency: A Kantian reply to Parfit. *Philosophy and Public Affairs*, *18*, 101-132.
Moran, R. (2001). *Authority and estrangement.* Harvard: Harvard University Press.
Parfit, D. (1984). *Reasons and persons.* Oxford: Oxford University Press.
Peters, R.S. (1973). *The philosophy of education.* Oxford: Oxford University Press.
Pettit, P. (1993). *The common mind. An essay on psychology, society, and politics.* Oxford: Oxford University Press.
Schechtman, M. (1996). *The constitution of selves.* Ithaca: Cornell University Press.
Wright, C., Smith, B., & Macdonald, C. (Eds.). (2000). *Knowing our own minds.* Oxford: Oxford University Press.

THE CONCEPT OF TRUTH IN EDUCATIONAL THEORY

Stefaan E. Cuypers

Introduction: Nietzsche's Truth-Nihilism in Post-Modern Philosophy of Education

In *On Truth and Lies in a Non-Moral Sense* Nietzsche asks an old philosophical question and gives a shocking new answer:

> *What then is truth? A movable host of metaphors, metonymies, and anthropomorphisms: in short, a sum of human relations which have been poetically and rhetorically intensified, transferred, and embellished, and which, after long usage, seem to people to be fixed, canonical, and binding. Truths are illusions which we have forgotten are illusions; they are metaphors that have become worn out and have been drained of sensuous force, coins which have lost their embossins and are now considered as metal and no longer as coins.* (Breazeale, 1979, p. 84)

In this early essay, Nietzsche denies the existence of truth. The belief in truth is fictitious – truth is but an all too human invention. As a young man, he straightforwardly rejected transcendent or metaphysical truth as a contradiction in terms. Although one can discern a later position in Nietzsche's thought about truth (Clark, 1990, chap. 4), I shall limit myself to his earlier position. Closely connected to this truth-nihilism is the attendant Nietzschean doctrine of truth-perspectivism (Poellner, 2001), of which one version or other emerges in contemporary so-called "post-analytical" social constructivism and feminist epistemology. Whereas truth-nihilism flatly denies truth, truth-perspectivism is less radical in that it relativizes truth to certain perspectives, e.g., the perspective of class or gender.

Nietzschean nihilism or, at least, scepticism about truth is, surprisingly perhaps, also present in much work in philosophy of education nowadays. Two recent books by Nigel Blake, Paul Smeyers, Richard Smith and Paul Standish (1998, 2000) are cases in point. Following the lead of post-modern deconstructionism (especially that of Lacan, Foucault, Derrida and Lyotard), it is argued that the concept of truth has no place anymore in current educational theory and, consequently, that truth-based or so-called "veritistic" epistemology is irrelevant to present-day thinking about education. In as much as such a veritistic epistemology is successfully attacked by the post-modernist, rationality as an educational ideal comes under fire too.

In light of this recent post-modern challenge to veritistic epistemology and its relevance to educational theory, I evaluate in this paper a key argument of one important defender of the concept of non-relativistic truth in contemporary philosophy of education, namely Harvey Siegel (1997, 1998). I argue that his defence of a veritistic epistemology – i.e., a theory of knowledge based on a realist conception of truth (section 2) – and its import for educational matters is trivial (section 3). I will then reflect on the prospects for a non-trivial defence of robust truth-realism which can be of assistance in theoretical as well as practical issues within educational theory (section 4). Crucial to this reflection will be considerations about the potential relevance of major analytical theories of truth and epistemic justification to contemporary philosophy of education. I conclude that, contrary to what the post-modernist wants us to believe, rationalist philosophy of education is still in good shape (section 5).

Siegel's Truth-Realism

Before evaluating Siegel's major argument for an educational veritistic epistemology, it is imperative to get clear about *what* veritistic epistemology precisely involves and *why* it is, according to him, important to educational theory. Let me begin with indicating why epistemological notions such as truth and justification are central to educational endeavours. According to Siegel, educators and philosophers of education start from:

> *the idea that it is possible, and desirable, for people to engage in, and take seriously the fruits of, rational inquiry, where such enquiry is understood to involve the pursuit of truth – concerning the natural world, or the human condition, or any other domain about which enquiry is possible. This presumes the legitimacy of talk of truth and falsehood, and of rational belief as belief that is based upon and appropriately related to relevant evidence.* (Siegel, 1998, pp. 19-20)

The related view concerning education then holds that:

> *it is educationally important that students gain knowledge, and the ability to engage in rational enquiry; ... students should be led, in their education, to value enquiry, and the justification that the evidence thereby produced offers to candidate beliefs, judgements and actions.* (Ibidem)

So Siegel subscribes to the traditional view that truth-based epistemology is of central importance to educational theory. Although not the sole ends of education, development of skills for rational inquiry and possession of justified, true beliefs are distinctive and pivotal aims. But, being so fundamental for educational endeavours, what exactly involves this veritistic epistemology? It is, firstly, a so-called "*S*-knows-that-*p*" epistemology. Veritistic epistemology starts from the so-called "standard" account of knowledge as *justified true belief*. According to this standard analysis, the concept of knowledge is analysed in terms of three individually necessary and jointly sufficient conditions:

- S *knows that* p, *if and only if,*
- *(i)* S *believes that* p,
- *(ii)* p *is true, and*
- *(iii)* S *is justified in believing that* p.

Independent of social context, power-structure or gender, this analysis gives the essence of knowledge. This is not to claim that the analysis is without difficulties, e.g., the notorious Gettier problem infects the standard analysis (Bernecker & Dretske, 2000, part I).

Secondly, and more importantly, veritistic *S*-knows-that-*p* epistemology is *realist*. With regard to the second necessary condition, (ii) *p* is true, "true" is here understood in the strong realist sense. Truth in a veritistic epistemology is objective, mind-independent and language-independent. As a consequence, truth cannot be defined as coherence within a system of beliefs or sentences; nor can it be construed pragmatically as something useful for the organisation of our experiences. Truth is not an internal but an external notion; it is not immanent but transcendent. The only theory capable of doing justice to such a strongly realist conception of truth is the *correspondence theory of truth*. According to this classical theory:

- p *is true, if and only if,*
- p *corresponds with the fact that* p.

Of course, the relation of correspondence, the notion of an abstract proposition (*p*) as well as the notion of an objective fact (the fact that p) independent of mind and language are fraught with well-known difficulties. However, the metaphysical burdens of a realist conception of truth can be made lighter by an appeal to a so-called "deflationary" theory of truth. I shall come back to this point below.

By sketching the contours of a realist truth-based *S*-knows-that-*p* epistemology, I have identified the scapegoat of Nietzschean truth-nihilism (in post-modern philosophy of education). According to deconstructionism, it is precisely this veritistic epistemology, or "representational theory" as it is sometimes called, which is the inseparable companion of the metaphysics of presence. It is this transcendent notion of truth of which Nietzsche says that it is an illusion which we have forgotten is an illusion. I now turn to Siegel's defence of such a veritistic epistemology against the post-modern attack.

True But Trivial

In line with Nietzschean truth-nihilism and truth-perspectivism, the post-modern credo holds that Truth-with-a-capital-T is fictitious and that all knowledge is perspectival. In his defence of the Enlightenment conception of knowledge and truth Siegel adduces the objection of inconsistency against this post-modern attack. In his opinion, the post-modern challenge to veritistic epistemology is self-defeating and thus inconsistent. The basic structure of this inconsistency argument is the following. In its denial of truth (not-T) the post-modern critique still presupposes truth (T) and hence contradicts itself (T and not-T). Siegel puts more flesh to this skeleton:

> *some of these [post-modern] criticisms of foundationalism, ..., face huge difficulties, as they appear to presuppose what they want to reject. For example, [the] post-modernist wants to reject the possibility of objective knowledge, but apparently regards it as an objective fact about the world that a subject's knowledge of that world is always "preinterpreted", and that knowledge is therefore never objective. ... Similarly, the post-modernist insistence that there is "no privileged position that enables philosophers to transcend the particularities of their own culture and traditions" seems itself an attempt to speak from just such a position, since it seems to be making an assertion concerning all philosophers, cultures and traditions. ... In short, there appear to be deep internal inconsistencies in the post-modern position ... .*
> (Siegel, 1998, pp. 30-31)

Siegel's reply to the post-modern challenge is, to my mind, correct but trivial. His response is trivial because, firstly, it only makes use of a purely formal strategy and as such it does not establish a substantial defence of veritistic epistemology. Secondly, it is not clear what the status of post-modernism's truth-denial is or has to be. Of course, robust truth-nihilism cannot, without contradicting itself, include the *truth* of the truth-denial. However, to avoid the problem of inconsistency, the post-modernist could opt for, what I call, a "regulative" truth-nihilism. He could claim then that there is no truth and, at the same time, coherently maintain that the status of this truth-denial is the same as that of a "regulative idea" which has no truth-value, i.e. which is neither true nor false. Thirdly, the objection of inconsistency itself presupposes the principle of non-contradiction (not-(T and not-T)). However, the post-modernist need not accept this principle in his radical critique of the "conservative" metaphysics of presence and its attendant veritistic epistemology. In case that the rejection of the non-contradiction principle sounds too wild to the analytically minded, remember that so-called "para-consistent logic" is a perfectly respectable research program in analytical philosophy (Priest, Routley, & Norman, 1989).

In addition, Siegel (1998, p. 31) says that "the post-modernist's argument against the possibility of objective knowledge is a strikingly weak one" and that it does not sufficiently argue against the central veritistic claim that truth is correspondence with the facts. However, even if the post-modern attack leaves this claim intact, the burden of proof still lies on Siegel's shoulders. Merely claiming that truth is correspondence with the facts is trivially true because, in one sense or other, it is acceptable to all theories of truth. Unless the relation of correspondence and the status of facts have been given a (controversial) interpretation, it is a truism of ordinary language that "is true" means "fits the facts" or "corresponds with the facts". Even the coherence and pragmatic theories of truth can accept this truism of ordinary language.

Against the post-modern challenge, Siegel (1987) defends a non-relativist or, what he calls, an "absolutist" epistemology based on a strongly realist conception of truth. However, although Siegel (1998, p. 32) asserts that veritistic epistemology is non-foundationalist and fully embraces fallibilism, he does not spell out *how* the correspondence theory of truth on its controversial realist interpretation can be compatible with rejecting or relaxing foundationalism and infallibilism.

Prospects For Robust Truth-Realism

Although I have been critical of Siegel's defence of the Enlightenment conception of knowledge and truth, I am in sympathy with his case against the post-modern attack. I do not dispute his premises nor the thrust of his conclusions, I only found his argument wanting in that it is trivial and so not compelling. Hence I have played the advocate of the devil since I myself subscribe to a version of veritistic epistemology and its relevance to educational theory.

In light of my foregoing discussion of Siegel's position, I now want to ask whether a non-trivial and more compelling defence of truth-realism in educational theory is possible. What are the prospects for a *robust* truth-realism to counteract the post-modern challenge? I shall limit myself here to sketching a general theoretical framework for a viable veritistic epistemology. My purpose, more specifically, is to show that a veritistic epistemology entrenched in such a sophisticated framework is immune to, or is at least less liable to be infected by, standard post-modern objections. To my mind, the essential ingredients of such a framework comprise Tarski's semantic theory of truth, the policy of fallibilism and the notion of verisimilitude or truthlikeness.

Firstly, veritistic S-knows-that-p epistemology as based on the classical correspondence theory of truth is an easy target for the post-modern attack. Not only the relation of correspondence but also the relata – propositions and facts – face serious difficulties. The relation of correspondence as congruence or isomorfism is terribly obscure. Wittgenstein's picture-theory (Wittgenstein, 1922), for example, explains the relation between propositions and facts in terms of the more basic relation between names and objects but it leaves the latter relation totally unexplained. Moreover, propositions as abstract truth-bearers, on the one hand, seem to imply an unacceptable Platonic realism while facts as mind-independent and language-independent truth-makers, on the other, seem to imply an intolerable metaphysics of an epistemically inaccessible ready-made world.

However, Tarski's semantic theory of truth can come to the rescue. This theory is called "semantic" because the concept of truth belongs to a cluster of other semantic concepts such as designation and satisfaction, which "speaking loosely, *deals with certain relations between expressions of a language and the objects (or "states of affairs") "referred to" by those expressions*" (Tarski, 1944, p. 345). According to Tarski, all semantic concepts can be defined in terms of the truth-concept, which in its turn can be defined in terms of the satisfaction-concept. Although the contemporary semantic theory is the legitimate heir of the correspondence truth-theory (Wolenski, 1999), it does not carry the metaphysical burdens of the classical theory. Tarski's semantic theory is not metaphysical but deflationary (or mimimalist). Though the property of being true is not substantial as in the classical correspondence theory, it is not eliminable either as in the redundancy theory (Ramsey, 1927). So truth is not robust but not nothing either: it is deflationary. According to Tarski, "… is true" is a meta-linguistic property of sentences:

> *Let us consider an arbitrary sentence [for instance, the sentence "Snow is white"]; we shall replace it by the letter "p." We form the name [the description] of this sentence and we replace it by another letter, say "X." We ask now what is the logical relation between the two sentences "X is true" and "p." It is clear that from the point of view of our basic conception of truth these sentences are equivalent. In other words, the following equivalence holds:*

(T)   X *is true if, and only if,* p.

> *We shall call any such equivalence (with "p" replaced by any sentence of the language to which the word "true" refers, and "X" replaced by a name of this sentence) an "equivalence of the form (T)." ... It should be emphasized that neither the expression (T) itself (which is not a sentence, but only a schema of a sentence) nor any particular instance of the form (T) can be regarded as a definition of truth. We can only say that every equivalence of the form (T) obtained by replacing "p" by a particular sentence, and "X" by a name of this sentence, may be considered a partial definition of truth, which explains wherein the truth of this one individual sentence consists. The general definition has to be, in a certain sense, a logical conjunction of all these partial definitions.* (Tarski, 1944, p. 344)

I set aside the technical details about the so-called "Convention T" as a metalinguistic criterion for the material adequacy of the truth-definition, as well as those about Tarski's complete definition of truth in terms of satisfaction by all sequences of objects. To make my point that a realist veritistic *S*-knows-that-*p* epistemology underpinned by a deflationary semantic truth-theory can withstand the standard post-modern attack, I only focus on a partial truth-definition which accounts for the truth of one individual sentence. Take for instance, the truth-definition of the English sentence "Snow is white":

"Snow is white" is true-in-English, if and only if, snow is white.

At the left-hand side of the equivalence the sentence "Snow is white" is mentioned on the meta-language level (indicated by double quotes) whereas at the right-hand side the same sentence is used on the object-language level. That is to say, the first occurrence of the syntactical string composed by the words "snow", "is" and "white" (in "Snow is white") mentions these words to name the sentence "Snow is white"; and the second occurrence of the same syntactical string uses the same words to ascribe the property of whiteness to snow. Where the meta-language (for example, English) differs form the object-language (for example, Dutch), the "use / mention" and "object-language / meta-language" distinctions are more perspicuous. Take for instance, the Dutch sentence "Sneeuw is wit":

"Sneeuw is wit" is true-in-Dutch, if and only if, snow is white.

If the Dutch sentence "Sneeuw is wit" is given the English meta-language name "S" (i.e., the abbreviation for the long English meta-language description "the Dutch sentence constituted by three words, the first of which consists of the 19th, 14th, two times the 5th, the 21st and 23rd letters, the second ..., and the third ... of the Dutch alphabet"), then the case is even more clear:

S is true-in-Dutch, if and only if, snow is white.

On Tarski's semantic truth-theory, the sentence "Snow is white" is true, if and only if, the property of whiteness can be predicated of snow. By contrast, on the classical correspondence truth-theory, the sentence "Snow is white" expresses the proposition *snow is white* which is true, if and only if, that proposition corresponds with the fact that snow is white. It is clear that the semantic truth-theory, and especially the closely related disquotational account of truth (Quine, 1992, pp. 79-82), has rid the correspondence theory of all metaphysical burdens. Truth is not a queer property of weird things anymore since the meta-linguistic property "... is true-in-language-L" is an uncontroversial attribute of sentences. No bizarre Platonic propositions have to be posited; no fanciful ready-made facts have to populate the world; and no odd relation of correspondence has to hold between such strange entities. Sentences, linguistic as well as worldly objects and properties will do the job. Consequently, a veritistic S-knows-that-p epistemology bolstered by Tarski's truth-deflationism cannot be ridiculed by post-modern straw men.

Secondly, veritistic S-knows-that-p epistemology as associated with foundationalism and infallibilism is likewise an easy target for the post-modern attack. Traditionally the correspondence theory of truth has been allied to the foundationalist theory of epistemic justification. True knowledge as well-founded and justifiable knowledge is certain. Certain knowledge as indubitable and incorrigible knowledge is infallible. Infallibilism is deemed necessary to deal with the challenge of epistemological scepticism, the doctrine that knowledge does not exist. Although there is a dispute between rationalists and empiricists about the kind of foundations (rational intuition or sense-impression), they all agree that infallible justification implies *ipso facto* absolutely certain and thus unshakeably true knowledge. It is well-known that foundationalism and infallibilism have come under fire, even within twentieth-century analytical epistemology (Rorty, 1980). Contemporary philosophy appreciates the possibility of error and the dynamics of knowledge, and vigorously disputes the so-called foundationalist "myth of the given" (Sellars, 1956). The post-modernist aligns himself with this devastating non-foundationalist critique of epistemic absolutism and dogmatism.

However, as Siegel (1998, p. 32) notes, veritistic epistemology need not be linked to these objectionable doctrines. It can embrace the policy of fallibilism (Siegel, 1997, p. 23). This policy starts from the acknowledgement that all knowledge is hypothetical and, accordingly, holds that justification on all available evidence does not imply certain knowledge. For example, on a fallibilist reading, mediaeval people were justified on the then available Ptolemaic evidence to believe – and hence they *knew* – that the earth stands unmoveable in the centre of the universe. Human knowledge is always fallible and corrigible when new evidence occurs: mediaeval people *thought* they knew the geocentric cosmology but now we know better. It goes without saying that fallibilism includes non-foundationalism because hypothetical knowledge lacks an unshakeable basis and definitely conclusive evidence. Non-foundational veritistic epistemology can then embrace either an internalist coherence theory of epistemic justification or, alternatively, an externalist reliability theory. As a consequence, the post-modern critique of veritistic S-knows-that-p epistemology is far off the mark since, by embracing fallibilism and non-foundationalism, veritistic epistemology itself abolishes all connections with epistemic absolutism and dogmatism.

Yet, another problem now looms large. Once certainty is abandoned, truth comes under pressure. And when truth is sinking, realism goes down the drain as well. At first sight, the policy of fallibilism brings a veritistic S-knows-that-p epistemology in danger. So embracing fallibilism is not so innocuous as Siegel (1997, passim) seems to think. There is a *prima facie* problem about *how* the semantic truth-theory, as the viable residue of the correspondence theory, can be made compatible with a fallibilist theory of epistemic justification. Let me explain. According to an infallibilist account of knowledge, a fourth condition has to be added to the standard analysis:

S *infallibly knows that* p, *if and only if,*
(i) S *believes that* p,
(ii) p *is true,*
(iii) S *is justified in believing that* p, *and*
(iv) p *is objectively certain (i.e., it is impossible that* p *is false).*

"It is impossible that p is false" is ambiguous between the impossibility of being in error about p and the necessity of p itself. Because p can be a contingent proposition, the fourth condition only excludes the epistemic possibility of not-p – not the ontological contingency of p itself. The impossibility of being in error about p (p's objective certainty) follows from either an infallible state of mind or an infallible justification. Now rejecting foundationalism and embracing fallibilism implies giving up this additional condition and acknowledging that

(iv) p is corrigible (i.e., it is possible that p is false).

But by admitting that *p* might be false, one admits at the same time that *p* might not be true. And by admitting this, one also, at least implicitly, admits that truth – the second condition – is not a necessary condition for fallible knowledge. So granting the possibility of not-*p* in fallibly knowing that *p* amounts to giving up the necessity of the truth-condition. As a result, the analysis of fallible knowledge does not need a truth-theory, let alone a (residue of the) correspondence theory. Hilary Putnam, for instance, substitutes (idealized) rational acceptability for truth in his fallibilist account of knowledge:

> *"Truth", in an internalist view, is some sort of (idealized) rational acceptability – some sort of ideal coherence of our beliefs with each other and with our experiences as those experiences are themselves represented in our belief system – and not correspondence with mind-independent or discourse-independent "states of affairs".* (Putnam, 1981, pp. 49-50)

Let me put this in the standard format of analyzing knowledge:

S *fallibly knows that* p, *if and only if,*
(i) S *believes that* p,
(ii) p *is rationally acceptable, and*
(iii) S *is justified in believing that* p.

Since rationally accepting *p* is nothing else than having justificatory evidence for *p*, there is no difference between the second and the third condition here, this analysis just says that

S *fallibly knows that* p, *if and only if,*
(i) S *believes that* p, *and*
(ii) S *is justified in believing that p (i.e.,* p *is rationally acceptable).*

This fallibilist account of knowledge is clearly *anti*-realist (internalist or perspectivist) since it lacks the truth-condition in terms of which strong realism can be defined. So the *prima facie* problem with embracing fallibilism for a veritistic epistemology is *how* to keep a truth-theory in service and thus to remain faithful to realism.

However, thirdly, the best way to defend a veritistic S-knows-that-p epistemology in the strongest possible realist sense, while at the same time keeping with the policy of fallibilism, is to invoke the Popperian notion of verisimilitude or truthlikeness in the analysis of knowledge. According to this realist fallibilist account, the concept of knowledge (that hypothesis h) comprises the concept of truthlikeness:

> S *fallibly knows that h, if and only if,*
> *(i') believes that h is truthlike,*
> *(ii') h is truthlike, and*
> *(iii') is justified in believing (i.e., has good reasons for claiming)*
> *that h is more truthlike than its rivals on available evidence.*
> (adapted from Niiniluoto, 1999, p. 84)

Although there never can be sufficient conclusive reasons to definitely accept that h is true, there always may be good reasons for claiming that h is superior or more closely similar to the truth than its rivals. There is no criterion for truth, yet there is one for being more closely similar to the truth or truthlikeness. Popper (1963, pp. 228-237) himself suggests that the degree of testability or corroboration of h – the degree to which h is falsifiable and has passed severe testing at time t – is an indicator of h's degree of verisimilitude. Hypothesis h is then more truthlike than all rival hypotheses because h has the highest degree of corroboration.

According to Popper, the theory of verisimilitude is in concordance with Tarski's semantic truth-theory:

> *Our idea of approximation to truth, or of verisimilitude, has the same objective character and the same ideal or regulative character as the idea of objective or absolute truth. It is not an epistemological or an epistemic idea – no more than is truth or content. (In Tarski's terminology, it is obviously a "semantic" idea, like truth, or like logical consequence, and therefore, content.)* (Popper, 1963, p. 234)

Whatever the difficulties with the notion of truthlikeness might be (Psillos, 1999), this notion is an essential instrument in the conceptual toolbox of realist fallibilism. Consequently, by making use of this toolbox veritistic S-knows-that-p epistemology can ward off the post-modern attack while at the same time embracing fallibilism and staying faithful to realism. In response to the post-modern challenge, Popperian verisimilitude can be used to indicate *how* the semantic truth-theory, or at least the directly related truthlikeness-theory, can be made compatible with a fallibilist theory of epistemic justification.

Conclusion: Rationalist Philosophy of Education

The general theoretical framework, comprising Tarski's semantic theory of truth, the policy of fallibilism and the notion of truthlikeness, that I have sketched, makes a veritistic S-knows-that-p epistemology immune, or at least more resistant, to standard post-modern criticisms. This framework is, I think, also more robustly realist then Siegel's trivial truth-realism since it offers an indication as to *how* a deflationary truth-theory can be compatible with radically rejecting foundationalism and thus fully embracing fallibilism.

In light of my outline of robust truth-realism in epistemology, let me briefly collect results for educational theory. Firstly, rationality – i.e., acquiring justified true belief – as an educational ideal is still defendable notwithstanding post-modern considerations to the contrary. This is, I submit, good news for so-called "critical thinking pedagogy" (Siegel, 1988). Secondly, and connectedly, social constructivist educational theory and other epistemological perspectivisms (such as feminism) cannot downgrade the importance of traditional formal instruction by specialists who place themselves and their students under the norm of truth(likeness) and the standards of rational inquiry. Thirdly, as a consequence, the role of narrative educational research is not so much constitutive of as heuristic for the "true story", i.e. the realist factual account beyond ever shifting interpretations and re-interpretations.

In sum, one thing is clear: contrary to the post-modernist's wishful thinking, rationalist philosophy of education is not yet dead.[1]

References

Bernecker, S., & Dretske, F. (Eds.). (2000). *Knowledge. Readings in contemporary epistemology.* Oxford: Oxford University Press.
Blake, N., Smeyers, P., Smith, R., & Standish, P. (1998). *Thinking again. Education after post-modernism.* Westport: Bergin & Garvey.
Blake, N., Smeyers, P., Smith, R., & Standish, P. (2000). *Education in an age of nihilism.* London: Routledge.

---

[1] I thank Wouter van Haaften, Ishtiyaque Haji, the members of the FWO research community *Philosophy and History of the Discipline of Education* and the members of the KU Leuven HIW *Centre of Logic* discussion-group for helpful comments and suggestions. An earlier draft was presented at the annual 2002 Oxford conference of the *Philosophy of Education Society of Great Britain*.

Breazeale, D. (1979). *Philosophy and truth. Selections from Nietzsche's notebooks of the early 1870's*. Atlantic Highlands / Hassocks: Humanities Press / Harvester Press.

Clark, M. (1990). *Nietzsche on truth and philosophy*. Cambridge: Cambridge University Press.

Niiniluoto, I. (1999). *Critical scientific realism*. Oxford: Oxford University Press.

Poellner, P. (2001). Perspectival truth. In J. Richardson & B. Leiter (Eds.), *Nietzsche*. Oxford: Oxford University Press.

Popper, K. R. (1963). Truth, rationality, and the growth of scientific knowledge. In K.R. Popper, *Conjectures and refutations. The growth of scientific knowledge*. London: Routledge & Kegan Paul.

Priest, G., Routley, R., & Norman, J. (Eds.). (1989). *Paraconsistent logic: Essays on the inconsistent*. München: Philosophia.

Psillos, S. (1999). *Scientific realism. How science tracks truth*. London: Routledge.

Putnam, H. (1981). *Reason, truth and history*. Cambridge: Cambridge University Press.

Quine, W.V.O. (1992). *Pursuit of truth* (rev. ed.). Cambridge, MA: Harvard University Press.

Ramsey, F. P. (1927). Facts and propositions. *Proceedings of the Aristotelian Society, Suppl. Vol. 7*, 153-170.

Rorty, R. (1980). *Philosophy and the mirror of nature*. Oxford: Basil Blackwell.

Sellars, W. (1959). *Empiricism and the philosophy of mind*. In R. Rorty & R. Brandom (Eds.). Cambridge, MA: Harvard University Press.

Siegel, H. (1987). *Relativism refuted. A critique of contemporary epistemological relativism*. Dordrecht: Reidel.

Siegel, H. (1988). *Educating reason. Rationality, critical thinking, and education*. New York: Routledge.

Siegel, H. (1997). *Rationality redeemed? Further dialogues on an educational ideal*. New York: Routledge.

Siegel, H. (1998). Knowledge, truth and education. In D. Carr (Ed.), *Education, knowledge and truth. Beyond the post-modern impasse*. London: Routledge.

Tarski, A. (1944). The semantic conception of truth and the foundations of semantics. *Philosophy and Phenomenological Research, IV*, 341-375.

Wittgenstein, L. (1922). *Tractatus logico-philosophicus*. In D. Pears & B. F. McGuiness (transl.). London: Routledge & Kegan Paul.

Wolenski, J. (1999). Semantic conception of truth as a philosophical theory. In J. Peregrin (Ed.), *Truth and its nature (if any)*. Dordrecht: Kluwer.

EXPERIENCING KNOWLEDGE
SOME PHILOSOPHICAL INSIGHTS FOR EDUCATIONAL RESEARCH

Kathleen Coessens[1]

The objective of this paper is to present a philosophical view on the experiencing of knowledge as the active involvement of a situated human being with knowledge. "Experiencing" is the fundamental mode of human existence. "Knowing" is one of its forms, beside the experiencing of "being" and of "meaning". As human beings we are thrown inescapably in a world of knowledge. Knowledge is a cornerstone of the human culture and being. Education is for a large part concerned with instructing, passing on knowledge, acquiring knowledge. But what happens between a potential knower and the achievement of his reaching, knowledge? And what components interfere in this process of knowing? This article will formulate some answers from a philosophical stance.

Experiencing

Experiencing is the inescapable activity of "being involved in and by the world": we are fundamentally "experiencing beings", engaged in a continuous and dynamic process that results in experience[2]. This broad definition of the concept of experiencing can be further refined into five points.

Experiencing is in the first place "being involved in and with the world". The first contact of the organism with the world and with life is established by experiencing. Experiencing, as Merleau-Ponty says, is always "experiencing the world" or "experiencing life": "L'expérience – c'est-à-dire l'ouverture à notre monde de fait (…) le fait que nous sommes au monde (…) notre expérience est l'expérience d'un monde" (Merleau-Ponty, 1945, p. 256). This "being involved" is a fundamental necessity from a biological point of view: the impact of the open world on the human being at an imma-

---

[1] Researcher at the University of Brussels (VUB) - Center for logic and the philosophy of science. The research for this paper is financially supported by the Flemish Fund for Scientific Research (FWO project G.0123.98)
[2] Only Vasilyuk (1991) and Gendlin (1962) use the concept "experiencing" consistently. Other authors use "experience" as a concept including as well "experiencing" in the sense of an activity or process, as "experience" in the sense of the result of that process. In this paper, "experience" will be used in its strict sense, but it should be borne in mind that in quotations from authors such as Dewey, Alexander or Strawson, it carries the broader meaning and may thus refer to "experiencing".

ture stage, when other animals still develop in an intra-uterine closed environment, necessitates an openness to and interaction with that world and leads to a specifically human way of "experiencing"[3]. That interaction is, on the part of the human being, an active exploration of and response to the ambiguities of the world: "interactions between the organic, habitual, and social structures the individual inherits from the past, his openness to the world, and the world itself" (Alexander, 1987, p. 32). As such, the interaction with the world involves the natural environment with its facts and laws as well as the human environment with its symbolic and epistemic systems.

Secondly, human existence implies the immediate and uninterrupted "experiencing" of life. This aspect is very prominent in Dewey's and Merleau-Ponty's theories. As Merleau-Ponty says, "Un jour et une fois pour toutes quelque chose a été mis en train qui, même pendant le sommeil, ne peut plus s'arrêter de voir ou de ne pas voir, de sentir ou de ne pas sentir, de souffrir ou d'être heureux, de penser ou de se reposer, en un mot de s'*expliquer* avec le monde" (Merleau-Ponty, 1945, pp. 465-466), or as Dewey has it, "Experience occurs continuously, because the interaction of live creature and environing conditions is involved in the very process of living" (Dewey, 1958/34, p. 35).

Thirdly, the result of "experiencing" is experience, the outcome of an active process. Experience proves that "experiencing" is not only an active and uninterrupted process, but that it carries a certain durability: "L'expérience n'est pas la répétition indéfinie du particulier; mais elle entre déjà dans l'élément de la permanence: elle est ce savoir vécu plus qu'appris, profond parce que non déduit, que nous reconnaissons à ceux dont nous disons qu'ils 'ont de l'expérience'" (Aubenque, 1963, p. 50). Each experience, as an instantaneous snapshot of experiencing, adds something to further experiencing and contributes to the next experience: experience contains a principle of continuity and as such accumulates into further experience: "Wholly independent of desire or intent, every experience lives on in further experiences" (Dewey, 1938, pp. 27-28).

The emergence of "experience" out of "experiencing" thus implies a transformation of all further experiencing. For Arnold Gehlen (1936) the unfolding of experiencing leads as well to further exploration of the world, as to further closure of the possibilities of exploring the world. Experiencing implies the continuous delimitation, confirmation or frustration of the human

---

[3] The theme of the specific openness of the world to the human being and of the human being to the world has been developed by Arnold Gehlen (1961), Max Scheler, Adolf Portman and Berger and Luckmann (1966). It is sustained by neurophysicians such as Edelman (e.g. Edelman & Tononi (2000).

being's projects, of his possibilities and capacities in relation to the world. The subsequent patterns of expectation lead to a more surveyable world, but at the same time to the shrivelling of never solicited capacities and of the human being's original flexibility. The child experiments a lot, it takes risks, tests new ways; the adult reutilises tested and proven patterns and tries out variants of these. Some degree of creativity and some capacities seem to be lost, but in compensation some risks and failures will be avoided. Dewey (1929) sees this process as the possibility of creating deeper and more specific experiences. A continuous interaction takes place between us and the world: our experience changes the world, but it changes ourselves too. We become better acquainted with the world and with ourselves as parts of that world, and the world becomes better suited for us.

Fourthly, this continuous "being involved in and with the world" is primarily not a conscious or purposeful act. Experiencing remains most of the time "unnoticed" and non-explicit: "It is something so simple, so easily available to every person, that at first its very simplicity makes it hard to point to. (...) We can put only a few aspects of it into words"(Gendlin, 1962, p. 11). It will not, cannot and must not totally be elucidated. Neither can it be passed on as a skill or knowledge: no manual or instructions exist. Every human being is uniquely and in its turn experiencing: "C'est au fils de recommencer le père et de devenir vieillard à son tour" (Aubenque, 1963, p. 60). As such, experiencing contains a pre-conceptual, pre-noetic or pre-verbal component, starting from the original contact with the world.

Finally, experiencing is an original primary fact of human life: life requires experiencing. The primacy of experiencing means that experiencing occurs as soon as there is a human being and occurs as long as human life lasts. As such, experiencing precedes all ontological, metaphysical or epistemological comprehension. As Merleau-Ponty says: "Mais d'où tenons-nous l'hypothèse, d'où savons-nous qu'il y a quelque chose, qu'il y a un monde? Ce savoir-là est au-dessous de l'essence, c'est l'expérience dont l'essence fait partie et qu'elle n'enveloppe pas. (...) Sous la solidité de l'essence et de l'idée, il y a le tissu de l'expérience, cette chair du temps" (Merleau-Ponty, 1964, pp. 147; 150). Experiencing is the ground for every interpretation, exploration or articulation of oneself and of the world. Experiencing is the ongoing basic practice of every human being.

Experiencing as a "being involved in and with the world" is multiple: it "has a range of possible ways of encountering the world, extending from the highly indeterminate, unlocalized feelings we have to the highly articulate symbolic manipulations of cognitive experience" (Alexander, 1987, p. 169). We can classify experiencing by distinguishing three dimensions: "experiencing being", "experiencing meaning" and "experiencing knowledge"[4]. "Being" is lived in the existential presence of the human being. It is the flow of experiencing that concerns one's emergence, one's appearance and one's being situated in the world, leading to primitive notions of and distinctions between the "I", the other and the environment. Once these interactions and notions are related to signs, symbols and interpretation, we are dealing with the experiencing of meaning: "Meaning is formed in the interaction of experiencing and something that functions as a symbol" (Gendlin, 1962, p. 8). Intention, meaning, interpretation, sense are elements which become grafted onto the experiencing of being. The third and last form of experiencing is "knowing", which is the object of this paper. Those three distinctions are constantly interwoven and sometimes difficult to discern in the whole of experiencing: "Experience is as much cognitive as sensory. It includes everything a bat or a new born baby can feel, and everything a great mathematician can experience in thinking"(Strawson, 1994, p. 4).

Knowledge-Experiencing

Knowing as a kind of experiencing differs from experiencing "being" and experiencing "meaning". Knowing mobilises specific human capacities such as reasoning, thinking, remembering and perceiving. Knowing is an act of "cognition", of the human capacities employed in knowledge processes. Moreover, it leads to "knowledge"; it has a result that is transferable, that can be passed on and communicated. Experiencing knowledge occurs when a relation is established between a "knower" and a "knowable" object[5] – be it a theory, a material or a thing.

Three elements distinguish experiencing "knowledge" from experiencing "being" and "meaning".

A first characteristic of knowledge-experiencing is the *substantiation and objectivation* of the relation with the world, in various manners. To begin with, knowledge-experiencing introduces a distance into the relation to the world. The immediacy of primary forms of experiencing, as "being", has disappeared and processes of the mental and the rational are inserted[6]. Next, this distance implies that some aspects of the flow of experiencing are extracted from the indeterminate mass of elements. Such an extracting from and focalising within a complex and charged context makes laboratory and parameter

---

[4] Dewey makes a different classification of experience: he differentiates between feeling, willing and knowing (1925).
[5] An object or material with a "knowledge-inscription", as Bruno Latour (1997) says.
[6] This distanciation explains the importance and virulence of spectator theories in knowledge.

settings possible. As a result of this, knowledge-experiencing engenders a result, independent of the original experiencing itself: knowledge with an autonomous status, accessible to others. Moreover, finally, this substantiation can go beyond the world by creating possible worlds, different logics, virtual theories and technologies.

A second characteristic of knowledge-experiencing is the *determination* of this relation with the world. The relation with the world will be determined, limited, verbalized, theorised, symbolized. One's "being situated", at first vague and undetermined, will be rendered explicit by way of establishing objects, focuses and methods. But each approach will be only one possible approach, from only one specific situation: "Knowledge then does not encompass the world as a whole. (...) it is not coextensive with experienced existence (...)" (Dewey, 1929, p. 296). But as Dewey further says: "Not all existence asks to be known" (Dewey, 1929, p. 296).

Determining the relation with the world equally implies an active transformation of situations and of experiencing in general: not only will the process of knowing alter the object of knowing, but the experiencing of a given situation will also be different once it happens in the "knowing" mode. This leads to two findings. In the first place, knowledge-experiencing is always parasitic on other experiencing: "All inquiry, regarded functionally, begins and ends with our involvements in the contexts of ordinary experience, no matter how abstract the actual inquiry may be" (Alexander, 1987, pp. 87-88). Secondly, knowledge-experiencing contaminates further experiencing and itself: "Experience always carries with it and within it certain systematized arrangements, certain classifications" (Dewey in Alexander, 1987, p. 46). Knowledge-experiencing implies as such a meta-level of experiencing: the object of knowledge-experiencing is always to some extent experiencing – or an aspect of it.

A third characteristic is that this determination is sustained by *systematisation and coherence*. This means organizing, classifying this relation with the world: "to bring a measure of order to our experiences and observations, as well as to make specific predictions about certain aspects of the world we experience" (Casti, 1992, p. 2). Here also there is an important meta-aspect: knowledge-experiencing will order, classify other experiencing, itself included. Systematisation and rules are introduced in mathematics as well as in traffic, classification in nature – the Linnaeus classification – as well as in sports. Everything that enters into contact with knowledge-experiencing will be rearranged, classified, ordered, systematised with the ultimate hope of coherence and closure.

From these three aspects we can conclude that knowledge-experiencing realizes a kind of meta-experiencing of our relation with the world, a form of extreme reflexivity towards the experiencing itself and that it is an instrumental way of experiencing. As Dewey says: "Knowing consists of operations that give experienced objects a form in which the relations, upon which the onward course of events depends, are securely experienced. It marks a transitional redirection and rearrangement of the real. It is intermediate and instrumental; it comes between a relatively casual and accidental experience of existence and one relatively settled and defined. The knower is within the world of existence; his knowing, as experimental, marks an interaction of one existence with other existences" (Dewey, 1929, p. 295).

Hammering and Stories

A carpenter uses a hammer. He doesn't have to think about its use. The tool is totally integrated in the act; the impact of the tool on the hand functions as an internal stimulus; the tool functions as an extension of the hand. The use of the hammer, as evident as it seems, is a multiple experiencing of knowledge. Beside the fact that the origin of the hammer already involves multiple knowledge-experiencing – invention and creation –, the use of the hammer – the hammering – is also knowledge-experiencing, taking place in a broader context of knowledge-experiencing – the construction of a chair, of a house. Those multiple levels of knowledge-experiencing are not always clearly present. The original acts of creating the hammer only come to the foreground once the hammer is defective, and the use of the hammer only when the hammer is improperly used[7].

The example of hammering throws more light on the web of knowledge-experiencing. Not only is any specific act of knowing part of a larger process and knowledge-experiencing, it also reflects as a micro-cosmos the whole range of the human processes of experiencing. The carpenter becomes conscious of this whole web when his tool does not function properly. The hammer suddenly becomes an object, different from him, useless, but maybe reparable. The carpenter suddenly situates himself in the whole project, realizes the bond between the hammer and the environment: the relation with the nails, the wood, the construction, as well as the relation between physical and social places. He realizes that, by way of his bond with the hammer, he can appropriate the world. The carpenter, the hammer and the world are united by knowledge-experiencing. As soon as any of these three elements disappears, the whole chain of multiple knowledge-experiencing is interrupted. But this chain of knowledge-experiencing present in the carpenter-hammer-world-

---

[7] See also Polanyi (1969), p. 127, and Heidegger (1927/1998), p. 98.

relation has extensions to other kinds of experiencing – plans of construction, dreams of living, projects, instruction, identity, choice.

The following example, narrative practices, points even more to the insertion of knowledge-experiencing in a broader web of experiencing.

In daily life, the child is submerged by stories and encouraged to participate in storytelling (Fivush, 1994). It grows up surrounded by narrative practices: "Narrative practices are the set of situated, socially conducted narrative activities that are meaningful within a specific culture and that bear a family resemblance to one another in their discourse form" (Miller, 1994, p. 165). A young child will be exposed to eight and a half stories per hour on average (Bruner, 1990, p. 83; Miller & Moore 1989). Those stories, some directed to the child, but most heard in conversations between others, are not always censured: death, violence, relational problems, aggression are part of the narrative luggage which offer the child explanations and knowledge of the world. This gives the child access to a lot of experiencing it could never live through itself: "These include temporally inaccessible experiences (such as those that happened before the child was born), spatially inaccessible experiences (such as those that occurred in places from which the child is excluded), and affectively/cognitively inaccessible experiences (such as bewildering experiences that the child has witnessed)" (Miller, 1994, p. 167). The child learns to situate, integrate or negotiate different experiences, facts and situations. Stories provide the child with the possibility of experiencing otherwise inaccessible knowledge.

But the teacher also uses stories for the integration of his diverging, fragmented and diverse theoretical and practical knowledge (Connelly & Clandinin, 1990, 1992; Beattie, 1995). The stories teachers tell about their experiencing and experiences cannot be reduced to pedagogical theories or methods. Teachers have to mediate between the inter-psychological and the intra-psychological (Wertsch, 1985; Vygotsky, 1962), between what they know and what they want to pass on, between what they know and what the student knows, between knowledge and meaning, between knowledge and being. They have to balance between acting and judging, between explaining and experimenting, between practice and theory, between reality and representation.

A such, narratives help the human being to cope with the complexity and fragmentation of the world (Fisher, 1995): to situate oneself on a temporal, spatial, social level, to negotiate conflicts and incoherencies in experiencing and to balance between personal freedom and social constraints. Narrative praxis integrates knowledge-experiencing in a broader web of experiencing.

Acts of Knowing in a Web of Knowledge-Experiencing

As the examples of hammering and narratives illustrated, each act of knowing is interwoven in the whole experiencing and presents itself as a micro-cosmos of that whole experiencing. It is part of a web of knowledge-experiencing – of the past, present and future – which defines as well as surpasses the knowledge-experiencing of a specific act and of a specific human being[8]. What are the components of such a web?

Following Polanyi, a first broad distinction can be drawn between a passive, implicit or tacit component and an active, more or less explicit component present in the act of knowing. Obviously an act of knowing involves an articulated statement of explicit knowledge from a focal awareness and from a critical position. Beneath all this, however, there is always a mass of tacit knowledge, which remains unarticulated, a-critical and of which the knower has only a subsidiary awareness[9].

This distinction can be further subdivided into, for the passive part, a pre-reflective component, a component of meaning, a cognitive component and a contextual component, and, for the active part, a heuristic, a performative and a reflexive component. This subdividing is not exclusive; its components are not wholly independent, can overlap each other and can be more or less explicit.

The first component of the passive aspect of an act of knowing is the pre-reflective component. Pre-reflective aspects of experiencing are predominant in experiencing meaning and being, but break through in knowing as well. We take for granted that we can walk, sit and eat as we do. We also orient ourselves, classify and even conceptualise by means of our body (Lakoff, 1987; Tversky, 1991). All knowing is grounded in pre-reflective, pre-verbal and pre-conceptual practices (Bourdieu, 1980): "prior to the universe of explicitly, consciously used meanings, there is a vast dynamic structure of prereflective involvement with the world which forms the tacit order against which consciousness emerges and which it uses as its material" (Alexander, 1987, p. 116).

The second aspect of the passive component involves the cognitive possibilities of the knower. It encompasses what the psychological concept of

---

[8] The act of knowing is the process, the activity which leads to knowledge. It is as such a whole of knowledge-experiencing in which a combination of different components can take place.

[9] I have further developed this model of Polanyi, drawing on the theories of Gilbert Ryle, H.H. Price, John Dewey and Galen Strawson.

"cognition" refers to. Any act of knowing is dependent on the characteristics of the knower at a certain moment with respect to perception, recognition, memory, understanding and reason – innate or achieved (Price, 1969). This cognitive component overlaps with the pre-reflective component because aspects of it recede into the pre-reflective. Experiencing in the world changes the cognitive component.

Third, each act of knowing contains also a contextual component: the broader context in which the subject is situated. This comprises the prevailing beliefs and ideologies, the social relations, the natural environment with their influence and constraints for any individual act of knowing.

Finally, there is an inherent component of meaning in all knowledge-experiencing because of the integration of prior experiencing and experience. This is the mostly evidential comprehension of how we have to react, respond and act in the world. It happens almost automatically: words of a known language have meaning for us, we can handle a mathematical rule, we can drive a car or a bike. Galen Strawson speaks of "understanding-experience": experiencing in which somebody "automatically and involuntary takes the sounds as signs, and indeed as words and sentences, that he automatically and involuntary understands as expressing certain propositions and as representing reality as constituted in certain ways" (Strawson, 1994, p. 6). Or as Ryle says: "the ability to do things in accordance with instructions necessitates understanding those instructions" (Ryle, 1949, p. 48). We "know" the meaning of what we are doing, of the things we handle; we have a kind of background knowledge: intellectual and practical knowledge, skills or competencies which are present to us and which are inserted into knowledge-experiencing. The "understanding-experience" is then the presence of implicit, tacit integration of prior knowledge-experiencing and intercedes with the cognitive and prereflective components.

An act of knowing also contains more explicit, active components: experimenting or inventing, performing or acting, thinking or reasoning. A heuristic component, a performative component and a reflexive component are part of the active effort of solving a problem, controlling a situation or just of being curious. Those three components interfere continuously.

The heuristic component implies the intellectual search and effort to close the gap between the as yet unknown and the known: "We have to cross the logical gap between a problem and its solution by relying on the unspecifiable impulse of our heuristic passion (...)" (Polanyi, 1958, p. 143). This effort is tributary to the domain of the passive and tacit aspects: "though we have never met the solution, we have a conception of it in the same sense as we have a conception of a forgotten name. (...) to look at the unknown really means that we should look at the known data, but not in themselves, rather as clues to the unknown; as pointers to it and parts of it" (Polanyi, 1958, pp. 127-128). Heuristic actions can occur in three different ways: in the first place as thinking, leading to invention and technology; secondly as observation, fostering classification and descriptive science; thirdly as understanding, by way of "indwelling". The development of sciences and technology has professionalized the heuristic action, though it is not the privilege of the scientist or researcher. Heuristic action is present in all anticipations of the unexpected in daily life: finding a lost object, missing a bus, understanding the conversation with the neighbour.

The performative component is the most apparent and active component: it is indeed the action itself, the being engaged with knowledge. It is the performance of Ryle's "knowing-how": "what it is for someone to know how to perform tasks" (Ryle, 1949, p. 28). It is also close to Austin's performative act within the whole of a speech-act: "what one is doing in saying something" (Austin, 1971, p. 22). This performative component is an intelligent performance, an action that is sustained by the component of meaning or understanding: "Understanding is a part of knowing how" (Ryle, 1949, p. 53). It is the unique adaptation, refitting, actualisation of dispositions, capacities, skills and habits in a situation containing new, specific and unexpected elements. An example is the performance of a piano player. On the one hand, the musician has acquired skills such as reading music or the coordination of both hands; on the other hand, each performance is unique, involving the pianist as well as the music itself. It can never be completely automatic. Such performative aspect accentuates the dynamic aspect or the aspect of process proper to all knowledge-experiencing: "It is of the essence of intelligent practices that one performance is modified by its predecessors. The agent is still learning" (Ryle, 1949, p. 42).

Finally there is always some aspect of reflexivity in an act of knowing. The human being is thinking what he is doing, when he is knowledge-experiencing: "'Thought' is not a property of something termed intellect or reason apart from nature. It is a mode of directed overt action" (Dewey, 1929, p. 166). This reflexive component is interwoven with the heuristic and the performative component: "To magnify thought and ideas for their own sake apart from what they do (except, (...) esthetically) is to refuse the lesson of the most authentic kind of knowledge – the experimental (...)" (Dewey, 1929, p. 138). The thinking can be a thinking while doing, but can also be a thinking of the doing – in some sense detached – and in that case function as an evaluation, a possibility of reorienting the heuristic and performative process in a broader view: "Just because these forms of thinking are 'free' and not 'tied', they avert our attention from the world around us" (Price, 1969, p. 106). In this sense it sustains the heuristic component by reflecting on other possibilities, on untouched sources or new concepts in case a knowing-act fails: "In thinking we are somehow referring to, in cognitive touch with, what we do not at the moment see or feel" (Price, 1969, pp. 253-254). The reflexive component not only brings new oxygen in the process of knowledge-experiencing, it also changes the broader context of experiencing: "In the course of experience, as far as that is an outcome influenced by thinking, objects perceived, used and enjoyed take up into their meaning the results of thought; they become ever richer and fuller of meaning" (Dewey, 1929, p. 168). An act of knowing can thus be considered as an act of commitment, a kind of meta-experiencing, containing the experiencing and the evaluation of experiencing.

The following scheme will recapitulate the different aspects of an act of knowing:

ACT OF KNOWING

tacit components	active components
pre-reflective component	heuristic component
cognitive component	performative component
contextual component	reflexive component
component of meaning	

Conclusion

This paper has tried to answer the question "How do we cope with the knowledge in the world?" The answer is that we do it by "knowing" as a specific, complex and dynamic form of experiencing. An important part of human living is indeed the knowledge searching, knowledge meeting and knowledge creating part which I have called knowledge-experiencing.

Bibliography

Alexander, T. M. (1987). *John Dewey's theory of art, experience and nature: The horizons of feeling.* Albany: State University of New York Press.

Aubenque, P. (1963). *La prudence chez Aristote.* Paris: Presses Universitaires de France.

Austin, J. L. (1979/1971). "Performative-constative". In J.R. Searle (Ed.), *The philosophy of language* (pp. 13-23). Oxford: Oxford University Press.

Beattie, M. (1995). New prospects for teacher education: Narrative ways of knowing teaching and teacher learning. *Educational Research, 73,* 53-70.

Berger, P. L., & Luckmann, T. (1966). *The social construction of reality.* Harmondsworth: Penguin Books.

Bourdieu, P. (1980). *Le sens pratique.* Paris: Les Editions de Minuit.

Bruner, J. (1990). *Acts of meaning.* Cambridge, MA: Harvard University Press.

Casti, J. L. (1992). *Reality rules: I. Picturing the world in mathematics*. New York: Wiley.
Connelly, F., & Clandinin, D. (1990). Stories of experience and narrative inquiry. *Educational Researcher* (June-July).
Connelly, F., & Clandinin, D. (1992). *Asking questions about telling teaching stories*. Paper presented at the Annual Meeting of the American Educational Research Association, San Francisco.
Dewey, J. (1963/1938). *Experience and education*. New York: Macmillan.
Dewey, J. (1958/1934). *Art as experience*. New York: Capricorn Books.
Dewey, J. (1929). *Experience and nature*. Allen and Unwin London.
Dewey, J. (1960/1929). *The quest for certainty: A study of the relation of knowledge and action*. New York: Capricorn Books.
Edelman, G. M., & Tononi, G. (2000). *A universe of consciousness. How matter becomes imagination*. New York: Basic Books.
Fisher, W. R. (1995). Narration, knowledge, and the possibility of wisdom. In W. R. Fisher & R. F. Goodman (Eds.), *Rethinking knowledge: Reflections across the disciplines* (pp. 169-192). Albany: State University of New York Press.
Fivush, R. (1994). Constructing narrative, emotion, and self in parent-child conversations about the past. In U. Neisser & R. Fivush (Eds.), *The remembering self – Construction and accuracy in the self-narrative*. Cambridge: Cambridge University Press.
Gehlen, A. (1961/36). *Anthropologische Forschung - Zur Selbstbegegnung und Selbstentdeckung des Menschen*. Reinbek bei Hamburg: Rowohlt.
Gendlin, E. T. (1962). *Experiencing and the creation of meaning*. New York: Macmillan.
Heidegger, M. (1998/1927). *Zijn en tijd*. Nijmegen: Sun.
Lakoff, G. (1987). *Women, fire, and dangerous things - What categories reveal about the mind*. Chicago: University of Chicago Press.
Latour, B. (1997). Where are the missing masses? The sociology of a few mundane artifacts. In W. E. Bijker & J. Law (Eds.), *Shaping technology/ Building society - Studies in sociotechnical change* (pp. 225-258). Cambridge, MA: MIT.
Merleau-ponty, M. (1945). *Phénoménologie de la perception*. Paris: Gallimard.
Merleau-ponty, M. (1964). *Le visible et l'invisible*. Paris: Gallimard.
Miller, P. J. (1994). Narrative practices: Their role in socialization and self-construction. In U. Neisser & R. Fivush (Eds.), *The remembering self – Construction and accuracy in the self-narrative* (pp. 158-179). Cambridge: Cambridge University Press.
Miller, P.J., & Moore, B. (1989). Narrative conjunctions of caregiver and child: A comparative perspective on socialization through stories. *Ethos, 17*, 43-64.
Polanyi, M. (1958). *Personal knowledge – Towards a post-critical philosophy*. Chicago: University of Chicago Press.
Polanyi, M. (1967). *The tacit dimension*. London: Routledge.
Polanyi, M. (1969). *Knowing and being*. London: Routledge & Kegan.
Price, H.H. (1969/1953). *Thinking and experience*. London: Hutchinson & co.
Ryle, G. (1990/1949). *The concept of mind*. London: Penguin Books.

Strawson, G. (1994). *Mental reality.* Cambridge, MA: MIT Press.
Tversky, B. (1991). Spatial mental models. *The Psychology of Learning and Motivation, 27,* 109-145.
Vasilyuk, F. (1991). *The psychology of experiencing.* Hertfordshire: Harvester Wheatsheaf.
Vygotsky, L.S. (1962). *Thought and language.* Cambridge, MA: MIT Press.
Wertsch, J.V. (1985). *Vygotsky and the social formation of mind.* Cambridge: Cambridge University Press.

WITTGENSTEIN AND CAVELL: REAPPRAISING SCEPTICISM IN EDUCATIONAL THEORY

Stefan Ramaekers

Scepticism has always been stirring emotions, in education no less than elsewhere. Here I focus on one position in educational philosophy that is particularly wary of scepticism in education – that of David Carr. Carr's concern for scepticism is a general one, with a specific attention for postmodernist scepticism that has been introduced in education over the last decades. In general, scepticism either has been incorporated into the process of theoretical scrutiny, or has been understood as a threat to its results (hence something to be combatted). Carr uses the same strategies to deal with postmodernist scepticism. In this chapter I argue for a way of dealing with scepticism in education and in educational theory other than in these either/or terms. This requires that we shift our perspective on scepticism away from a philosophical position or methodological tool to an understanding of it as inherent to our human lives with language – an understanding for which I draw on the writings of Stanley Cavell. This shift of perspective can invigorate educational theory in the sense of being better attuned than before to the concerns of practice rather than being worried over (a defense of) foundations.

First, I briefly sketch the basics of Carr's position contra (postmodernist) scepticism. Second, I indicate some problems with this position and link this up to the Wittgensteinian-Cavellean shift of perspective concerning scepticism I have in mind here. Thirdly, I return to Carr, indicate in what sense Carr himself can be taken to be a sceptic, and draw some positive outlines for a different understanding of educational theory.

Craving for Certainty: David Carr's Educational Philosophy

Carr places himself in a tradition of analytical philosophy going back to Plato, Socrates and Aristotle. Characteristic of this tradition is an ongoing concern for epistemological enquiry as central to the philosophical enterprise, for "rational enquiry into the formal character of knowledge and truth" (Carr, 1998a, p. xi). It is important that we see what lies behind this concern: from the beginning this philosophical tradition is marked by a desire for absolute stability and timeless truths. This implies, simply, that Carr's conception of knowledge and truth in education relates to this desire. Put otherwise, against the background of a pursuit of foundational certainty and its accompanying desire for rational justification, it is not hard to see that Carr is particularly wary of what are, in his view, the pernicious consequences of scepticism for educational theory and practice, more particularly of the fact that scepticism even jeopardises education itself. For Carr, postmodernism is an example of such scepticism.

Carr is concerned about "the spread of non-realist or anti-realist conceptions of knowledge and truth" (Carr, 1998b, p. 12) – which are promoted, Carr argues, within (ironically, we could say) analytical philosophical movements such as the "meaning as use theory" in line with Wittgenstein, as well as within postanalytical or postmodernist philosophical currents such as pragmatism and poststructuralism (Carr, 1998b, 1999). In his understanding, precisely these postmodernist currents have led to a widespread scepticism about the value of epistemological theorising in educational philosophy and in extreme cases even about the very possibility of epistemology itself (Carr, 1994, 1998a). As he puts this:

> *[...] it seems to have become almost* de rigueur *to be "incredulous about metanarratives" and to prefer the relativist – or at least pluralist – language of rival traditions or narratives to any absolutist talk of objective knowledge and truth.* (Carr, 1999, p. 442)

For Carr, this is, educationally speaking, very troublesome. Siegel puts this view by saying that it is uncontroversially and pre-philosophically so that education aims at imparting knowledge to students (Siegel, 1998). So what are we to make of teaching, learning, the curriculum, understanding without reference to epistemological notions such as knowledge, truth, justification, rationality? Moreover, it seems to be widely held, Siegel continues, that rational enquiry and the pursuit of truth such enquiry involves are considered to be educationally important (ibid.) – which makes it altogether even more astonishing that such epistemological notions have been undermined so vigorously.

In the interest of education, Carr therefore commits himself to rehabilitating some conception of objective knowledge and truth, through a rational critique of postmodern(ist) currents in educational theorising. Knowledge according to Carr should be understood as

> *the grasp of an independent objective order by an epistemic agent who, in his attempts to apprehend it, observes certain rational canons and procedures of disinterested and impartial enquiry.* (Carr, 1994, p. 224)

This notion of objective truth is simply indispensable as a goal of human enquiry "if we are to have any confidence that our enquiries may actually take us somewhere by way of an understanding of that which exists beyond the otherwise uncertain contents of our own minds" (Carr, 1994, p. 225).

It is insightful to briefly pause here and notice how Carr puts the issue as a dualism. Either our understanding refers to something independent of us, human beings, or we are confined to the contents of our own minds. The latter denotes subjectivism, a variant of relativism. And, Carr gives us to understand, we clearly do not want that. Therefore we should stick to (what seems to present itself to Carr as) our only alternative: if we are to make sense, our understanding must be conceived of as grasping something beyond our own minds. What lies beneath this dualistic construal is that, in Carr's view, postmodernist currents in educational theory are a species of relativism. In fact, he recently (2001) charged the postmodernist critique of the value neutrality of testing with relativism of the worst kind. Moreover, according to Carr these currents do not account for knowledge in terms of a grasp of an independent objective order either and thereby open the door for anti-realism.

For Carr, postmodernism entails "that there can be *no* common theoretical or practical discourse enshrining cross culturally applicable canons of rationality, knowledge and truth" (Carr, 1998b, p. 3), which leads to an overall scepticism about the very possibility of objective knowledge and truth. However, this yields potentially devastating consequences for education, he argues. The following passage captures the spirit of his concerns:

> *If there are no objective truths or facts of any matter – if all is matter of individual or socio-historical construction of more or less persuasive models of reality and there can be no rational basis, other than convenience or utility, for preferring one perspective to another – what price any notion of education as initiation into truths, virtues and values that are significant in ways that transcend convenience and utility? And what becomes of curriculum planning? If there is no more than personal preference or cultural prejudice to someone's judgement that Mozart is musically more rewarding than Madonna, what justification can there be for including one rather than the other in any school curriculum?* (Carr, 1998b, p. 13)

Education as initiation cannot be conceived of properly without objective truths; education as initiation demands objective truths, values and virtues. To be sure, Carr does not argue that one needs a *definitive* theoretical account in order to be able to educate at all. Though his project of rehabilitation of objective knowledge and truth should be understood on realist terms, this does not imply "absolute or bedrock metaphysical and other truths" (Carr, 1994, p. 236). It requires only a minimal realist account and a minimal sort of correspondence (Siegel, 1998). He explicitly rejects the position "which would require the subject of knowledge to adopt some inconceivable Archimedean epistemological standpoint" (Carr, 1994, p. 225) and opts for what he calls a "modest Aristotelian correspondence": "it is speaking truly to say of what is, that it is, and speaking falsely to say that it is of what is not" (Ibid.). Nonetheless, it is important that we see that what he does commit himself to – since he sets his own position up as an anti-sceptical one – is to provide a minimal theoretical guarantee in order to ensure himself he is educating in truth, and not in illusion. An educator's confidence in her educational practices is enhanced if educational theory can provide certain knowledge – hence the need for rational enquiry in any domain of human interest and for the notion of objective truth as a significant goal of such enquiry.

It is interesting to note that, by arguing for this minimal realist requirement, Carr considers himself to be meeting some postmodernist objections, particularly those against a realism of the metaphysical kind. At times Carr does not dismiss postmodernism as advancing relativism, but grants that it teaches us a lesson, viz. a fallibilist one. It teaches us that much, if not all, human knowledge is inescapably provisional (Carr, 1994, 1998a). In line with (what he understands to be) the fallibilist insights of postmodernism, he readily concedes that "important questions about the nature and meaning of knowledge and truth are by no means finally settled" (Carr, 1999, p. 445). As such then, Carr would not consider himself to be a foundationalist, or at least certainly not in the traditional sense. One does not need to have *settled* epistemological questions before education can take a start (Carr, 1999). Similarly, it is the acceptance of this fallibilism which makes clear that the sort of *rational* critique Carr argues for should not be understood as a (rather naïve) return to some absolute sovereignty of reason alone (Carr, 1998b). Nevertheless, we need to acknowledge that what clearly underlies his conception of knowledge and education is a foundationalist tenacity. This means that since education can, in his view, only be properly conceived of if there are objective truths or facts of the matter which children can be initiated into or at least be acquainted with, we need to direct our investigative efforts towards finding such truths and facts. Scepticism, in sum, is therefore either to be combatted, or to be incorporated into the quest for certainty (for instance in the form of a fallibilism).

Shifting the Scene: Towards an Existential Interpretation of Scepticism

There are, however, some problems with Carr's way of dealing with (postmodernist) scepticism, two of which I will indicate briefly here. First, his assessment of postmodernist scepticism is not entirely correct in the sense that it does not apply to all instances of postmodernism in education. Elsewhere (Ramaekers, 2002) I have discussed the idea of postmodernist scepticism and its challenge to educational theory. Briefly, what Carr effectively does is reducing postmodernist scepticism to (what we could call) a scepticism-against-the-background-of-certainty. This means that postmodernism is construed as being primarily concerned with the epistemological constitution of a claim purporting to be knowledge. Insofar as Carr understands postmodernism as a relativism, this more specifically implies that he takes it as consistently denying the possibility of rational justification. Insofar as he construes it as a fallibilist lesson, it is restrictively incorporated into the usual business of the justification of claims to knowledge, which allows him to preserve his view of objective truth as the proper goal of educational theory, and, particularly, of objective truth as presupposed in any conception of education (as initiation).

Though some instances of postmodernism in educational theory can rightfully be understood as such scepticism-against-the-background-of-certainty, in general postmodern doubt is to be distinguished from this type of scepticism (see Ramaekers, 2002). The relevant distinction here is the one between scepticism about grand narratives, and scepticism about the purported certainty of knowledge. The latter is a scepticism that operates within the parameters set out by the project of modernity; the former questions that very project. Unlike Cartesian doubt, postmodernist doubt is not a doubt in the cause of attaining certainty (Burbules, 1996). Postmodernism is about doubting "whether doing more and more of what we are doing, even when it might be a *good* thing, will solve our problems, settle questions of truth or right and wrong, or make people's living better" (Burbules, 1996, p. 41). Concerning education it points to elements that cast doubt upon, for instance, the self-evidence of the idea of knowledge as emancipatory, the idea that knowledge, amassed in a particular (scientific) way, serves the end of freeing people through learning.

Second, Carr's quest for certainty (or at least his case for a reappraisal of epistemology) is based upon the line of thought that when certainty is abandoned, truth comes under pressure as well, which in turn opens the door for anti-realism. It is the very connection certainty-truth-realism and the way this is embedded in the idea of rational justification that leads into problems here. Against this background, the quest for certainties in education can only appear as problematic for the very substantive idea of (quasi)-unified truth that it entails. Despite a resort to fallibilism, the charge of essentialism (or of absolutism, or of dogmatism) is hard to avoid. In view of the multiplicity and diversity of perspectives in an evergrowing multicultural world, neither the appeal to an objective or inherent "good" of some kind, nor the appeal to some objectively working or quasi-pure reason (in a neo-Kantian vein) is acceptable these days. On the other hand, it needs to be acknowledged that, at least at first sight, Carr seems to have something going for the concern that scepticism invites relativism in education. There is not much argument needed here that educational practitioners (parents, teachers) do not like (cannot bear) the thought that truth is something an individual constructs by and for herself, or that "what's true for you" is one thing and "what's true for me" is another. Moreover, and put stronger, we should also acknowledge that the practitioner herself demands certainty. What she desires is not just any answer to the educational questions that trouble her mind, but (preferably) the correct answer, the one that with most certainty will solve the educational problems she is confronted with. However, it is not obvious at all that engaging in a quest for certainty is the appropriate way for the educational theorist to go here.

What the brief presentation of Carr's ways with scepticism above teaches us here is that, if anything, debates over certainties in education stand in danger of becoming polarised to a point where neither side is capable of disengaging from the argument by virtue of being one side of the debate. Typically, this has been so in much literature on postmodernism in education. Such polarisation is dangerous, or at least unfruitful, "it lends itself to the creation of bugaboos", as Smith and Standish put it (1997, p. ix). The net result of this is that one refrains from actually entering the scene of debate over particular contents for the purpose of holding on to one's position, and that accordingly attention is paid to defending or demolishing foundations more than to the practical concerns of education itself.

What is needed here, I suggest, is not a reappraisal of epistemology against, or in order to counter or to tame and incorporate, the sceptical challenges, but rather a reappraisal of scepticism itself. In fact, such a reappraisal seems to present itself to us by the very nature of education as this emerges in the discussion until here. That is, we seem to be stranded in a situation where we feel that the nature of education makes us see that we cannot simply deny nor simply accept the sceptical conclusions. What suggests itself here then is a way of dealing with scepticism in education other than in the traditional either/or-terms of debates between (so-called) foundationalists and anti-foundationalists.

The shift of perspective on scepticism I have in mind here is exemplified by Cavell's understanding of scepticism as he sees this emerging in Wittgenstein's philosophising. According to Cavell, Wittgenstein "does not negate the concluding thesis of scepticism", but "affirms that thesis, or rather takes it as *undeniable*, and so shifts it weight" (Cavell, 1979, p. 45). The final part of this quotation is the crucial one. According to Cavell, Wittgenstein tries to convey the thought that our relation to the world and to others in it is more intimate or closer than can be expressed in terms of "belief" and "knowledge". What this means is that Wittgenstein shifts the weight from epistemology to what is entailed in his idea of agreement in judgements or in criteria while at the same time accounting for scepticism in this very idea of agreement. Allow me to explain.

For Wittgenstein, agreement in judgements is not agreement "about" something – as in convention: coming together to decide on some issues – but means "being in agreement throughout, being in harmony, like pitches or tones, or clocks, or weighing scales, or columns of figures"; it means being "mutually voiced", "mutually *attuned* top to bottom" (Cavell, 1979, p. 32). This implies that the "nature" of a human being's initiation into a community is not one of coming to agree "about" some things – as if a child should give her consent to what she is initiated in – but one of entering in agreements "that were in effect before our participation in them" (Cavell, 1988, p. 40). Most importantly, the nature of agreements is that they do not require rational justification, or further philosophical explanation, or grounding in something else. For Wittgenstein, "nothing is deeper than the fact, or the extent, of agreement itself" (Cavell, 1979, p. 32).

It is important to see that what we have here is not the epistemological certainty the epistemologist is looking for. Firstly, the closeness or intimacy Wittgenstein has in mind here is a non-epistemic one. Rather than being something that can be neatly expressed (explained, categorised), it is something that shows itself, for instance, in the mastery of our mother-tongue and in the ordinary things we do and do not do. Secondly, this does not prevent the sceptical question from being raised. In fact, Cavell repeatedly stresses that for Wittgenstein scepticism is inherent to the ways in which we possess language:

> *a mark of the natural in natural language is its capacity to repudiate itself, to find arbitrary, or merely conventional, the lines laid down for its words by our agreement in criteria, our attunement with one another (which is to say, in my lingo, that the threat of skepticism is a natural or inevitable presentiment of the human mind).* (Cavell, 1988, p. 48)

In this sense, Wittgenstein's return to the ordinary, to our agreements, should be read as a continual struggle with or "response to the threat of skepticism" (Cavell, 1979, p. 7). Scepticism is not something to be denied or defeated, but something which needs to be given a place in the human mind. Taking words back to their everyday use (Wittgenstein, 1953, §116) is not something to be done once and for all, but each time "when language goes on holiday" (Wittgenstein, 1953, §38).

It is important to see that this broadens the content of what we take to be scepticism. As Cavell understand this,

> *the very raising of the question of knowledge in a certain form, or spirit, [constitutes] skepticism, regardless of whether a philosophy takes itself to have answered the question affirmatively or negatively.* (Cavell, 1979, p. 46)

This brings scepticism and dogmatism under the same denominator. For Cavell, sceptical doubt and dogmatism are alike in their repudiation of ordinary language. Both the attempt to metaphysically align one's ordinary concepts to something in the nature of things and the questioning stance that continually undercuts the understanding provided by our ordinary concepts count as scepticism.

On this account, scepticism can be understood as the expression of a dissatisfaction with our ordinary ways of expressing our knowledge about the world and other minds:

> *The dissatisfaction with one's human powers of expression produces a sense that words, to reveal the world, must carry more deeply than our agreements or attunements in criteria will negotiate.* (Cavell, 1988, p. 60)

This attempt to go further, or deeper, than what our ordinary words express goes back to a (human-all-too-human) sense that meaning might evaporate and therefore ought to be fixed in something else. Scepticism, then, is the intellectual interpretation of an existential fear which can be understood as a fear about whether anything means what we think it means. That is, dogmatism is the intellectual attempt to dispel that fear by trying to fix the relation between mind and world, for instance by resort to universals, or "superlative facts" (Wittgenstein, 1953, §192), while epistemological scepticism is the intellectual denial of that attempt. Both intellectual instances fail to address the existential undertones of the problem.

Scepticism in Educational Theory: Responsiveness to the Ordinary

It is not difficult to see in what sense discussed here Carr himself can now be taken as a sceptic. The sort of questions he asks in educational philosophy are *modi* of the form or spirit of question Cavell understands as scepticism. This sceptical spirit is clear, for instance, in the question of the musical authority of Mozart over Madonna (quoted above). Carr's insistence on rational justification amounts to an appeal to something other than, something beyond, what he calls personal preference or cultural prejudice – namely extra-personal and extra-cultural objective considerations. For Carr, the fact that we include Mozart and not Madonna in the curriculum cannot be intelligibly accounted for by resorting to agreement in judgements. In his view it marks an absence of foundations, and is *therefore* to be called preference or prejudice.

Returning to Wittgenstein's idea of agreement, we can see that Carr resembles the sceptic who cannot cope with the *human* element in that fact of agreement. Pivotal in Wittgenstein's concept of agreement is individual responsibility for maintaining the shared criteria as our means of making ourselves intelligible. Carr seems to be unable to cope with the truism that, in a deep sense, "Concepts ... are the expression of our interest" (Wittgenstein, 1953, §570). He therefore rejects (what presents itself to him as merely) cultural criteria to decide the matter of musical authority. Here Carr is like the sceptic who seeks constraints on what it makes sense to say that are external to (what presents itself to him as the messy stuff of) human discourse, dialogue and debate. If anything, this is what marks the search for foundations in education. It is a search for something which is deemed to be more stable than we, "merely" human beings, can deliver, something which does not demand our engagement and responsibility, but which speaks for itself, which literally "goes without saying". What Carr seeks is a justification for including Mozart rather than Madonna in the curriculum for which the individual in the end is no longer accountable.

Carr seems to fear that with the emphasis of this human element through the concept of agreement rationality is lost. However, this is a misunderstanding of agreement in the sense that although Wittgenstein resists resorting to something independent of the fact of agreement, he does not deny rationality. What is denied is Rationality-with-a-capital-r, not rationality-with-a-small-r. Wittgenstein foregrounds the notion of individual responsibility in maintaining what is rational and what is not. Rationality is something which, in order to exist, needs to be exercised (expressed). The functioning of rationality depends on our continued willingness to sustain the practices we call rational. When for some reason this willingness is withdrawn, what is at stake is not merely the idea of rationality, but the very idea of a community, the existence of which depends on a commitment to the shared criteria of its practices.

This implies an acknowledgement of the (human-all-too-human) anxiety that what we collectively, and I individually, uphold as rational may not be received as such by others. What is rational needs to be applied into each new context, it needs to be projected into those contexts. Wittgenstein's point is that this is not a matter of top-down application of a set of more or less definitive rules. The emphasis lies on judgements, not on rules. What he tries to convey is that "no universal can relieve us of the anxiety and responsibility involved in making those projections" (Hammer, 2002, p. 20).

Something of this anxiety and of the failure to acknowledge individual responsibility is captured in Carr's ideas about moral progress:

> *[...] just as we know – in the light of what human progress there has been – that past personal and social moral sensibilities seriously failed to register real human needs and interests, so we can be sure that other moral needs, currently beyond our present ken, await discernment through further sensitive reflection and interpersonal engagement.* (Carr, 1998c, p. 125)

The spirit in which Carr puts this suggests that "our present ken" is somehow a determination of our moral needs that is not correct enough – as if what we call moral now is somehow not morally real enough, and as if our moral sensibilities need to be refined to pierce what seems to be the shallowness of current morality in order to discover other, more real moral needs. My point is not that there is something deeply wrong with the fact of this disappointment with "our present ken" – in fact, this sceptical move is an inherent possibility of the human condition. What is wrong, in my opinion, is the suggestion of a solution by constructing a "beyond". This very construal marks a failure to take issue with the limits that are inevitably drawn by our moral practices.

What is needed here is a sense of humility that marks a willingness to see the limits that are drawn as *our* limits, and accordingly to take responsibility for these limits of our understanding. This is not a denial of moral progress. It is to say that the construal of a beyond is not a condition required for the idea of moral progress to be meaningful. The task is not to judge "our present ken" by some standard of morality invoked by the appeal to a beyond. Rather, it is our moral horizon itself, with its inevitable limitations, that forms our task. Sensitive reflection and interpersonal engagement is not something we need in order to direct ourselves to moral needs as yet awaiting further discernment – which amounts to a distraction from the actual moral concerns of educational practice. What is needed is sensitive reflection on and interpersonal engagement in our present ken itself. This will allow us to shift the emphasis of (moral) education from a worry about foundations (objective moral values) and its concomitant fixation on justification, to a concern for an educational activity that touches upon particular issues between particular persons with particular questions that need careful attention in each particular case in which they arise. At the same time it allows us to highlight the importance of exemplarity in moral education – exemplarity in what might be called the thick sense of the word, as a coming down on one side or the other, as an acknowledgement of one's colours, hence as an acceptance of vulnerability and of the possibilities of change (moral progress, if you will) that that entails.

Put otherwise, and in conclusion, the challenge for educational theory lies in attempting to be responsive to the ordinary. In view of what has been said above about scepticism as inherent to the human life with language, this also implies being perceptive to those instances in which language goes on holiday. Instead of being seduced by the (granted, appealing, but nevertheless illusory) peace of foundations in education, what Cavell's understanding of scepticism brings out in education and in educational theory is – to adopt the sense of this expression to be found in Blake *et al.* – the politics of knowledge. Blake *et al.* argue that

> *With a conscious postfoundationalism comes renewed responsibility to the politics of knowledge, no longer seen as an excuse for the arbitrary, but a demanding intertwining of the normative and epistemic realms.* (Blake et al, 1998, p. 31)

What educational philosophers such as Carr all too easily conclude is that the ordinary is the arbitrary, and that with this resort to (what they think to be) the arbitrary, truth is expelled from the educational picture, and that this in turn leaves education without grounds, hence lost. We have seen with Wittgenstein and Cavell that the scene has shifted. The foundationalist's fear of loss of truth is exposed as the convenient guise of a deeper, more important fear, viz. the fear of one's own responsibility concerning what it makes sense to say – a fear of *voicing* what is true, hence a fear of vulnerability.

References

Blake, N., Smeyers, P., Smith, R., & Standish, P. (1998). *Thinking again. Education after postmodernism.* London: Bergin & Garvey.

Burbules, N. (1996). Postmodern doubt and philosophy of education. In A. Neiman (Ed.), *Philosophy of education 1995* (pp. 39-48). Urbana: Philosophy of Education Society.

Carr, D. (1994). Knowledge and truth in religious education. *Journal of Philosophy of Education, 28*, 221-238.

Carr, D. (1998a). Preface and acknowledgments. In D. Carr (Ed.), *Education, knowledge and truth. Beyond the postmodern impasse* (pp. x-xiii). London: Routledge.

Carr, D. (1998b). Introduction. The post-war rise and fall of educational epistemology. In D. Carr (Ed.), *Education, knowledge and truth. Beyond the postmodern impasse* (pp. 1-15). London: Routledge.

Carr, D. (1998c). Moral education and the objectivity of values. In D. Carr (Ed.), *Education, knowledge and truth. Beyond the postmodern impasse* (pp. 114-128). London: Routledge.

Carr, D. (1999). Toward a re-evaluation of the role of educational epistemology in the professional education of teachers. In S. Tozer (Ed.), *Philosophy of education 1998* (pp. 439-447). Urbana: Philosophy of Education Society.

Carr, D. (2001). Educational philosophy, theory and research: A psychiatric autobiography. *Journal of Philosophy of Education, 35*, 461-476.

Cavell, S. (1979). *The claim of reason. Wittgenstein, skepticism, morality, and tragedy.* New York: Oxford University Press.

Cavell, S. (1988). *In quest of the ordinary. Lines of skepticism and romanticism.* Chicago: The University of Chicago Press.

Hammer, E. (2002). *Stanley Cavell. Skepticism, subjectivity, and the ordinary.* Cambridge: Polity Press.

Ramaekers, S. (2002). Postmodernism: A "sceptical" challenge in educational theory. *Journal of Philosophy of Education, 36*, 629-651.

Siegel, H. (1998). Knowledge, truth and education. In D. Carr (Ed.), *Education, knowledge and truth. Beyond the postmodern impasse* (pp. 19-36). London: Routledge.

Smith, R., & Standish, P. (1997). *Teaching right and wrong. Moral education in the balance.* London: Trentham Books.

Wittgenstein, L. (1953). *Philosophische Untersuchungen/Philosophical investigations* (G. E. M. Anscombe, Trans.). Oxford: Basil Blackwell.

CAUSALITY AND (IN-)DETERMINISM IN EDUCATIONAL RESEARCH

Paul Smeyers

Introduction

The need to apprehend the world one lives in is a fundamental part of the human condition. This apprehension includes understanding the meanings of various forms of expressions (concepts, symbol, art objects, rituals), of feelings and emotions, of actions in the world of human activity past and present (in terms of purposes, aims and more functional explanations), and last but not least, the understanding of natural phenomena. In the context of the physical world one may want to distinguish a style of explanation from a mechanical kind. The former explains in terms of basic comprehensive principles (for instance in biology: selection, mutation, heritability of traits), how in other words phenomena fit into an overall scheme; the latter answers questions of how things work (sometimes understood as what they are made of), where what one is looking for is a causal kind of explanation. As will be argued later, both of these forms of explanations are by no means incompatible.

It is evident that one wants to understand how society at large functions, what other people do, and who one is. "Understanding" here refers to knowing how things are, so that they can be taken into account in what one does later on. But in many circumstances, the concept of "causality" seems to pervade our thinking about ourselves and others, our environment, even the entire universe we live in. Causal explanations are fundamental to the intellectual understanding of physical systems, living organisms, and in our practical deliberations in these contexts. They are involved in the use of technology (where we attempt to achieve particular effects while avoiding undesirable ones) and in our everyday practical planning and dealings. Not only physicists and engineers, but social scientists have since the Enlightenment been occupied with finding causes in order to be able to manipulate particular outcomes. Psychologists and educational researchers are no exception to this general tendency. Here, for many, to explain an event is to identify its causes.

There is of course a strand of criticism against the use of "cause" in the sphere of human explanations. This is not to deny that human beings are exempted from causal interactions generally; no one seriously denies that, for instance, bodily functions are subjected to physical and biochemical laws and processes. Nevertheless, once it is suggested that our behaviour itself can be made clear either partly or exhaustively by these kind of processes, human scientists and philosophers generally protest. Philosophers of human action in the continental and analytical traditions such as Dilthey, Gadamer, Ricoeur, in addition to Wittgenstein, Winch and Taylor, have argued to the contrary that human beings *give* meaning to their lives. It behoves us to ask then, whether causal explanations still have significance or not, and in what sense, and for which contexts? And is it correct that if one accepts causal explanations of human behaviour there looms the threat of the disappearance of ethical issues, thus inviting us to live "beyond freedom and dignity"?

Necessary and Sufficient Conditions, Determinism and Indeterminism

Perhaps the most obvious place to begin a discussion of the proposed regular nature of causation is Hume's *A Treatise of Human Nature*. Hume's example is of one billiard ball lying on the table and another moving toward it with rapidity. His basic insight is that formal reasoning cannot reveal causation because we cannot deduce the nature of an effect from a description of the cause, or the nature of the cause from a description of an effect. One can imagine for instance that someone had screwed the second ball to the table. In this case the first ball will most likely return where it came from. As deductive logic cannot provide the answer, Hume turns to empirical investigations. On the basis of his observations he concludes that in situations where we believe that there is a causal relation, there is a temporal priority of the cause to the effect. There is furthermore a spatio-temporal contiguity of the cause to the effect and finally, on every occasion on which the cause occurs, the effect follows–there is constant conjunction. As there is, in his opinion, no physical connection between the cause and the effect (the connection does not exist outside of our own minds), the relation between cause and effect is to be found in custom and habit. As Hume could not find a necessary connection between cause and effect, neither in formal reasoning nor in the physical world, his lesson answers the question whether and how we can explicate the concept of causality in terms that do not surreptitiously introduce any occult concepts of power or necessary connection, which is exactly what he wanted to do.

The form philosophical discussions of causality take is usually as follows: there are two facts (or types of) C and E or two events (or types of) C and E between which there is a relation R. Questions are raised whether C and E should be taken to refer to facts or events, further, whether to individual facts or events or classes of them. Sometimes the logical structure of the relation is discussed in terms of necessary or sufficient conditions or a combination of both. Given the interaction of several conditions this leads to complex schemes to understand particular occurrences. Consider for instance the following example in which a cause is defined as a condition. If a barn burns down this might have been caused by a careless smoker, by embers from a nearby forest fire falling on it, by a stroke of lightning, or even from spontaneous combustion engendered by fermentation of fresh hay. None of these is a necessary condition, but any of them might be sufficient. Moreover, no fire will occur unless some additional factors are present (for instance, in the case of the incident of the cigarette, that it falls on some flammable material and that it goes unnoticed). These other conditions, however, would not suffice to start a fire. Each of them is a condition that is an Insufficient but Non-redundant (necessary) part of a condition that is Unnecessary but Sufficient (an INUS-condition). The dropping of the burning cigarette is an example thereof. Such a clear example is helpful in order to make the particular points concerning causality. As matters of "meaning" are always involved where examples from social sciences are concerned, an analogous case from that context cannot easily be given. We will continue a bit longer in the area of natural phenomena before refocusing on the human world.

The success of the development of more sophisticated experimental and mathematical techniques has extended the application of Newton's laws to new phenomena. The 19th century deterministic worldview has in some ways been confirmed and extended by 20th century science, for instance in the field of molecular biology, where the mechanisms of heredity are explained exclusively in chemical terms. Thus scientists find themselves just one step away from explaining learning in terms of specific chemical changes that occur in the brain cells and from chemical understanding of feelings and emotions in the field of psychology. To the determinist, the fact that we are unable to make perfect predictions in all cases is the result of human ignorance and other limitations, not because nature is lacking in precise determination – clearly, prediction is irrelevant to determinism. There is, however, also another evolution that uses a different frame, i.e., one of indeterminism. The challenge of the relativity theory is not simply that quantum mechanics is *prima facie* non-deterministic, but that under plausible constraints, no deterministic completion of the quantum theory is possible. In view of this it seems inadvisable to accept determinism as an *a priori* principle – and of course the truth or falsity of quantum mechanics is a matter of physical fact. Concerning this it would not make much sense to step, as Wittgenstein would call it, outside of our form of life, i.e., to allow that our concepts are seen as no more than whimsical social constructions. Doubts about the possibility of finding causes for everything either on the basic of logical or empirical considerations and the relativity theory, have made clear that determinism is not the only option. Incidentally, the debate between determinism and indeterminism belongs to philosophy; different kinds of metaphysical systems were offered and the metaphysical question itself was posed in various ways. I will now move on to the implications of all of this for our understanding of scientific explanation and consequently for educational research.

Statistical and Functional Explanation, Causal and Pseudo-Processes

There are, of course, different sorts of explanation. A popular kind is the one where specific conditions obtaining prior to the event are cited (initial conditions) and general laws. Let me make this point clear. It is stated that the occurrence of the event to be explained follows logically from those premises. One can distinguish between deductive explanations that incorporate universal laws (which hold without exceptions) and inductive explanations which employ statistical laws (which hold for most or many cases). According to Hempel scientific explanation consists in deductive or inductive subsumption of that which is to be explained under one or more laws of nature. This is referred to as the deductive-nomological model (D-N). For him, however, inductive-statistical explanations are essentially relativised to knowledge situations – he suggested the requirement of total evidence that took the form of the requirement of maximal specificity, where all possibly relevant knowledge is available. If there were an inductive-statistical explanation whose law-like statistical premise involved a genuinely homogenous reference class then we would have an instance of an inductive-statistical explanation simpliciter, not merely an inductive-statistical explanation relative to a specific knowledge situation. However, as there are according to Hempel no inductive-statistical explanations simpliciter, ideally inductive-statistical explanation would have no place in his position. There is a striking similarity between this kind of explanation and Laplace's formulation of determinism. In view of this close relationship it is tempting to conclude that events that are causally determined can be explained, and those that can be explained are causally determined. And from this it is just one more step to say that when human actions and decisions can be explained, they are determined; this leads on to the conclusion that to explain human behaviour and choices is to show that they cannot be free (in which case moral responsibility disappears). However, it should be noted that in many cases *we do not have enough facts to be able to construct an explanation and we can never be sure that a new condition might not turn up* (one that in principle could not have been taken into account previously), that will jeopardise our D-N construction. Again, to put this in other words, one can never exclude whether a further relevant subdivision of a reference class might be necessary on the basis of additional knowledge. This parallels what was noted in the discussion of the INUS-condition. Furthermore, *the inferential conception suffers from the fact that it seriously misconstrues the nature of subsumption under laws.* Explanation requires a sufficient condition that is based on empirical evidence that something actually happened. Inference on the other hand refers to something in the future. To infer something that lies in the future not only presupposes determinism, but also relies on the fact that everything had to be been taken into account – a matter one can never be logically sure of. When we relinquish the assumption of determinism the asymmetry becomes even more striking. Doubts about the fact that explanations are essentially arguments may follow from the impossibility of prediction as a consequence of the lack of all the facts and/or asymmetry of inferences – though this does not mean that we must give up the covering law conception, subsumption under laws can take a different form.

Examples from the atomic and subatomic world show us that there is a limit to the joint precision with which two so-called complementary parameters can be known: there is an inescapable uncertainty if one attempts to ascertain the values of both the position and momentum of a particle, and similarly for energy and time. Ascertaining the position of an electron with great precision, makes us unable to ascertain its momentum very exactly and conversely[1]. To offer an explanation here is something different: it comes down to the assembling of a total set of relevant conditions for the event to be explained, and citing of the probability of that event in the presence of these conditions. The explanation is in this case not an argument (a logical structure with premises and conclusions governed by some rule of acceptance), but rather *a presentation of the conditions relevant to the occurrence of the event, and a statement of the degree of probability of the event given these conditions.* Evidently, a persistent statistical correlation – a genuine statistical-relevance relation – is strongly indicative of a causal relation of some sort, but

---

[1] More precisely: when a photon strikes an electron, the direction in which the electron will go is not determined. There is a probability distribution over all possible directions. Furthermore, in this collision the amount by which the frequency of the photon will change is not determined. A probability distribution over all possible amounts exists. Because of the conservation of energy and of momentum, there is a perfect correlation between the direction of the electron and the change in frequency of the photon. The pair of values is however not determined. Incidentally, it is important in this context also to refer to problems with our instruments of measurement as well. The click that results from a genuine photon detection is utterly indistinguishable from the click that results from a spurious count. And finally, there is of course the presumption that conditions surrounding this particular occurrence can be specified in enough detail to establish the existence of a unique necessary and sufficient cause. (This example is discussed in Salmon, 1998)

one should not confuse statistical correlation with genuine causation. This would be to conflate symptoms with causes.

When two types of events, A and B are positively related to each other, we hunt for a common cause C that is statistically relevant. The statistical-relevance relations must be explained in terms of two causal processes in which C is causally relevant to A and C is causally relevant to B. This is the heart of the matter where it is claimed that a statistical explanation is based on causality. Now the question is, why should we prefer for explanatory purposes the relevance of C to A and C to B over the relevance of A to B which we had in the first place? The answer is that we can trace a spatio-temporally continuous causal connection from C to A and from C to B (while the relation between A and B cannot be accounted for by any such direct continuous causal relation). One will recall that causal explanations present us, according to Hume, with a problem. Nevertheless, his criticism needs to be qualified. Indeed, it seems that Hume overlooked an important aspect of causality, i.e., that causal processes are capable of transmitting information.[2] A proper understanding of this will make it possible to distinguish between causal processes and pseudo-processes. This distinction emerged from Einstein's special theory of relativity which claims that no signal (no process capable of transmitting information) can travel faster than light. The so-called "at-at" theory of causal transmission is an attempt to remedy Hume's criticism. The basic thesis about mark transmission can be stated as follows: "A mark that has been introduced into a process by means of a single intervention at point A is transmitted to point B if and only if it occurs at B and at all stages of the process between A and B without additional interventions" (Salmon, 1998, p. 197).

Thus, Zeno's paradox can be solved as follows: to move from A to B is simply to occupy the intervening points at the intervening moments. It consists in being at particular points at the corresponding instants. There is no question as to how the arrow gets from point A to point B. (There is no zipping through the intermediate points at high speed.) The arrow is at the points between them at the corresponding moment. And there can be no question about how the arrow gets from one point to the next, for in a continuum there is no next point. "Mark transmission" is the proposed foundation for the concept of propagation of influence. The ability to transmit a mark is the criterion of a causal process; pseudo-processes may also exhibit persistent structure, but this structure is transmitted not by means of the process itself but by some other agency. The basis is thus *the ability of the causal process to transmit a*

---

[2]   The development as before is mainly based on the position of Salmon (cf. Salmon, 1998).

modification in its structure resulting from an interaction (a mark) without appealing to any of Hume's secret powers.[3] Whether the result of the interaction will be transmitted is a question that can in principle readily be settled by experiment (thus one will investigate whether the resulting modifications in the process are preserved at other stages of the process). The patterns in which we fit events and facts that structure our world we wish to explain, are statistical and causal relations. Causal processes play an important role for they are mechanisms that propagate structure and transmit causal influence. This together with the "at-at" theory answers Hume's question about the nature of the connections between causes and effects. One can therefore conclude that causal processes exist *besides* probabilistic or statistical causality. In indeterministic settings it appears that necessary causes have at least some degree of explanatory force, but sufficient causes do not. According to the causal conception, we explain facts (general or particular) by exhibiting the physical processes and interactions that bring them about, but such mechanisms need not be deterministic to have explanatory force, they may be irreducibly statistical. Thus a scientific explanation of a particular event is not rigidly determined by general laws and antecedent conditions.

To this different picture of causal processes and statistical explanation, finally another kind of explanation has to be added: *functional explanation*. An illustration of this is the following example from biology. Jackrabbits that inhabit the hot regions in the south western part of the U.S.A.

---

[3] The following example may illustrate this. Consider a rotating spotlight, mounted in the center of a circular room, that casts a spot of light on the wall. A light ray travelling *from* the spotlight *to* the wall is a causal process: the spot of light moving around the walls constitutes a pseudo-process. The former process occurs at the speed of light; the latter "process" can go on at arbitrarily high velocities, depending on the size of the room and the rate of rotation of the light source. The speed of light places no restrictions on the velocity of the pseudo-process. The fact that the beam of light travelling from the light source to the wall is a causal process can be revealed by a simple experiment. If a red filter is interposed in the beam near its source, the color of the spot of the wall will be red. This "mark" is transmitted along the beam. It is obvious how the transmission of such marks could be employed to send a message:
Red if by land and blue if by sea.
And I on the opposite shore will be
Ready to ride and spread the alarm
To every Middlesex village and farm.
It is equally evident, I believe, that no information can be sent via the moving spot on the wall. If you are standing near the wall at one side of the room, and someone else is stationed at a diametrically opposite point, there is nothing you can do to the passing sport of light that will convey any information – e.g., "The British are coming!" – to the other person. Interposing a red filter may make the spot red in your vicinity, but the "mark" will not be retained as the spot moves on. (Salmon, 1998, pp. 194-195)

have extraordinarily large ears. They constitute an effective cooling mechanism. There are of course many devices that can fulfil this function. It can be shown therefore deductively (or at least with a high inductive probability) that such animals will have some mechanism or other that enables them to adapt to the extreme temperatures, but it does not follow that the jackrabbit must have developed large radiating ears (nor that it is probable that it would do so). Explaining this particular cooling device (as opposed to explaining why it has some mechanism or other that fulfils this function) demands therefore a different kind of explanation. That explanation is labelled "functional".

In the study of social institutions by sociologists, anthropologists and other social scientists, many of these kind of explanations may be found. Again, it might be claimed that functional explanations are always illegitimate, or at best incomplete. But it is not clear why they should be ruled out on logical grounds. They offer a particular *kind* of explanation that the received view of scientific explanation (deductive certainty or high inductive probability) cannot account for, without necessarily invoking teleological and anthropomorphical elements – criticisms that are usually brought against this position. In this approach, difficulties with Hempel's model (where there is always a demand for a sufficient condition) are overcome (the functional explanation provides a necessary condition). The epistemic value of such an explanation is measured by the gain in information provided by the probability distribution over the partition. Similarly, in the statistical-relevance model it is the amount of relevant information that counts; it consists of a probability distribution over a (maximum) homogeneous partition of an initial reference class. Thus a unified style of explanation (using basic comprehensive principles) can be accommodated with explanations of a mechanical kind (how things work). Both of them may be compatible for a particular problem. Because of its insistence on what is intelligible, this kind of explanation (i.e., functional) resembles understanding and description as used in the human sciences. The general conclusion must be that if indeterminism is a feature of the atomic and subatomic world (causal indeterminacy – the truth or falsity of (in)determinism is a matter of physical fact), and if it cannot be ruled out on logical or metaphysical grounds, there is no reason to use determinism as the paradigm *par excellence* (or the only paradigm) for other domains of understanding – moreover, as our everyday concept of human action tells us differently: it refers to freedom and accepts responsibility for what we do in normal circumstances.

Implications for the Human World and for Educational Research: Ethics and Particularity

What follows from this account of scientific explanation for the world we live in, give meaning to, and investigate as educational researchers? Given that we cannot predict the future even in the presence of our best causal investigations does the mode of explanation really matter? Must indeterminism lead to indifference? Or is the conclusion that, though we may not live in a deterministic universe, the best we can aim for is the identification of necessary or sufficient conditions, for causal processes and statistical regularity?

In some sense the answer to the latter question must of course be positive, at least in as far as our investigations concern the question how things work – whether we are concerned with metals or with the functioning of òur brains. Moreover, it is imperative that we consider the uses to which such research can be put in order to achieve particular policies or programmes. Given that precise outcomes cannot be predicted with absolute certainty, what we do will always invoke some kind of *practical reasoning*. To decide what to do in this or that particular situation only based upon scientific knowledge is not enough. Moreover, human behaviour can be described in different ways: one may focus on its *mechanistic side or on its intentional aspect*, and both need not necessarily be seen as rivals. Though surely much more about this can be said, it may suffice to refer here to the fact that a particular mechanism on the basis of which we are able to act may not only be a necessary condition for particular actions, it will also characterise human activities more generally. It is only because we can get hungry or thirsty that it makes sense to invite someone for a meal or a drink. And because what people generally do in particular circumstances is not irrelevant either, quantitative research surely has its point. That this does not answer the question why people do what they do in terms of reasons, goes without saying – as that is a different question. How else, then by asking someone can we know, what her reason for doing something is? Understanding what something is, or rather "what it is like" (which is typical of causal explanations) should not be confused with understanding what something is in the sense of "what it means" or "what it signifies" (typical for a teleological explanation).

Educational theory can I think confidently rely on four kinds of educational research: philosophical, interpretive (which includes historical and qualitative research), quantitative (statistical) and causal. At the one extreme one may find common ground with literature (fiction), and at the other with bio-chemical research. These different kinds of investigations make it possible to do justice to the full array of educational questions and the various functions research has to fulfil. Educational research will naturally reflect – as philosophy in general does – the spirit of its time. That means it nowadays may as well focus on the one hand on *phronesis* (or praxis dealing among other things with "ends") on the other as partly directed, i.e., means-end reasoning (which refers among other things in these days taking into account too the demands of performativity). This implies that "skills" and "outcomes" are as much part of education as an initiation into the discussion of ends and what is more generally worthwhile that philosophers of education have traditionally focused on. Neither philosophers nor non-philosophical educational researchers can ignore this spectrum with impunity. They may therefore want to expose the hidden mechanisms and manipulations of our society, that presupposes the gathering of relevant data and studying the influence of the constraints in which we live and operate. They may want to point to the limits of manipulative forces in the context of education or investigate what is culturally worthwhile to cherish and pass on. Concerning these latter aspects, it may be argued that it will bear the mark of the evocative, not surprisingly though, it is indeed about education (cf. Blake, Smeyers, Smith, & Standish, 2000, for a development of this and the "conversion" aspect of education). It can neither be astonishing that philosophers are forced to accept a strong insistence on description as well. Likewise for philosophical and empirical research the focus is on *what* is to be described, how this should be done, the *kind of things* one wants to draw attention to in this description, and finally on the *way* in which the description is offered.

None of this implies that quantitative research whether statistical or causal has no point whatsoever. What is clear however is that causal mechanisms neither threaten human freedom nor generally take away our responsibility. Complete determinism thus reveals itself as just another version of the transparency claimed by some advocates of the project of modernity either on societal, intersubjective or personal levels. The result of our investigation is not spectacular: we are familiar with the idea that as well conceptual inquiries as research of facts are both constitutive of understanding. Causality of course exists. Regularities in human action can be informative. The kinds of research that spring from these notions explain what people do; that agents usually have particular intentions when they do what they do; that sometimes they act out of habit or are just irrational; and even that people may remain a mystery for others and for themselves. None of this should surprise educational researchers. And all of it explains human behaviour. What follows of course is that educational researchers should take all of it into account, and should not turn their head and pretend they do not see.

This parallels Wittgenstein's insistence on the relevance of "following a rule" to understand what people say and do. Both point to the insufficiency of a strict rational model, be it either concerning the application of deductive rules to predict certain outcomes concerning natural phenomena, or to understand why it is that people do what they do. The human mind does not seem to function as a calculus of which language and action bear overwhelmingly witness, neither in its physiological nor in its meaning-giving aspect. Certain social scientists in general have opted for a rationalistic and deterministic model to understand society and individuals. They have taken a wrongheaded picture of nature for their pre-eminent example. Nature has taught us a lesson: to give up this idle talk, to search again for "friction" (cf. Wittgenstein, 1953, § 107), to abandon the metaphysical castle of air, and to take instead into account the multiplicity of reality and the various kinds of explanations we need to understand its complexity. This is the ultimate reason why responsibility is at the heart of research, why always in whatever we do or say and thus in our investigations of these, deep held commitments are at stake. Thus the ethical presses itself upon us in a way that is not limited to the domain of the moral; it thus becomes clear, how, in other words, normative demands are always at stake. "Good" educational research, be it empirical or conceptual, should reflect these insights in its endeavour for an educational theory that speaks of education to its practitioners and is therefore necessarily occupied with values and the nature of "the good life".

References

Blake, N. , Smeyers, P., Smith, R., & Standish, P. (2000). *Education in an age of nihilism*. London: Falmer Press.

Salmon, W.C. (1998). *Causality and explanation*. New York: Oxford University Press.

Wittgenstein, L. (1953). *Philosophical investigations/Philosophische Untersuchungen* (G.E.M. Anscombe, Transl.). Oxford: Blackwell.

IV. EDUCATIONAL RESEARCH: ETHICAL CONSIDERATIONS
(Section Editor Lynn Fendler)

THEORISING EDUCATIONAL PRACTICES: THE POLITICO-ETHICAL CHOICES

Michael A. Peters[1]

Introduction

The notion of *practice* figures as an unanalysable given in educational literature and activity. Practices are seen as the bedrock of a set of educational activities that are widely regarded as self-evident. The presuppositions of the term are not analysed or clarified and rarely is it acknowledged that theories of practice not only shape what we accept as "true" and "normal" but also implicitly constitute a set of politico-ethical choices. In education the term practice is used frequently. In fact, *practice* is part of a new orthodoxy in education prioritising the practical over the theoretical, "practitioner knowledge", "the reflective practitioner", "situated learning", "communities of practice", "effective educational practices" and the like. This paper comprises four related parts: first, it maps some of the uses of the term *practice* as it figures in educational discourse and theory; second, it considers the turn to practice in contemporary theory; third, by reference to the work of Hubert Dreyfus, it outlines and develops a typology of five competing views of practice, elucidating their politico-ethical implications; and finally, it highlights the elusiveness of practice as a concept and the difficulties it presents for accounts of professional practice and learning.

The Elusiveness of *Practice:* Turner's Challenge

Stephen Turner's (1994) *The Social Theory of Practices* poses a challenge to contemporary theory. He claims that practices "are the vanishing point of twentieth-century philosophy" (p. 1). While the term is widely employed in literary criticism, feminist scholarship, history, anthropology, and social theory, he suggests that the concept of practice is "deeply elusive" (p. 2) and he questions what is being referred to when, for example, Wittgenstein talks of "the inherited background", or social theorists talk of "tacit knowledge" or "presuppositions". Practices, he maintains, are ascribed mysterious properties of being "social" or "shared". To what extent should we take this language seriously, he asks? He tracks out the history of practices in a range of kinship terms of tradition, custom, mores and habits and goes on to claim:

---

[1] I would like to thank Lynn Fendler for a set of constructive criticisms of this paper.

> *In postfoundationist writings in the humanities, the diversity of human practices has become a place-holder or filler in the slot formerly occupied by the traditional "foundationalist" notions of truth, validity and interpretive correctness. Truth, validity, and correctness are held to be practice-relative rather than practice-justifying notion. (p. 9)*

His complaint is that when we move away from first principles in traditional philosophy to practices as a way of grounding our framework we are in fact substituting something, which is neither explicit nor universal. He examines the causal aspects of practices allegedly showing that causes do not identify practices nor explain them. To identify or attempt to explain practices as "shared presuppositions" suffers from a circular reasoning, he claims, and the major problem facing any account of practice is that there is no available model that accounts for transmission. As he says: "The concept of shared practices ... requires that practices be transmitted from person to person" yet every causal account to establish sameness where the same practice is reproduced in another person, leads to ludicrous results.

There are two problems concerning the notion of practice, especially relevant for educational theory. First, if, indeed, as Turner indicates, practice is a slippery concept and that it demands an account of its *shared* nature which implies its transmittance, then for professional practice and development, especially the education of teachers, this becomes an importance problem. How do we *educate* beginning or novice teachers in the practice of teaching when there is no viable model of transmission?

Second, and associated with this difficulty, there are two related difficulties. If current phenomenological accounts based on Heidegger, Wittgenstein and Dreyfus are accepted then professional practice and learning must be considered noncognitive, nonconceptual, and prelinguistic. Under these conditions, how can practice be learned or transmitted? Van Manen (e.g., 1999) provides us with one possible answer in terms of forms of noncognitive knowing. Similarly, "reflection in action" accounts of professional practice and learning face objections nicely put by van Manen concerning the paradoxical nature of reflective practice: if it is "retrospective or anticipatory reflection" it is unoriginal but likely; if it is "reflection in action" or contemporaneous, it is original but unlikely.

Mapping the Meanings of Educational *Practices*:
Culture, Social, Bodily, Applied Knowledge

The concept of *practices* is, perhaps, *the* neglected underlying concept that signals a whole host of elements concerning the so-called "new pedagogy", a term used by a report for the Tavistock Institute as part of a rview of current pedagogic research and practice (Cullen et al, 2002). The notion of educational practices includes the emphasis on social construction and postmodern theory (if I can use this abbreviation) that gels with a constellation of new emphases in educational studies more generally. It reflects the central importance of culture – the importance of "cultures" in the plural (e.g., learning and knowledge cultures, evidence-based cultures, organisational cultures) and of "cultures" in the sociological literature that attempt to identify elements of "sub-cultures" especially in relation to youth. The term also implies a central focus on "the practitioner" and practitioner knowledge, as it is written into programmes of "the reflective practitioner" dating from the work of Donald Schön (1987, 1995) and Chris Argyris (1974, 1978, 1999). This use is carried over to so-called "communities of practice" (e.g., Wenger, 1998) as it has become known in a burgeoning literature together with associated notions of "situated learning" (Lave & Wenger 1991). In relation to both these developments – the cultural turn and the reflective practitioner – the term has been used to signal the priority of the practical over the theoretical in educational activities. This means, among others things, that education activities are primarily engagements-with-others-in-the-world; it implies that learning and teaching are fundamentally social activities, "doings" or performances without "inner" processes. The stress on practices also accords with and partially explains the currency of the now taken-for-granted distinction between Mode 1 and Mode 2 knowledge first proposed by Gibbons *et al* (1994) with its emphasis on applied knowledge and contexts of use. Less obviously, perhaps, these overlapping tendencies in philosophy and social theory that have infiltrated education tend to focus on the increasing importance of an understanding of the body to education, not just the emotions or embodied knowledges or rationalities, but also the body as formations of self and social order. Finally, the use of *practices* also highlights pragmatics in general, both in linguistic and cognitive theory (i.e., practices as pragmatically-grounded). These theoretical tendencies, I will argue, derive from a largely unexamined shift in philosophy and social theory to focus on *practices* as the underlying concept of cultures and communities, which brings social order and structures social reality.

While we can map these overlapping uses and family resemblances (Wittgenstein, 1953) of the term practices in relation to education and social theory, it is not the cases that the term is used deliberatively or purposively with these meanings or understandings explicitly in mind. Rather the term has been adopted in use without much reflection and when it is used it is often done so without sufficient attention to what the term implies.

Let me provide some recent prominent and influential examples. Herbert J. Walberg and Susan J. Park (2000) have written a booklet an entitled Effective educational practice, which appears in the Educational Practices Series developed by the International Academy of Education and distributed by the International Bureau of Education (available at http://www.ibe.unesco.org). Neither the series nor Walberg and Park theorise the underlying notion of practice. It a concept that is taken for granted and regarded as a given.[2]

Another example, this time from the field of organizational science which has appropriated the term practice in so-called "communities of practice". John Sharp (1997) provides the following definition:

> *A Community of Practice (COP) is a special type of informal network that emerges from a desire to work more effectively or to understand work more deeply among members of a particular specialty or work group. At the simplest level, CoPs are small groups of people who've worked together over a period of time and through extensive communication have developed a common sense of purpose and a desire to share work-related knowledge and experience.*

He discusses the work of John Seely Brown and Paul Duguid in their study of Xerox. He writes:

> *The notion of "practice" is critical in CoP, pointing out that the group concentrates on learning that emerges only though working, or actually practicing one's craft. CoPs supplement the book and classroom learning of many trade and professional workers. To learn how one does work in this organization, or in this area,*

---

[2] They write, for instance: "The practices described in this booklet can generally be applied to classroom subjects in primary and secondary schools ... As with all educational practices, of course they can be effectively or ineffectively planned and conducted ..." The booklet goes on to talk of "powerful" and "consistent" practices in promoting academic learning, clearly assuming that there are good and bad practices. In terms of effective practices, then, we are told that research demonstrates that "learning is enhanced when schools encourage parents to stimulate their children's intellectual development" or "students learn more when they complete homework that is graded, commented upon and discussed by their teachers." We do not need to pursue this example here as it is clear that the term practice is employed with little reflection on the status or meaning of practices.

that goes beyond the official "canonical" training for that activity implies that a key part of learning how to work is learning how to communicate and share information within the community of practice. In this sense, learning is about work, and work is about learning, and both are social.

Again, while the term is used it is not theorised. Practice refers loosely to planned collaboration that is meant to generate a common, shared understanding of events and an action orientation for dealing with such events the next time they arise.[3]

A final introductory example: the Tavistock Institute recently made its final report to the British Economic and Social Research Council, entitled *Review of Current Pedagogic Research and Practice in the Fields of Post-Compulsory Education and Lifelong Learning* (Cullen et al, 2002) as part of its synthesising analysis that was commissioned as necessary background to the Council's Teaching and Learning Research Programme, Phase III – Emerging Themes (see http://www.ex.ac.uk/ESRC-TLRP/). The Institute was interested in providing an overview, identifying the key research questions, and locating the gaps as a basis for its conclusions and recommendations.

In one sense its conclusions are not surprising. In the Preamble the Review itemises a set of realities that underlie pedagogic research and *practice*:

firstly, there is little established "evidence based culture" in teaching and learning. Secondly, pedagogic understandings are shaped by different – and sometimes conflicting – patrimonies across each sector. Thirdly, however, there has been significant – and complex – degree of "inter-breeding" between the sectors of post-compulsory education, and it is often difficult to attribute a particular set of pedagogic "outcomes" to particular sources of evidence. Fourthly, practices are either grounded in day to day minutae of "chalkface" learning delivery (and hence ungrounded in theory), or, conversely, are tied to a particular "grand learning theory" and are unsubstantiated in practice (p. 4).

---

[3] CoP entails collaboration and common understandings. The use of the term shifts the epistemology of learning away from the psychological realm and a transfer theory of learning into a sociological realm but does not entail a future oriented perspective that might enable practitioners for dealing with such events next time. CoP is one example of the 'new pedagogy.' I am grateful to Lynn Fendler for this observation.

In this short summary the concept of practice figures implicitly in the notion of "evidence based culture" and explicitly in the final sentence, yet no attempt to made to distinguish the concept or indicate the theoretical stakes in different accounts.[4]

With all three examples we can clearly see an instrumental focus on the concept of practice as something that indicates a kind of bedrock, beyond which we cannot go. The implicit assumption behind the uses of the concept practice is that both learning and pedagogy are fundamentally *shared social activities* that can be identified, unpicked, observed and improved. The notion of learning and pedagogical practices as shared social activities sometimes takes on an explicit constructivist construction as in "communities of practice" where the underlying assumption is that organisationally it is possible to create or construct communities based on shared practices and that it is possible to design group learning strategies in organisational settings.

The emphasis on practice in education takes many different and related forms (see Table 1 below). I draw a distinction between those forms that are relatively well theorised and those that are not. In the former case we can distinguish among various related notions of practice advanced directly by theorists or drawn from the work of others outside education. We can identify, for instance, a pragmatic notion of practice as it figures in the work Dewey, a praxical notion of practice, influenced by Marx and the Frankfurt school that shapes Freire's work, and a notion of practice that informs the work of Bourdieu. We might also acknowledge scholars working in education who have begun to import the notion of practical reason from Aristotle focusing on his notion of *phronesis* or from Wittgenstein, in terms of "meaning as use", rule-following and "background practices". We might also mention in this context the work of life-world phenomenologists, strongly influenced by Schutz (1972) and Berger and Luckmann (1967) in sociology but ultimately

---

[4] The main elements of the new pedagogy are itemised in the Executive Summary (pp. 11-17) of the Tavistock Institute's Review which indicate that its constitutive elements are largely a combination of constructivism and postmodernism, generating a range of new practices. This new pedagogy views not only knowledge but also the whole educational enterprise differently and while the societal context has changed the "core issues and propositions about learners, learning and teaching have not altered" (p. 12). "Performativity" is singled out for special attention for it is "creating tensions between the social and the highly individualistic consumer ethic identified as the key to post-modernity, and between the rediscovery of learning as a *social activity* and the rise of self-directed and virtual (web-based) pedagogies" (p. 12, my emphasis). Finally, "The reconfiguration of the 'learning setting'" has meant that pedagogies are "much more concerned with: the de-centering of knowledge; the valorisation of other forms of knowledge and ways of knowing; supporting the learner as consumer; working with knowledge as 'social', distributed rather than individualised; learning rather than education" (p. 13).

springing from Husserl and Heidegger. Yet even with these theorised accounts in education rarely is the notion of practice analysed or clarified. There is no systematic approach to these theorised accounts or to the ethico-political implications of the theory of practice embraced. Any account of practices in education first would need to systematically differentiate among these different accounts.

Table 1. *Theories of Educational Practice*

Practice as *problem-solving* (e.g., Dewey)
Practice as *praxis* (e.g., Marx, Freire)
Practice as *lived experience* (e.g., lifeworld phenomenology)
Practice as *reflection in action* (e.g., Schön)
Practice as *phronesis* or practical judgement (e.g., Aristotle)
Practice as *lebensformen* (forms of life) (e.g., Wittgenstein)
Practice as *habitus* (e.g., Bourdieu)
Practice as *noncognitive knowing* (e.g., van Manen)

The Contemporary Turn Toward *Practices*

The present emphasis on practices – the contemporary turn to practices – can be traced, perhaps, to the contemporary "turn" to Aristotle, to the continuing influence of Marx, and to the currency of both Heidegger and Wittgenstein.[5] Theory of practice is embedded in the priority of practical engagement with the world, a materialist social ontology and a view of language as practice-based. This broad view has its origins in an account of practical reason beginning, perhaps, with Aristotle (2000), who in the *Nicomachean Ethics* (Book VI) talks of *phronesis* as the ability to use the intellect practically. Practical reason is to be distinguished from theoretical reason in that the former is directed to a practical and especially a moral outcome and results in an action rather than a proposition or new belief (see Dunne, 2001).

It is not possible to talk of practices without the mention of Marx for his materialist social ontology has influenced thinkers like Heidegger as well as contemporary practice theorists like Bourdieu (1977, 1990, 1998) and Freire (1972). His texts are strewn with references to the priority of the practical. The second thesis on Feuerbach reads: "The question whether objective truth can be attributed to human thinking is not a question of theory, but a *practical* question" (1969, p. 283). His point is that we are practically bound up with the world we are contemplating and therefore already part of a whole

---

[5] While the Kantian inversion of Cartesian epistemology makes Heideggerian relationality thinkable I restrict myself to the philosophers mentioned.

set of social relations and material conditions. The touchstone for Marx is, of course, the concept of labour, broadly considered as the means of self-realisation and creative self-development. In Marx's anthropology the concept of labour pre-figure the human body as the source of social life. Thus, Marx "does not explain practice from the idea but explains the formation of ideas from material practice" (1947, p. 58). The materialist view of history that Marx embraces holds that "social being" determines consciousness: as he writes "Life is not determined by consciousness, but consciousness by life" (1947, p. 47) or "it is not the consciousness of men that determines their being, but on the contrary, their social being that determines their consciousness" (1963, p. 182). Yet as he says in *The Eighteenth Brumaire*: "Men make their history, but they do not make it just as they please; they do not make it under circumstances chosen by themselves, but under circumstances directly encountered, given and transmitted from the past" (1968, p. 97). Language is also practical and historical practices lie at its foundation.

Heidegger was to emphasise the practical over the theoretical and also claimed to find his source for firsthand practical understanding in Aristotle (Sheenan, 1993, p. 81). As Harrison Hall (1993, p. 128) notes "The practical world is the one that we inhabit first, before philosophizing or engaging in scientific investigation" and "The world in the traditional sense can be understood as derivative from the practical world". Heidegger's emphasis on the priority of the relational context of practical activity is also mounted as a critique of traditional Cartesian ontology which pictures the world as comprising subjects as minds whose mental representations (ideas) attempt to capture an independent (material) reality. Philosophy and science on this view is concerned with ways of guaranteeing the accuracy of our representations. We can only avoid the problem of knowledge (scepticism) and the problem of value (how things have value) by avoiding traditional Cartesian metaphysics which wants to privilege the thinking subject (Hall, 1993, p. 129). In particular, Heidegger questions the claim made by Plato that moral knowledge must be explicit and disinterested. As Hubert Dreyfus (1993, pp. 293-294) argues:

> *Heidegger questions both the possibility and the desirability of making out everyday understanding totally explicit. He introduces the idea that the shared everyday skills, concerns, and practices into which we are socialized provide the conditions necessary for people to make sense of the world and of their lives. All intelligibility presupposes something that cannot be fully articulated – a kind of knowing-how rather than a knowing-that. At the deepest level such knowing is embodied in out social skills rather than our concepts, beliefs, and values. Heidegger argues that our cultural practices can direct our activities and make our*

lives meaningful only insofar as they are and stay unarticulated background practices. As Heidegger puts it in a later work, "The Origin of the Work of Art," "Every decision ... bases itself on something not mastered, something concealed, confusing; else it would never be a decision".

Wittgenstein too came to accept in his later work that philosophy, like language, was, as Rorty (1993, p. 344) expresses the point "just a set of indefinitely expansible social practices". Rorty (1993, pp. 347-348) goes on to making the comparison between Heidegger and Wittgenstein explicit:

Early Heidegger and late Wittgenstein set aside the assumption (common to their respective predecessors, Husserl and Frege) that social practice – and in particular the use of language – can receive a noncausal, specifically philosophical explanation in terms of conditions of possibility. More generally, both set aside the assumption that philosophy, might explain the unhidden on the basis of the hidden, and might explain availability and relationality on the basis of something intrinsically unavailable and unrelational.

David Bloor (2001) explains that rationalism is the philosophical tradition which accords priority to theory over practice and conservatism is the tradition sometimes referred to that accords practice priority over theory. I prefer Bloor's alternative descriptions – Enlightenment and Romantic – for the reason that not all accounts of the priority of practice are conservative, witness, for instance, the accounts by Bourdieu and Foucault. As Bloor indicates rule-following would seem to be a paradigm case of rationalism yet for Wittgenstein rule-following is a practice and its normative aspect derives from the consensus between different rule-followers which can be understood only in naturalistic terms as facts about our "natural history".

Both Heidegger and Wittgenstein are important because with their emphasis on background practices – how the present, and our skills and understandings always take place against a cultural background that in principle is not intelligible or able to be articulated in a principled way – the very project of the "reflective practititoner" becomes problematic. The contemporary turn to practices in education not only reflect the broader turn to practices in philosophy and social theory but in the mainstream it turns to practices naively and generally without theoretical sophistication. Indeed, we might hypothesise the "reflective practitioner" had become ideology and as its ideological force has grown so the institutional ossification of the doctrine becomes more obvious and more dangerous.

In the Introduction to a recent edited collection entitled *The Practice Turn in Contemporary Theory* Theodore Schatsky (2001) indicates that underlying the adoption of the term *practice* in contemporary theory is the desire to move away from dualistic ways of thinking. He characterises the philosophical work of Ludwig Wittgenstein, Hubert Dreyfus and Charles Taylor (both heavily influenced by Heidegger) as an attempt to overcome the object/subject dualism and to "highlight non-propositional knowledge and illuminate the conditions of intelligibility" (p. 1). Talk of practices for sociologists such as Pierre Bourdieu, Anthony Giddens and the ethnomethodologists, he advises us, is a way of avoiding the dualism of action and structure as well as the determinism of objectified social structures and systems. In the hands of "cultural theorists" like Michel Foucault and Jean-Francois Lyotard, Schatzki maintains, *practices* provide a means for theorising language as a discursive activity against structuralist and semiotic notions of language as a structure or system. Social scientific studies of science that picture science also as an activity (in the work of Andrew Pickering and Joseph Rouse) use the notion of practices to counter representational accounts of science and to challenge "humanist dichotomies between human and nonhuman entities" (p. 1). Clearly, there has been a major paradigm shift in contemporary thought linked to the theorisation of practice. While there is, Schatzki claims "no unified practice approach" (p. 2) most theorists identify practices as fields of human activity defined as the skills, or tacit knowledges or presuppositions that underlie activities. And while most theorists focus on *human* activities there is a significant posthumanist trend especially in science and technology studies that wants to construe practices as involving an interface with machines and scientific instruments. Finally, Schatzki (2001, p. 2) contends:

> *most practice theorists would agree that activity is embodied and that nexuses of practices are mediated by artefacts, hybrids and natural objects, disagreements reign about the nature of embodiment, the pertinence of thematizing it when analyzing practices, the sorts of entities that mediate activity, and whether these entities are relevant to practices than mere intermediaries among humans.*

As he elaborates, forms of human activity are anchored in accounts of the body and typically theorists will maintain "bodies and activities are 'constituted' within practices" (p. 2). In so doing practice theorists tend to adopt a materialist social ontology emphasising the way human activity depends on shared skills or understandings, typically viewed as embodied. The fundamental philosophical claim involves the assertion of the priority of practical engagement and understanding of the world over any form of theoretical contemplation, understanding or speculation. The priority of practical engagement and understanding follows from an emphasis on the body and on embodied knowledge, rationality and understanding, which takes place through the skilled body, through the acquisition of shared embodied know-how (see Peters, 2003). If actions are embedded in practices and individuals are constituted within practices, then practice theory pits itself against contemporary theoretical approaches that privilege the individual, language as a signifying system, the life world, institutions or roles, structures or systems in defining the social. These phenomena can only be correctly elucidated and analysed through the field of practices, which Schatzki defines as "the total nexus of interconnected human practices" (p. 2). He also addresses the problem of social order in terms of practices but raises the question of what orders the field of practices itself.

These meta-questions concerning the kind of ontology constituting accounts of practices leads to further questions concerning the ethics and politics associated with these accounts, which are crucial to identify in theories of professional practice and development.

Dreyfus and Five Competing Views of *Practices*

Following the American phenomenological philosopher Hubert Dreyfus, it is possible to identify five competing views of practice and the extent to which they are unified or dispersed, and integrated or disseminatory. The outline of these five approaches sets up a rich set of connections between theories of practice and the ethico-political commitments they embody. Perhaps, what is required in pedagogical theory and practice, above all, is an account of *practices*.

The following five points are taken from an essay by David Stern (2000, pp. 67-68) and based upon a handout, as Stern indicates in a footnote (fn 33, p. 358), provided by Dreyfus at the NEH Summer Institute on Practices on July 24 1997, under the title "Conclusion: How background practices and skills work to ground norms and intelligibility: the ethico-political implications":

1. Stability. (Wittgenstein, Bourdieu) the practices are relatively stable and resist change. Change may be initiated by innovators, or be the result of "drift", but there is no inherent tendency in the practices for this to happen. The consequent is either a conservative acceptance of the status quo or revolutionary prescription of change.
2. Articulation. (Hegel, Merleau-Ponty) the practices have a telos of clarity and coherence, and become increasingly more refined as our skills develop. This leads to political progressivism and whiggish history, albeit with the recognition that the path to progress will not always lead in that direction.

3. Appropriative Gathering, Ereignis. (Dreyfus's reading of later Heidegger) When practices run into anomalies, we make an originating leap, drawing on marginal or neighbouring practices and so revising our cultural style. This supports those who can best bring about such change within a liberal democratic society, such as entrepreneurs, political associations, charismatic leaders, and culture figures.
4. Dissemination, Difference. (Derrida) there are many equally appropriate ways of acting, and each new situation calls for a leap in the dark. The consequence is a sensitivity to difference, to loosen the hold of past norms on present and future action, and to become aware of the leaps we make rather than covering them up with whiggish history.
5. Problematization. (Foucault) Practices develop in such a way that contradictory actions are felt to be appropriate. Attempts to fix these problems lead to further resistance. This leads to a hyperactive pessimism: showing the contingency of what appears to be necessary and engaging in resistance to established order.

Dreyfus develops a typology of five competing account of practices. I think it is possible to add to these by recognising contributions from the Aristotelian, Kantian, pragmatic (Dewey) and analytic traditions.

The central question is to determine whether and the extent to which these different accounts necessarily overlap in their definition of practice or share similar assumptions. In educational theory, for example, Van Manen (1999) has addressed the question of practice, noting how the term is used in many different contexts – professional practice, education practices, reflective practice and the like – and suggests that this usage which focuses on preferred ways of acting, tacit knowledge, presuppositions, traditions and so fort, differs from the traditional meaning of practice as "practical" or "applied theory". Van Manen (1999) argues that case of reflectivity in teaching has been made unreflectively. Teaching is rarely if ever based on "reflection in action", van Manen maintains, and he disputes Schon's (1983, p. 54) claims that "we can think about doing something but that we can think about something while doing it". He suggests that the notion of reflective practice, considered in Schon's sense as a practice of reflecting-about-doing-something-while-doing-it is open to two objections: "the relational structure of the interaction, and the temporal dimensions of the practical contexts in which the action occurs."

Van Manen argues "Phenomenologically it is very difficult, if not impossible, for teachers to be emersed in interactive or dialogic activities with their students while simultaneously stepping back from the activity." He argues, by contrast, that the practice of teaching involves a form of noncognitive knowing that inhere in our body, in our actions, in the things around us, and in our relations with others. It is a kind of silent practice that cannot be captured in words or propositions and made theoretical explicit. As he argues:

> *This noncognitive knowledge is like a silent practice that is implicit in my world and in my actions rather than cognitively explicit or accessible to critically reflection. What Wittgenstein, Heidegger, Dreyfus have suggested is that this silent practice cannot necessarily be translated back into words, propositional discourse. Heidegger proposed provocatively that while Rede ordinarily means "talk" in the sense of reason, not all Rede manifests itself through words. Dreyfus uses the term Articulation to refer to this nonreflective implicit knowing. He says, "one does not have words for the subtle actions one performs and the subtle significations one Articulates in performing them." And Wittgenstein suggested that this practical domain of our actions is ultimately nonconceptual, prelinguistic, noncognitive.*

Dreyfus' Heideggerian approach to practices is the most developed contemporary example of the phenomenological position and perhaps the most influential approach in education that provides a clear basis to challenge the orthodoxy of the "reflective practitioner" and especially cognitivist approach best exemplified by Schön. Yet on the basis of this preliminary analysis, we may begin to distinguish between at least seven broad theoretical approaches to educational practices, all of which must be analysed in relation to one another to reveal the ethico-political choices implicit in their accounts. We might identify these Approaches to Educational Practices as: (1) Phenomenological (Wittgenstein, Heidegger, Dreyfus): practices as noncognitive, nonconceptual, and prelinguistic; (2) Marxist (Bourdieu and Passeron): practice as telic or praxical; (3) Positivist: practice as "practical" or "applied theory"; (4) Cognitive: practice as "reflection in action" (Schön); (5) Ethical (Aristotle, Kant): practice as practical judgement or engagement; (6) Deweyean pragmatism: practice as problem-solving; (7) Poststructuralist: practice as problematization (Foucault) or difference (Derrida). There remains the very difficult task of sorting out the differences.

References

Argyris, C., & Schön, D. A. (1974). *Theory in practice: Increasing professional effectiveness*. San Francisco: Jossey-Bass.

Argyris, C., & Schön, D. A. (1996). *Organizational learning*. Reading, MA: Addison-Wesley. (Orig. 1978)

Argyris, C. (1999). *On organizational learning*. Malden, MA: Blackwell Business.

Aristotle (2000). *Nicomachean ethics* (R. Crisp, Ed. and Trans.). Cambridge/New York: Cambridge University Press.

Berger, P., & Luckmann, T. (1972). *The social construction of reality: A treatise in the sociology of knowledge*. London: Penguin.

Bloor, D. (2001). Wittgenstein and the priority of practice. In T. Schatzki, K. Knorr Cetiona, & E. Von Savigny (Eds.), *The practice turn in contemporary theory* (pp. 95-106.). London/New York: Routledge.

Bourdieu, P. (1977). *Outline of a theory of practice* (R. Nice, Trans.). Cambridge/New York: Cambridge University Press.

Bourdieu, P. (1990). *The logic of practice* (R. Nice, Transl.). Cambridge: Polity.

Bourdieu, P. (1998). *Practical reason: On the theory of action*. Stanford, CA: Stanford University Press.

Dreyfus, H. (1993). Heidegger on the connection between nihilism, art, technology, and politics. In C. Guignon (Ed.), *The Cambridge companion to Heidegger* (pp. 289-316). Cambridge: Cambridge University Press.

Dunne, J. (2001). *Back to the rough ground; Phronesis and techne in modern philosophy and in Aristotle*. Notre Dame, IN. University of Notre Dame Press.

Freire, P. (1972). *Pedagogy of the oppressed* (M. Bergman & R. Harmondsworth, Trans.). London: Penguin.

Gibbons, M. et al. (1994). *The new production of knowledge: The dynamics of science and research in contemporary societies*. London/Thousand Oaks, CA: Sage.

Hall, H. (1993). Intentionality and world: Division I of *Being and Time*. In C. Guignon (Ed.), *The Cambridge companion to Heidegger* (pp. 122-140). Cambridge: Cambridge University Press.

Lave, J., & Wenger, E. (1991). *Situated learning: Legitimate peripheral participation*. Cambridge/New York: Cambridge University Press.

Marx, K. (1969). Theses on Feuerbach. In L. S. Feuer (Ed.), *Marx and Engels: Basic writings on politics and philosophy*. London: Collins.

Marx, K. (1963). *The eighteenth Brumaire of Louis Bonaparte*. In L. S. Feuer (Ed.), *Marx and Engels: Basic writings on politics and philosophy*. London: Collins.

Marx, K. (1974). *The German ideology*. In C.J. Arthur (Ed.). London.

Rorty, R. (1993). Wittgenstein, Heidegger, and the reification of language. In C. Guignon (Ed.), *The Cambridge companion to Heidegger* (pp. 337-357). Cambridge: Cambridge University Press.

Rouse, J. (2001). Two concepts of practices. In T. Schatzki, K. Knorr Cetiona, & E. Von Savigny (Eds.), *The practice turn in contemporary theory* (pp. 189-198). London/New York: Routledge.

Schatzki, T. (2001). Introduction: Practice theory. In T. Schatzki, K. Knorr Cetiona, & E. Von Savigny (Eds.), *The practice turn in contemporary theory* (pp. 1-14). London/New York, Routledge.

Schatzki, T., Knorr Cetiona, K., & Von Savigny, E. (Eds.). (2001). *The practice turn in contemporary theory*. London/New York, Routledge.

Schön, D.A. (1987). *Educating the reflective practitioner: Toward a new design for teaching and learning in the professions*. San Francisco: Jossey-Bass.

Schön, D.A. (1995). *The reflective practitioner: How professionals think in action*. Aldershot, UK: Arena. (Orig. 1983, Basic Books)

Schutz, A. (1972). *The phenomenology of the social world*. (G. Walsh & F. Lehnert, Trans., with an introduction by G. Walsh). London: Heinemann Educational.

Sheenan, T. (1993). Reading a life: Heidegger and Hard Times. In C. Guignon (Ed.), *The Cambridge companion to Heidegger* (pp. 70-96.). Cambridge: Cambridge University Press.

Turner, S. (1994). *The social theory of practices: Tradition, tacit knowledge, and presuppositions*. Chicago: University of Chicago Press.

Turner, S. (2001). Throwing out the tacit rile book: Learning and practices. In T. Schatzki, K. Knorr Cetiona, & E. Von Savigny (Eds.), *The practice turn in contemporary theory* (pp. 120-130). London/New York: Routledge.

Van Manen, M. (1995). On the epistemology of reflective oractice. *Teachers and teaching: Theory and practice* (Vol. 1, pp. 33-50). Oxford.

Van Manen, M. (1999). The practice of practice. In M. Lange, J. Olson, H. Hansen, & W. Bünder (Eds.), *Changing schools/changing practices: Perspectives on educational reform and teacher professionalism*. Leuven, Belgium: Garant.

Wenger, E. (1998). *Communities of practice: Learning, meaning, and identity*. Cambridge/New York: Cambridge University Press.

Wittgenstein, L. (1953). *Philosophical Investigations* (G.E.M. Anscombe, Trans.). New York: Macmillan.

PERSONAL AUTONOMY, AUTHENTICITY AND THE INTRINSIC VALUATION OF NATURE

Dirk Willem Postma

Contemporary proposals for environmental education, such as those labelled "Education for Sustainable Development" and "Education for Sustainability", are generally articulated within the conceptual language of liberal education. This paper concentrates on a fundamental tension underlying this coalition between liberalism and environmentalism. I will argue that the environmental need for an intrinsic valuation of nature conflicts with the anthropocentric striving for personal autonomy, inherent to liberal education. In order to illuminate this tension, the first section of this paper will offer an analysis of the liberal ideal of personal autonomy, and its implications for our identification of value. In the second section I will clarify what we mean when we refer to the "intrinsic value of nature". Furthermore, I will explore what kind of attitude towards nature is implied by this recognition of intrinsic value, and mark the contrast with the autonomous attitude required by liberal education.

It would be hard to exaggerate the importance of the ideal of personal autonomy for the practice and theory of contemporary education. Education seems to appeal to the human striving for "authorship" or self-direction in life. In particular, liberal philosophers of education value education as a vehicle for the acquisition of knowledge, skills, virtues, and attitudes required by this moral imperative. Liberal education eventually aims at a certain way of life, a life of self-examination, inspired by Socrates' adage that "an unexamined life is not worth living". Adult, autonomous people will make sure that the opinions, convictions, and judgements they develop are "their own" and not the result of some kind of indoctrination, coercion, or irrational temptation. Children should be stimulated to become aware of the rules, conventions, powers, and habits that structure their lives and subject them to rational reflection and criticism. By doing this, it is argued, children will gradually develop their own codes of conduct, their own personal styles of thinking, judging, and acting. For Kant, a person acts autonomously when she is inclined to judge and act in accordance with a self-chosen law. For this law to be a moral law, it should be accepted on universally held, rational grounds. In line with the first formulation of the categorical imperative, one should be able to ensure that the maxim underlying one's will could function simultaneously as a guideline for universal legislation. In line with the second categorical imperative, one is supposed to respect every human being as a person of intrinsic worth. That is, one should never treat other persons merely as means to an end, but always as ends in themselves (cf. Peters, 1973; Dearden, 1972).

Although contemporary philosophy captures a wide variety of conceptualisations of this ideal, on further examination, every concept of autonomy turns out to be comprised of two related, though distinct ideals. That is, to be called an autonomous, a person must meet at least two necessary conditions: first, there is the *condition of authenticity*. The condition of authenticity requires that my desires, beliefs, ideas, and choices are actually "mine" and not enforced, indoctrinated, seduced, or coerced by some other person or external conditions. This is the condition of "ownership". Second, there is the *condition of reflection*, demanding of the autonomous person that she subject her desires, beliefs, ideas and choices to rational reflection. Furthermore, she must be willing to act in accordance with her reflective judgement.

Liberal philosophers of education, like R.S. Peters (1973) and Dearden (1972), tend to focus primarily on the reflective conditions of autonomy. However, when it comes to the condition of authenticity, they veil themselves in rather vague terms. Peters and Dearden do recognize which kinds of identifications are ruled out by the condition of authenticity – those involving indoctrination, violence, seduction, and so on – but are not very clear about what authenticity implies. Peters does recognize that children have to develop "a sensitivity to considerations which are to act as principles to back rules – e.g., to the suffering of others" (Peters, 1973, p. 132). Now the question remains how children develop this sensitivity, how they come to identify certain goods as intrinsically worthwhile. According to Stefaan Cuypers (1992), underlying this liberal ideal of authenticity is a conception of (self-)identification in terms of choice: we choose the things that really matter to us. This conception implies a hierarchical model of the moral person's volitional structure, as articulated by Dworkin and Frankfurt (1988): "Persons typically not only have desires of the first order, X desires that p, but also desires of the second order, X desires or doesn't desire that X desires p" (Cuypers, 1992, p. 6). Now, the autonomous person should be willing to subject her desires of a first order to the desires of a second order. If there is conformity between first and second order desires, then a person can be said to have acted autonomously. Environmental spokespeople and educators often appeal to such conformity: we should be willing to make our "shallow desires" – our desire for a long morning shower, for cheap meat and vegetables, or for frequent holidays by air – subordinate to our decisive commitment to a sustainable future.

However, I agree with Cuypers that this picture of self-identification in terms of choice is untenable or at least one-sided. In the first place, such a hierarchical model of personal autonomy necessarily leads to a regressus ad infinitum because it is never clear whether or not there is a desire of a yet higher order to pursue (Cuypers, 1992, p. 8). How can the environmentalist consumer, for instance, be sure about the higher order status of the principle of sustainability? It is not inconceivable that this particular kind of environmental awareness is being manipulated by governmental campaigns and commercial lobbies, thereby distracting our attention from the prevailing economic and social structures underlying the environmental crisis. As long as it remains unclear how we should determine the relative status of desires, every distinction between lower and higher order volitions is blurred because they are all shaped by social interaction and disciplined by external powers.

In the second place, Frankfurts picture of self-identification in terms of choice does not do justice to our fundamental intuitions. We experience our identifications and commitments not merely as things we actively and intentionally seek, but, to a certain extent, as positions we find ourselves in. Instead of choosing our object of identifications, it chooses us, so it seems. This fundamental intuition gives rise to a completely different view of the nature of self-identification. Surprisingly, an alternative conception is given by Frankfurt as well. Contrary to his previous notion of self-identification in active terms of deciding, Frankfurt explores an alternative account of self-identification in terms of "caring about something". Crucial to this alternative notion is the insight that, in our daily actions and judgements, we are guided by persons, communities, ideals, projects, stories, paintings, natural spots, ..., we did not choose, but we found to be an object of our respect.

This process of "finding oneself in a relation of care" is mainly passive of kind; our authentic identifications escape the conscious intentions we express for having them. In contrast with the reflective distance required by the activity of choosing, in this view, identifications spring from a close involvement and contact with the things we care about. We experience the influence of a strange kind of necessity, a necessity which is not under our voluntary control: "The moral person feels that he cannot help caring so much about this or that as he does. He feels that he cannot bring himself to will otherwise than he does" (Cuypers, 1992, p. 10). Frankfurt refers to this compelling appeal as a "volitional necessity". This is not like the compulsive desires of an addict, nor like the intrusion of an alien force. On the contrary, the notion of a "volitional necessity" indicates a desire, the moral person is unwilling to resist. In fact, he finds this desire to be constitutive of his identity (Cuypers, 1992).

When we understand self-identification as a subjective act of choosing, then every valuation of nature appears as an act of projection and appropriation. Natural entities are valuable insofar as they fit the reflective criteria and categories that enable us to choose them as "useful", "valuable" or "worthwhile". Within this form of identification all values are in a sense instrumental because they are the product of a rational evaluation of things according to standards that are external to them. Especially within a framework of instrumental rationality – pervasive in late-modern consumer society

– our natural environment tends to be appreciated and protected only insofar as it contributes to human survival and well being. Animals, plants and things are merely regarded as resources for human consumption, production and exploitation, rather than valued for their intrinsic qualities, as sources of meaning, beauty, play, imagination, consolation, and wonder.

Understanding identification in terms of care seems to do more justice to the object of identification, to the value inherent or intrinsic to nature. The "caring subject" seems to be more receptive to the value embodied by natural entities themselves. But how should we understand the proclaimed "intrinsic value of nature" and how do we, human agents, come to recognize nature as intrinsically worthwhile? What kind of attitude towards nature is implied by this caring recognition and how does this attitude relate to the educational ideal of autonomy? These questions will be dealt with in the remaining part of this paper.

On the Intrinsic Value of Nature

There are different conceptions of "intrinsic value" depending on the particular discourse in which the term is used. Within the discourse of environmental ethics, for instance, the phrase "intrinsic value of nature" is generally employed in order to mark the contrast with the *instrumental* value we often attach to our natural environment in virtue of the human resources and economic commodities it provides us with. X is regarded to have intrinsic value if and insofar as the value of X is not limited to the instrumental use we make of X. X is valued, not (merely) as a means to some further end, but as an end in itself. Henceforth, I will refer to this meaning of intrinsic value in ordinary language as "intrinsic value in the weak sense". Within the discourse of meta-ethics, on the other hand, intrinsic value is generally defined in opposition to *extrinsic* value: one can only speak of the intrinsic value of X, if and insofar as the value of X is established independent of human valuation. To argue that our natural world is of intrinsic worth in this strong sense, is to make a meta-ethical or epistemological claim: the claim that the value of nature should not be located in the subject doing the valuing, but in the natural object itself. An objectivist stance like this would imply that value is "discovered" in nature rather than "attached" by human beings (O'Neill, 2001).

Few philosophers will deny the possibility of an intrinsic valuation of nature in the weak sense. Nearly all are convinced that animal species, plants, landscapes and so on should be protected and appreciated not only because of their usefulness for human purposes, but because of their non-instrumental qualities as well. However, since modern subjectivism reigns within analytic ethics, there has been a tendency to deny the possibility of an intrinsic valuation of nature in the strong sense. The subjectivist argument runs as follows:

every value is contingent upon a human activity of valuation. "There can be no value apart from an evaluator (...) all value is as it were in the eye of the beholder" (Callicot, 1989, p. 27). So, apparently, in this view we cannot escape extrinsic value. Therefore, the intrinsic valuation of nature should be regarded as a logical impossibility, a *contradictio in terminis* (Brown, 1987, p. 49; Li, 1996). In my view, however, we can – or even should – speak of the intrinsic value of nature in both senses. The weak and strong concepts of intrinsic value are in fact two sides of the same picture of human valuation (though they point to different levels). As I will illustrate in the remaining part of this section, a close look at the use of the weak concept of intrinsic value in ordinary language leads to recognition of the intrinsic value of nature in the strong sense.

If we take the weak sense of intrinsic value (i.e., non-instrumental value) as a starting point for our analysis, then the question rises: what exactly constitutes the difference between instrumental value and intrinsic value? One might argue that, in the end, all human valuation is of an instrumental kind. Take for instance the beautiful landscape that inspires an artist to paint a watercolour. Though, we would not hesitate to ascribe an intrinsic value to this landscape on the basis of its aesthetic qualities, one might argue that the artist "uses" the landscape as a "means" or "instrument" for pursuing her own artistic end. The same goes for my Sunday afternoon walk in a nearby forest. One might argue that the value I attach to this forest is nothing more than an instrumental value: walking in the forest satisfies my aesthetic or contemplative "needs". Obviously, these examples point to the limits of instrumental valuation; speaking about aesthetic, existential or spiritual values in terms of needs, ends or interests is highly counterintuitive. In our experience, there is a major difference between consumer needs or economic needs on the one hand, and "needs" of imagination, contemplation, inspiration, consolation and spirituality on the other. Apparently, a radically different attitude is implied in these ways of relating to our natural environment.

In contrast with instrumental valuation, Burms and De Dijn (1995) argue that the recognition of intrinsic value rests on an experience of transcendence. Intrinsic value emanates from our involvement in meaningful "wholes", larger realities that exceed the limits of our contingent existence and valuation. This existential feeling of interconnectedness, of being part of a significant reality we did not choose gives meaning to our world and ourselves. Experiences like these necessarily imply an awareness of negation; inevitably, something eludes our picture of nature, its value is always beyond our grasp, as if nature resists every human attempt to appropriate, to value, to categorize, or utilize. In other words, that which brings about an experience of meaning, beauty, wonder, imagination, or inspiration transcends the experience itself. The awareness of an elusive surplus is often articulated as the experience of a call; we experience a call from those things that go beyond our limited existence: a beautiful layer of clouds, a frightening storm, or the amazing flight of an eagle apparently appeal to our desire for a meaning and beauty (Burms & De Dijn, 1995, p. 8).

Almost unnoticed, we have moved from a weak to a strong concept of intrinsic value. This is not surprising, since we have seen that intrinsic valuation in the weak sense (i.e., non-instrumental valuation) rests upon an experience of transcendence; intrinsic valuation of nature can be understood as our response to a transcendent call. This being accepted, the subjectivist might insist that "natural value" in this sense still results from *our* subjective responses; every individual will respond to this call by applying her own personal value to nature. However, *pace* the subjectivist, I would like to stress that it is not *my* response or *your* response, but *our* response that is intrinsically meaningful. As we can delineate from the insights of the later Wittgenstein, nature can only be significant or meaningful to us within a shared language and culture. There is no such thing as a private language, in which we express our most inner and individual impressions of nature, without appealing to a *sensus communis*, a common-sense appreciation of nature. Every expression of value solicits an understanding in agreement. In other words, we find ourselves constantly negotiating for a personal appreciation of nature with an audience imagined as a tribunal whose understanding, if not whose approval, is necessary for our experience of intrinsic value (Blake et al., 2000, p. 136; Altieri, 1994). So, from the outset, the value of nature is embedded in the intersubjective level of our language community. Intrinsic value is neither intrinsic to the subject – the evaluator – nor to the object of valuation – nature itself – but rooted in ordinary language.

Whereas human beings are not necessarily at the centre of this valuation process, their presence is required, and – more importantly – their "possession" of language is fundamental to the very possibility of valuation. For this reason, I defend a moderate anthropocentric view of the concept of nature. Nature should not be defined in opposition to "culture" – in terms of what is left untouched by human beings. On the contrary, natural entities such as plants, animals, rocks and landscapes are meaningful only if they are somehow fostered in our human practices and inserted in our cultural web of meanings and relationships. In this sense, nature is a dimension of reality, intrinsically part of our human world, rather than a separable entity. Even if we speak of "wilderness" or "pristine nature", we draw on those images of "untouched nature" as we have seen on *Discovery Channel*, on a safari-tour in a zoo, or we draw on the fantasies evoked by reading Daniel Defoe's *Robinson Crusoe* or Rudyard Kipling's *The Jungle Book*.

However, one might ask, if those values are all captured within our common language, what then constitutes the experience of a transcendent call? In my view, our response to a transcendent call should be understood in a twofold sense. First, we are incited by our fellow-language speakers to take responsibility for the things we say and do, for their meaning and consequences. By taking responsibility, we respond to an appeal emanating from our language community, its norms, ideals and expectations. Similarly, we seek recognition for our appreciation of nature by articulating the pleasure and beauty we find in nature in a way that can be recognized by the language community (cf. Altieri, 1994). We generally experience a call in this secular-psychological sense, however, there is a second sense in which we feel we have to respond to a call. This feeling does not originate from our sense of belonging to a language community, but goes beyond language. In his *Kritik der Urteilskraft,* Kant refers to this experience of nature as the experience of the sublime. Whereas "ordinary" aesthetic judgement deals with matters of taste and pleasure, the experience of the sublime opens up a sense of the absolute. This experience is marked by ambivalence: a strong sense of unease, tied to a sense of intense pleasure. For instance, if we are forced to take shelter from a powerful thunderstorm or bear witness to a volcanic eruption, we are likely to realize our human vulnerability and futility in a kind of uncomfortable, perhaps even painful way, while we are simultaneously overwhelmed by a profound experience of beauty. Therefore, some speak of the sublime as a sense of "delightful terror" or "negative lust". However, this experience cannot (yet) be represented or expressed in ordinary language. Initially, we are faced with a notorious speechlessness. The sublime constitutes a transitional category, indicating the experience of that which is on or just beyond the boundaries of our language and *ipso facto* our world (Hargrove, 1989, p. 88).

In my view, the transcendent call we experience (in the second sense) emanates from a tension between that which is significant and meaningful to us, and that which is not (yet). As a result of this tension, we feel like something is questioning us; we are called to give meaning to nature, to find words for the unspeakable. Now, the objectivist might argue that we are in fact implying an objectivist notion of value; we respond to a call that arises from our contact with nature, and try to find words for the value intrinsic to our natural environment. Though this might sound plausible, in my view, it is not correct. In line with Heidegger's notion of expressive language, I will argue it is not Nature that speaks to us, but indeed, it is *language speaking* ("Die Sprache spricht"). For Heidegger the essence of human language is couched in the concept of *Lichtung* (clearing); in our language we disclose a world in which things appear to us as meaningful for the first time. That is, language does not represent a pre-existent reality. Rather, language creates an expressive space in which the essence of things can reveal themselves to us. If we speak for instance about the breathtaking panorama we have enjoyed from the top of a hill, we are not (merely) *bringing to light* this experience – describing the height, the palette of colours, distances, the species of trees we could descry and so on. We will also find ourselves *bringing about* an experience of natural beauty, evoking within ourselves and our audience a feeling of admiration, desolation, fear or whatever. However, this expression is not a matter of self-expression (so not subjectivist either), but a response to a call emanating from language itself. Charles Taylor underlines in his paper *Heidegger, Language and Ecology*:

> *So language, through its telos, dictates a certain mode of expression, a way of formulating matters which can help to restore thingness. It tells us what to say, dictates the poetic or thinkerly word, as we might put it. (....). This is how I think we have to understand Heidegger's conception of language speaking. It is why Heidegger speaks of our relation to language in terms of a call (Ruf) we are attentive to. "Die Sterblichen sprechen insofern sie hören". And he can speak of the call as emanating from a silence (Stille). The silence is where there are not yet (the right) words, but where we are interpellated by entities to disclose them as things. Of course this does not happen before language; it can only happen in its midst. But within language and because of its telos, we are pushed to find unprecedented words, which we draw out of silence.* (Taylor, 1995, p. 124)

So, whereas the "impulses" originate from outside language (the interpellating entities), the transcendent call (to disclose them as things) itself can only be heard in the midst of words. We draw the words out of silence, but the silence Heidegger speaks of is a silence surrounded by language. Apparently, poetic or evocative language makes us responsive to a transcendent reality, in a way that enables us to experience and express the intrinsic value of nature. The ideas of Heidegger indicate that this value can neither be reduced to a subjective experience of awe, nor to an objective quality or voice that speaks to us. Rather, it is by virtue of our language, and its "telos", that we disclose a world of things that speak to us and demand our respect. Because of its telos, we cannot deploy this language simply as a means to our own ends and purposes. The words transcend my purposes and by that resist any instrumental appropriation of its meaning and value. Moreover, the words require us to listen and care. They engender an attitude of solicitude.

Conclusion

The listening attitude inherent to our recognition of intrinsic value contrasts strongly with the imperative of active choice that is at the heart of the liberal ideal of personal autonomy. Even more, our solicitude runs the risk of being corrupted and suppressed by this striving for appropriation of value. In order to safeguard our "authenticity" the ideal of personal autonomy requires us to control all "external influences" by means of rational reflection. Paradoxically, we thereby seem to seclude ourselves from the very sources of authentic identification, among them, the silence, beauty, and inspiration we find in our natural environment. One could say that we must lose ourselves in nature in order to find its intrinsic value. Now it is clear that Kantian liberal theory mainly neglects this passive and non-intentional nature of (self-)identification, it is not hard to see how this ideal might contribute to an instrumentalisation of our identification of natural value. Liberal theory urges us to subject our intuitive relationship with nature to rational reflection. Thus, the ideal of personal autonomy requires us to distance ourselves from our natural environment, whereas an authentic identification of nature's intrinsic value – at least partly – requires us to be means that we are? receptive to the transcendent reality and value that thrust itself upon us. I want to argue that, more than our reflective abilities, we need a kind of receptivity in order to distinguish our authentic commitments from those that are imposed on us in an inauthentic way. By hammering solely on personal autonomy in terms of rational reflection and choice, liberal education leaves little room for a transcendent call to be heard. In contrast to the ideal of personal autonomy the educational ideals of care and authenticity imply that sometimes we should give up our striving for autonomy, and lose ourselves to that which speaks to us.

References

Altieri, C. (1994). *Subjective agency. A theory of first-person expressivity and its social implications*. Oxford: Blackwell.

Blake, N., Smeyers, P., Smith, R. & Standish, P. (1998). *Thinking again: Education after postmodernism*. New York: Bergin and Garvey.

Brown, L.M. (1987). *Conservation and practical morality. Challenges to education and reform*. New York: St. Martins Press.

Burms, A. & Dijn, H. de. (1995). *De rationaliteit en haar grenzen. Kritiek en deconstructie*. Leuven: Leuven Universitaire Pers.

Callicot, B. (1989). *In defense of the land-ethic*. Albany: State University of New York Press.

Cuypers, S.E. (1992). Is personal autonomy the first principle of education? *Journal of Philosophy of Education, 26*(1), 5-17.

Dearden, R.F. (1972). Autonomy and education. In R.F. Dearden, P. Hirst, & R.S. Peters, *Education and the development of reason*. London: Routledge & Kegan Paul.

Frankfurt, H. (1988). *The importance of what we care about: Philosophical essays*. New York: Cambridge University Press.

Hargrove, E. C. (1989). *Foundations of environmental ethics*. Englewood Cliffs, NJ: Prentice Hall.

Li, H. (1996). On the nature of environmental education. In *Philosophy of Education Society Yearbook 1996*. University of Illinois.

O'Neill, J. (2001). Meta-ethics. In D. Jamieson (Ed.), *A companion to environmental philosophy* (pp. 163-176). Oxford: Blackwell.

Peters, R.S. (1973). Freedom and the development of the free man. In J.F. Doyle (Ed.), *Educational judgements* (pp. 119-141). London: Routledge and Kegan Paul.

Taylor, C. (1995). *Philosophical arguments*. Cambridge: Harvard University Press.

EQUAL RECOGNITION: IDENTITY POLITICS AND THE IDEA OF A SOCIAL SCIENCE

Paul Standish

In the closing plenary session of a recent conference (2000) on citizenship in Europe run by *Politeia*, Thomas Meyer, Director of the Akademie der politischen Bildung der Friedrich-Ebert-Stiftung, spoke on the theme "Media society, globalisation and citizenship education – 21st century Europe before global changes and national challenges"[1]. Meyer's presentation was admirably clear and cogent. As his argument developed, he addressed more directly the topic of identity politics, on which he had recently published a book, and advanced some trenchant criticisms. Sympathetic though I was to some of these criticisms, I waited for his position to be deepened by a more measured appreciation of the complex issues involved here, but none was forthcoming. Justice is justice for individual citizens, he emphasised, and this, for those in the European Union at least, is enshrined in the rights that are given to individuals, rights that all citizens of member states have as citizens. Identity politics is always a matter of special pleading – a means to further the interests of a particular group in a manner that exceeds the bounds of fair and equal treatment. It is the unjust advancement of self-interest.

If the rather strident turn his paper seemed to take left anyone in doubt as to Meyer's position, his response to the first questioner, who happened to be a Philipino woman, was clear: it was not just identity politics in the hands of a lunatic fringe that he was condemning. Just as proper names have no place in any principle of universalisability in ethics, so here too any claim advanced in the *name* of a particular group must be unwarranted. Hence, it seems to follow, movements such as Stonewall, or campaigns on behalf of gypsies in Germany, or the Civil Rights marches in the US in the 1960s, all become suspect in this way. For while it might well be retorted that some, if not all, of these campaigns could perhaps be legitimated solely in terms of claims of universal justice, it is surely the case that the substance of those campaigns has depended on, or has brought with it, something more specific than this: that is, a sense of the particularity of the group concerned that claims in those terms are apt to obscure. It was precisely because (individuals in) such groups had not been granted sufficient recognition as human beings (and not just universal human beings, but people living at that particular socio-historical juncture), the argument might run, that campaigns on their

---

[1] At the time of writing his paper is not available in print but a brief account of it, in German, can be found at: http://www.politeia.net/seminar/Konferenzbericht.htm.

behalf in the light of their particular plight were made. As far as I can see, the logic of Meyer's argument requires him to condemn these movements, along with the lunatic fringe.

What are the grounds for suspicion of identity politics? A first problem, the one that Meyer makes clear, is the way that more universal concern for justice, understood as the fair and equal treatment of individuals, seems to be overshadowed by the desire to protect the interests of a particular group. There is usually no difficulty in seeing why it is that this or that particular group regards itself as oppressed or deprived in some way. Sometimes though the suspicion is that commitment to the cause has deprived its advocates of sensitivity to more universal considerations. If the worry here is the neglect of universal values, there is also a second cause for concern, at what seems to be the other end of the spectrum. That is to say, the commitment to achieve justice for members of the group in question may depend on the group having a certain mass or muscle, so to speak. They need this in order for their voices to be heard. So what, we are left wondering, of those smaller groups or non-groups – ordinary people in the endless variety of their particular lives? Here also then, from the perspective of the particular as opposed to the universal, there seems to be a danger of neglect, a failure of representation, and so injustice. This can prompt a further doubt, moreover, about the way in which a concern with group identity, and with the claims of justice that ensue, can encourage in members of that group a misconception of their own identity whereby the specific characteristics that make them members of that particular group come to assume an excessive importance in their conception of themselves – excessive in the sense, particularly, that this is false to the nature of human being. Hence there is the suspicion that the very idea of human being, inextricably implicated in any conception of ethics, is skewed.

I have indicated that in order to understand these campaigns, it is not sufficient to refer simply to the principles of universal justice. At the heart of the case that such groups have made there has been a plea for recognition of the particular circumstances of the group, of how they are different and why this is significant. In contemporary policy and practice in education such arguments have become familiar enough, especially in the contexts of equal opportunities and multiculturalism, and research in education is often based on acceptance, tacit or explicit, of such principles. There is now greater awareness of the ways in which a liberal commitment to justice – based on principles of universality and assumptions of a universal human nature – can issue in policies and practices that are insensitive to the interests of those who are not part of the dominant mainstream. It can take, for example, the form of so-called colour-blindness. Hence those committed to multiculturalism or to equal opportunities now cultivate a sensitivity to difference. There is an attempt to reflect this in various forms of recognition.

The ways in which Meyer's position relates to citizenship education are plain enough. I want to develop the present argument more broadly in connection with questions of equality and recognition in educational practice, and also in relation to the idea of a social science (hence *a fortiori* an educational science).

Difference and recognition have received an immense amount of attention in educational theory, and often the emotive nature of the topic has had adverse effects on the clarity of the arguments, making the serious attention that these issues warrant all the more difficult to attain. One of the most celebrated attempts to address these matters in philosophy is Charles Taylor's essay "The Politics of Recognition" and the collection of essays in response with which it is published (Taylor, 1992). I want to take Taylor's essay as advancing something like a best case for a politics of recognition.

Taylor draws attention to the massive subjective turn that takes place roughly from the eighteenth century, especially with Rousseau. We come to think of ourselves as beings with inner depths, depths that are the source of our authenticity, our true or real selves, in a way that is at the heart of modern consciousness and notions of identity. Just as autonomy can be a characteristic of individuals or of social groups (institutions, states, etc.), so also can authenticity be considered in a related way, and it is such a shift that helps to locate ideas of authenticity in more communitarian ways of thought. Taylor begins his essay "The Politics of Recognition" with remarks about personal authenticity but goes on to explore Herder's application of the concept to cultural groups:

> *There is a certain way of being human that is my way... being true to myself means being true to my own originality, which is something only I can articulate and discover. In articulating it, I am also defining myself. I am realising a potentiality that is properly my own. This is the background understanding to the modern ideals of authenticity, and to the goals of self-fulfilment and self-realisation in which the ideal is usually couched. I should note that Herder applied his conception of originality at two levels, not only to the individual person among other persons, but also to the culture-bearing people among other peoples. Just like individuals, a Volk should be true to itself, that is, its own culture* (Taylor, 1992, pp. 30-31).

If earlier hierarchical societies determined a person's identity in terms of social position, the forces of democracy now combine with the ideal of authenticity to found identity on something more inward. But, Taylor argues, the fundamentally dialogical character of human life means that this process cannot be exclusively inward. We need rich human language and other modes of intercourse as means of expression through which our identities can take shape: our identities depend on our dialogical relations with others. The point is not that this dependence is a regrettable feature of the modern world, a product of the disintegration of more stable and strictly ordered societies; on the contrary it was always there, though at times when social stratification was such that identity and recognition were too unproblematic to be thematised as such, this was scarcely apparent. Moreover, the relation with others within a culture, which provides the dialogic medium through which identity is expressed and worked out, is compromised where, in plural societies, that culture is not itself adequately *recognised*. It is the fact that recognition can fail in the modern world that gives a more acute sense of its importance:

> *On the social plane, the understanding that identities are formed in open dialogue, unshaped by a predefined social script, has made the politics of equal recognition more central and more stressful. It has, in fact, considerably raised the stakes. Equal recognition is not just the appropriate mode for a healthy democratic society. Its refusal can inflict damage on those who are denied it, according to a widespread modern view.* (Taylor, 1992, p. 36)

The egalitarian multicultural politics Taylor advances here is based on a subtle and penetrating analysis of the modern construction of the self, elaborated most fully in *Sources of the Self* (1989). There is no doubt that this latter text offers a rich exploration of the idea of the culturally situated self. As such it joins a number of major philosophical critiques of the fallacies that have been commonly found in celebrations of the sovereign subject. These critiques do not leave untouched the very concept of the human.

Before raising questions about Taylor's position, I want to digress slightly in order to associate the views put forward here with Taylor's broader position regarding the idea of a social science, a position in which a visual imagery of cognition is played out in the ideas of perspicuous contrast, the fusion of horizons, and definition. In the earlier essay, "Understanding and Ethnocentricity", he defends what he calls the *interpretive* (or *verstehen*) view, the thesis that social theories are about practices, against two other conceptions. The first is the *natural science* model, his target throughout, and the second, more complex position is the view that "misconstrues interpretation as adopting the agent's point of view", a view he associates in part with Peter Winch (Taylor, 1985, p. 123). He calls the latter the *incorrigibility* thesis on the grounds that, in requiring that we explain each culture in its own terms, it rules out the possibility of our showing that that culture's beliefs are confused or deluded or simply wrong. Taylor sees the interpretive view of social science, in contrast, as resting on the possibility of finding a language in which

> *we would formulate both their way of life and ours as alternative possibilities in relation to some human constants at work in both. . . Such a language of contrast might show their language of understanding to be distorted or inadequate in some respects, or it might show ours to be so (in which case, we might find that understanding them leads to an alteration of our self-understanding, and hence our form of life – a far from unknown process in history); or it might show both to be so.* (Taylor, 1992, pp. 125-126)

The cogency of this view rests precisely on its language of contrast, through which it steers clear of the presumptions of the transparency or the opacity of other cultures associated respectively with the rejected viewpoints. Moreover, while it can call into question our self-definitions, this view itself rests on a background of self-definition, one that embeds it inextricably into the complex and multifarious practices of our cultural heritage. Taylor believes that emphasising practice in this way can help to free social science from the kinds of bogus explanation and specious knowledge that encourage us to look for technological solutions to our deepest problems. It can help us to see how "explaining another involves understanding him, and at the same time, it can give us some insight into the complex relations that bind explanation and self-definition, and the understanding of self and other" (Taylor, 1992, p. 130).

This seems to show that a connection can be made between Taylor's account of the theoretical basis of a social science and his conception of the ethics of authenticity and recognition: both concern self-definition. Furthermore, the dialogical aspect to the self-definition of an individual or a cultural group is echoed in the language of contrast upon which social science must rely. I shall not dwell on the problems of ethnocentricity that may arise in Taylor's reference to "human constants" or in the perhaps more universal understanding of the language of perspicuous contrast to which dialogue may be thought to lead. For present purposes, let me take issue with Taylor's account of recognition (and the implications of this for ethics and education), and follow on to suggest problems with the related understanding of a social science.

I do not want to contest the importance of dialogue in the construction and sustaining of human identity. What is worth questioning here, however, is the way that this is then understood in terms of a kind of reciprocity – the need for equal recognition. My suspicion is that, very much in spite of the intentions of those who advocate these views, such a way of thinking secures the position of the agent (or the subject) in such a way as to prevent the openness to the other that is necessary. That is, it involves a fundamental distortion of the ethical. One problem here is the principle of *reciprocity*. Another is the understanding of the relation to the other primarily in terms of *cognition*. There are aspects of poststructuralist thought that show a way beyond this.

Emmanuel Levinas offers a way of addressing the precarity of the human that goes beyond the terms of both liberals and communitarians, and he does this in terms that avoid the emphasis on reciprocity and cognition. Crucially this involves going beyond the question of the nature of the *being* of human beings, the question that divides these ways of thinking, and he does this by putting ethics before ontology.

Levinas wants to overturn the primacy of ontology, and he wants to do this by showing that fundamental to our being, indeed prior to our *being*, is our responsibility to the Other[2]. Levinas characterises this responsibility in terms of the contrast between our awareness of things through sensible experience and the epiphany of a face. When confronted with the face I see something that necessarily goes beyond anything my senses can determine. For what I see to be a face something must be revealed of the interiority of the Other – perhaps no more than that interiority is there. And that interiority always exceeds any possibility of knowing that I may have. Moreover, for the face to be a face, it must reveal a being whose ultimate vulnerability and need always put me in a position of obligation, and this, it will be his claim, is a responsibility that will deepen the more that I answer to it. Levinas famously quotes *The Brothers Karamazov*: "Each of us is guilty before everyone for everyone, and I more than the others" (Levinas, 1998b, p. 146). Before the Other I am individuated in my obligation – this is not something I can pass up or pass on – and before the Other my obligation is absolute. This is wholly other to any calculus of efficiency and satisfaction, of need and fulfilment. As John Llewelyn puts this, "Ethical Desire is not the correlate of satisfaction. It is Absolute relation that disturbs all correlation, bad conscience that provokes consciousness, the itch of the other under my skin. Every apology *pro vita mea* is ever increasingly lame" (Llewelyn, 2000, pp. 121-122).

If there is something scandalous about this to the canons of our accustomed thinking in ethics, it is because it exceeds the kind of economy of thought that is presumed to be essential. This is a wholly different kind of

---

[2] The capitalisation of "Other" denotes a relationship of a different order from the kind of otherness that is definitional of items in a categorisation. This Other is not different from me in virtue of any perceivable characteristic or quality but because of its invisible interiority, its irrevocable exteriority to me.

economy, or, perhaps better, an *aneconomy*. But it is important for this not to be imagined to involve a kind of romanticism of particularity. While the relation delineated here is strikingly asymmetrical, it in turn correlates with the symmetry of a different order. There is a profound incomparability, more than an inequality, in the relation between me and the Other; but between other others, those I speak of in the third person, there is comparability and equality. This latter order of the third person is the realm of systems, contracts, legislation, principles. It is not prior to my relation to the Other but rather is itself sustained by that relation. The "concrete abstraction" of the face is "torn up from the world, from horizons and conditions" (Levinas, 1981, p. 91); it

> *subtends society, which begins with the entry of the third man. In it my response prior to any problem, that is, my responsibility, poses problems, if one is not to abandon oneself to violence. It then calls for comparison, measure, knowing, laws, institutions – justice. But it is important for the very equity of justice that it contain the signification that had dictated it.* (Levinas, 1981, p. 193, fn. 33)

The poignancy of my relation to the Other is in turn deepened by the rift between its limitless obligation, its particularity, and the institution of a system of justice that the third person order makes possible. This unavoidable paradox is at the heart of what has been called Levinas' "universal particularism". It is there in the relation of the saying to the said. It is there in the arrival of the Stranger, there in the event. As Llewelyn puts this,

> *My responsibility calls for third personal justice, the institutionalized system within which competing claims are to be judged; and such judgements are made within an instituted linguistic system. What is said in these judgements, their dit, is addressed to a being with a face. That is to say, the said calls to be unsaid by being resaid as a to-say, a dire. Justice would be primary violence without this repeated reconversion of the said into saying, without the tie to fraternity, without the manifold of claims and symmetrical counter-claims being refolded back to the asymmetry of the face to face.* (Llewelyn, 1995, pp. 140-141)

One consequence of such a perspective is the realisation of an alienation other than that which could be resolved by any recognition, of something beyond the reach of egalitarian politics. This would be alien in the sense that Judaism is alien, not assimilable, to Western thought, alien in the sense that the particularity and absoluteness of my responsibility cannot be accommodated within the economy of any *system* of ethics.

In certain respects circumstances of multiculturalism, or of the asylum-seeker at our gate, present to us in relief the kinds of ethical imperative that is Levinas' concern. In *Totality and Infinity* he writes of the figure of "the Stranger who disturbs the being at home with oneself" (Levinas, 1969, p. 39). This disturbance suggests something other than the equilibrium of reciprocity, for it defies any kind of calculus, any economy, of needs and satisfaction or of the *scales* of justice. It shows, *par excellence*, the way that the ethical implicates me from the start in responsibility. But this disturbance, however much it may superficially be imagined to be a threat, is the very possibility of transcendence: "The relation between the same and the other, metaphysics, is primordially enacted as conversation, where the same, gathered up in its ipseity as an "I", as a particular existent unique and autochthonous, leaves itself" (Levinas, 1969, p. 39). There is no doubting the primacy of conversation, or something like the dialogical, in Levinas' views. What is markedly at odds with Taylor is the way that dialogue involves not a reciprocity or mutual equilibrium but a fundamental disequilibrium: this is the condition of ethics.

The concern with reciprocity and the tendency to give primacy to the cognitive relation – tied as knowledge is to ontology, to what is the case – involve misconceptions of the ethical, bringing in ethics, as it were, after the event. In this they involve a misconception of the very nature of human being. They gravitate towards a way of thinking that conceives of things in terms of the naturalism of desire and satisfaction, in terms that Levinas will characterise as totality. The understanding of ethics in terms of the contractual (from Hobbes to Rawls) is the epitome of this. Although Taylor's views are so very much more enlightened and nuanced, the emphasis on reciprocity and recognition reveals the extent to which they are still cast in such a way of thinking. Levinas' conception of ethics involves transcendence and, in contrast to totality, infinity. It is in the light of transcendence and infinity, in the light of this relation to the Other, that human being is to be understood.

In remarks on the work of Claude Lévi-Strauss and Maurice Merleau-Ponty regarding the understanding of other cultures, Levinas writes: "The most recent, boldest and most influential enthnography maintains the multiple cultures on the same plane. The political work of decolonization is thus attached to an ontology – to a thought of being, interpreted in its multiple and multivocal cultural meaning" (Levinas, 1998, p. 86). In giving primacy to the ontological they in effect block the possibility of the ethical, as properly realised. So too are the horizons of Taylor's thought set by notions of self-definition that are fundamentally ontological.

Those horizons, I have tried to show, determine not only his conception of authenticity and his defence of a politics of recognition; they are at the heart of his account of the possibilities of a social science. If Levinas is right, it is not only that ethics, and its relation to a politics of recognition, must be reconceived: it is that this in turn must recast the very idea of a social science. It is understandable that this kind of study should, *qua* science, be conceived in terms of systematised and institutionalised thought. But especially insofar as it is a *social* science, one that deals with human beings, it needs to maintain within itself a sense of the rift between that institutionalisation and the nature of the relation to the Other, which must somehow, however silently, be at the very heart of what is studied, which must paradoxically be somehow there in that "science". This would not rule out the kind of egalitarian politics upon which much social scientific (including educational) research is predicated. But it would radically alter this through its disruption of that economy of equality – with the totalising rhetoric in which it thrives and is trapped; by its acknowledgement of a sense of the ethical that defies those terms. In the end, standing in relation to such an asymmetry, this would be a more profound and more cogent study, and it would both sustain and be sustained by a more credible kind of equality.

There are then serious weaknesses in the politics of recognition, even in the "best case" that Taylor provides. There is something feeble or unconvincing at the heart of its expression to which liberal universalism reacts, something that does scant justice to the justice that it otherwise seeks. This is a feebleness that I have indentified in terms of reciprocity and recognition. But the views of Meyer, it should be clear, are woefully inadequate. His tacit acceptance of the onward march of globalisation allows him a kind of missionary zeal about the liberalism he espouses. John Gray has recently lamented the dominance of similar sentiments in the liberal market philosophy that, in the 1990s, was hailed by some as the end of history (Gray, 2001). The resolution of alienation promised by such eschatologies is forever at variance with the resistance to total assimilation and the absolute responsibility that Levinas sometimes refers to as Jewish particularism (where this is emphatically not confined to the experience of Jews – see Levinas, 1990, pp. 114ff). Amongst the delusions of globalisation there may also be the idea that equality and recognition – in the manner that these are widely conceived and as Taylor eloquently defends them – must be the common measures of civilisation. If the theoretically and practically demanding views of Levinas on these matters are right, familiar educational practices that attempt to do justice to multiculturalism and equality seem to be irrevocably compromised, and the possibilities of citizenship distorted from the start. Educational research that ignores these complexities needs radically to be reconceived.[3]

---

[3] Parts of this paper were presented in different forms at the recent EERA conference in Lille, 2001, and at the University of Hiroshima in 2003, and I thank those present for their response. I am grateful to Naoko Saito for suggestions regarding the reading of Taylor.

References

Gray, J. (2001). The era of globalisation is over. *New Statesman*, 24 September.

Levinas, E. (1969). *Totality and infinity: An essay on exteriority* (A. Lingis, Trans.). Pittsburgh, PA: Duquesne University Press.

Levinas, E. (1981). *Otherwise than being, or beyond essence* (A. Lingis, Trans.). Pittsburgh, PA: Duquesne University Press.

Levinas, E. (1990). *Nine Talmudic readings* (A. Aronowicz, Trans.). Bloomington/Indianapolis: Indiana University Press.

Levinas, E. (1998). *Collected philosophical papers* (A. Lingis, Trans). Pittsburgh, PA: Duquesne University Press.

Llewelyn, J. (1995). *Emmanuel Levinas: The genealogy of ethics*. London/New York: Routledge.

Llewelyn, J. (2000). *The hypocritical imagination: Between Kant and Levinas*. London/New York: Routledge.

Taylor, C. (1985). *Philosophy and the human sciences*. Cambridge: Cambridge University Press.

Taylor, C. (1989). *Sources of the self*. Cambridge: Cambridge University Press.

Taylor, C. (1992). *Multiculturalism and "The politics of recognition": An essay*. Princeton, NJ: Princeton University Press.

ETHICAL PROBLEMS OF COMMUNITY IN EDUCATIONAL RESEARCH

Lynn Fendler

Community building is all the rage. From broad curriculum theories to classroom micro-practices, educators are exhorted to build community for promoting democracy, moral development, better learning, and citizenship. Definitions of community that circulate through educational research have implications for ethical questions about inclusion/exclusion, equity, and political governance. In order to build a community, it is necessary to designate what is not community: the outside, the other. To analyze what community means – what a "community" looks like – is to examine how the discourse of community normalizes and delimits our thinking about educational possibilities. Nikolas Rose (1999) writes:

> *To analyse, then, is not to seek for a hidden unity behind this complex diversity. Quite the reverse. It is to reveal the historicity and the contingency of the truths that have come to define the limits of our contemporary ways of understanding ourselves, individually and collectively, and the programmes and procedures assembled to govern ourselves. By doing so, it is to disturb and destabilize these regimes, to identify some of the weak points and lines of fracture in our present where thought might insert itself in order to make a difference.* (pp. 276-277)

In this analysis, I highlight three constituent strands that make community seem like such a desirable aim to strive for in educational research. The first aspect of the current discourse on community is its Third Way appeal. As popularized by Tony Blair, Anthony Giddens, and Amitai Etzioni, community building is seen to provide an alternative to the two unsatisfactory options – a way between state control and free-market individualism, and between communitarianism and liberalism. The second strand infusing community discourse is the trope of solidarity. Based in the assumptions of labor union activism, community is promoted as a strategic weapon that promises empowerment and ability to effect changes. The third strand is an appeal to emotion, a provision that is often couched in terms of safety. Community is advocated on the grounds that it makes people feel welcome and comfortable. In my critical appraisal of the effects of community, I am not arguing that community is a bad thing or that it should be avoided in educational research projects. Rather, I argue that these strands supporting community also produce effects of assimilation and normalization; community is dangerous when community-building practices function to perpetuate existing inequities and censor possibilities for difference.

Third Way

The U.S. spokesperson for the third way, Amitai Etzioni (2000) defines the concept by saying:

> *It is correctly stated as neither a road paved by statist socialism nor one underpinned by the neoliberalism of the free market. It tilts neither to the right or [sic] to the left. (In the US – which has had no significant social tradition – the Third Way runs between a New Deal conception of the big state, which administers large-scale social programmes and extensively regulates the economy, and a libertarian or laissez faire unfettered market.)* (Etzioni, 2000, pp. 13-14)

Third-way thinking is fashionable in many circles, and educational research circulates third-way logic in the discourse of community by arguing that: 1) commonality has been a harmful and exclusionary basis for community building in education; and 2) anything-goes liberal pluralism is equally unsatisfactory because it affords no way of recognizing or distinguishing ethically irresponsible approaches.

One approach to theories of community that inscribes the third-way appeal is Etienne Wenger's (1998) *Communities of Practice*. Perhaps the most widely cited reference on community in U.S. educational research, Wenger's book develops a line of inquiry that he and Jean Lave inaugurated in *Situated Learning* (1991). Community as constructed in Wenger's text is less normatively defined than in most other research, and Wenger does not assume that communities are a good thing: "Communities of practice are not intrinsically beneficial or harmful. They are not privileged in terms of positive or negative effects" (Wenger, 1998, p. 85). Rather, Wenger's analysis posits that communities are inevitable among people who work together, but that the presence of certain criteria – engagement, imagination and alignment – can transform those communities of practice into sites of learning (see esp. pp. 173-187).

Wenger's argument is an example of third-way thinking because its overall project negotiates a middle ground between the individualism of psychology and the collectivism of sociology. Lave and Wenger's work on communities was innovative in educational psychology because it proposed an alternative to the transfer theory model of learning. Transfer theory explains learning as a set of cognitive skills that can be applied or transferred to an array of disparate tasks. As such, transfer theory explains learning in highly individualistic terms, without regard to social circumstances. In contrast, Wenger's theory of learning in communities of practice does not rest on assumptions of individualism, and it explains learning as a product of social interaction. At the same time, communities of practice are not understood as collectivities or sociological structures. In that sense, communities of practice constitute a third way between collectivism and individualism.

The rhetoric of the third way is seductive because it appears to bypass the compromises of communitarianism and the selfishness of liberal individualism. However, third-way thinking embodies its own disciplinary mechanisms (Nisbet, 1953/1990). Nikolas Rose's critique of third-way thinking focuses on the construction of the citizen as a moral subject, an examination of what he calls "ethopolitics" (Rose, 2000). Rose explicates a "double movement" in the shifts in governance patterns from the society to the community:

> *Organization and other actors that were once enmeshed in the complex and bureaucratic lines of force of the social state are to be set free to find their own destiny. Yet, at the same time, they are to be made responsible for that destiny, and for the destiny of society as a whole, in new ways. Politics is to be returned to society itself, but no longer in a social form: in the form of individual morality, organizational responsibility and ethical community.*
> (Rose, 1999, pp. 174-175)

The discourse of community then, becomes a vehicle of self-governance by which educational researchers can envision their participation in ways that appear apolitical. Third-way thinking paves the way for community to be installed as a new site for government, while appearing to operate outside the structures of government. Membership and participation in any given community enacts the simultaneous processes of inclusion and exclusion (Popkewitz, 2001; 1998); however, third-way thinking appears to be an inclusive middle ground, so its mechanisms of exclusion, censorship, and normalization are obscured. Nowhere is the normalization impulse of community more blatant than in Thomas Sergiovanni's (1994) widely cited book, *Building Community in Schools*, where he writes: "Community building is the secret weapon that can help domesticate the wild cultures that now seem so omnipresent in our schools" (p. xiv).

Solidarity

Generally speaking, educational researchers recognize the homogenizing tendencies of melting-pot theories of community. Nevertheless, critical theories in educational research still promote solidarity as a model of community. In community-as-solidarity, many kinds of people with various allegiances can combine efforts for strategic purposes toward a mutually beneficial end. This vision rests on the same assumptions as labor union organizing: solidarity is good, and fragmentation is bad. Solidarity is widely endorsed to be the best or only strategy of empowerment, especially when research is conducted within structural assumptions of dominance and oppression.

Community-as-solidarity theorists also argue against cultural assimilation. Culturally autonomous communities are good for purposes of solidarity and empowerment in the face of a different dominant culture. The theoretical stance that promotes solidarity and decries assimilation implies complicated tensions. One implication is that culturally autonomous schooling is appropriate for minorities and under-represented people, but such communities would not be seen as appropriate for people with assumed privilege. For example, when critical theorists argue in favor of sex-segregated or race-segregated schooling, they mean to support women and racial minorities; they do not intend to support exclusive schools for rich, White, heterosexual males. It is assumed that wealthy, White, able-bodied, heterosexual males already have a de facto community and its corresponding access to resources. So in this sense of community, culturally autonomous solidarity re-inscribes a deficit model, based in the assumption of compensatory opportunities, although this implication of the program is seldom articulated. The intended goal of culturally autonomous schooling is to compensate for the deficits of some homogeneous populational groups, and the only groups who are exhorted to build communities are those who are perceived to be in need. Presumably, this sort of community building is only supposed to be a means to an end. The community advocated in this example of culturally autonomous schooling is not supposed to be applied to everyone in the society. That is, the need for community does not apply to the society at large, but rather to isolated cultural groups, providing a platform for access to power and full democratic participation in society.

Most solutions that rely on means-to-an-end thinking lend themselves to easy critique, and culturally autonomous schooling is no exception. In this promotion of community-for-solidarity, it is unclear what should happen when the cultural sub-group reaches power and full democratic participation in society. At what point will the sub-group be considered ready for admission to the society at large? And then, on what grounds should that larger entity be called a community? Will the differences eventually wither away? Conversely, by what means is the possibility for cultural (or other) differences maintained in the context of the larger society?

This discourse of community-as-solidarity reiterates existing hierarchical power relations. Some groups are positioned as deficient and in need of remediation, and other groups are seen as normal and acceptable as they are. This is an example of deficit-model thinking in which those who are excluded from the community are regarded as lacking, in need of assistance, or deserving of support from those more fortunate. At the same time, the group that is seen as forming an acceptable community is not regarded as pathological or in need of therapy or intervention in any way. As Skutnabb-Kangas (1990) argues, "This static and ethnocentric view, where the whole burden of integration is on the incomer alone, and where the dominant group's values are presented as somehow 'shared and universal,' rather than particularistic and changing, like all values are, still prevails in many countries" (p. 87). So in this model, the status of the included is affirmed and maintained, and the status of the excluded is also affirmed and maintained.

In the view of community-as-solidarity, diversity is good up to a point, but for purposes of political mobilization, solidarity is ultimately required. However, this assumption that empowerment requires solidarity has ironic consequences. The leap to a solidarity requirement prescribes and circumscribes possibilities for participating in community, and ultimately undermines the prospects for acknowledging difference.

Again, visions of solidarity, regardless of how comprehensive, cannot avoid establishing exclusions of some sort. As Mouffe (1992) writes:

> *the idea of the common good specifies what we can call...a 'grammar of conduct' that coincides with the allegiance to the constitutive ethico-political principles of modern democracy: liberty and equality for all. Yet, since those principles are open to many competing interpretations, one has to acknowledge that a fully inclusive political community can never be realized. There will always be a 'constitutive outside,' an exterior to the community that is the very condition of its existence. It is crucial to recognize that, since to construct a 'we' it is necessary to distinguish it from a 'them,' and since all forms of consensus are based on acts of exclusion, the condition of possibility of the political community is at the same time the condition of impossibility of its full realization.* (p. 30)

Here, Mouffe concisely summarizes the analytical argument for problematizing community-as-solidarity. Insofar as educational research denies the constitutive outside, that research has turned a blind eye to pervasive practices of exclusion that are inherent in all attempts at inclusion. Such a stance not only denies the practices of exclusion, but also foregoes a critical perspective that might address the mechanisms by which exclusion is exercised.

In another critique of solidarity, Laclau (1992) historicizes the relationship of the universal to the particular, asserting that the "integrationist" assumption of liberal democratic community was "originally conceived for far more homogeneous societies" and that "this theory was based on all kinds of unexpressed assumptions that no longer pertain" (p. 89). This point suggests that educational research may profit by exploring the ways community platforms reiterate unintended impulses toward commonality.

Affect, Emotion, and Caring

Recognizing the complexities inherent in theorizing community, the trend of recent writing has been toward integrating the affective aspects of community, especially the notion of caring (Noddings, 1995; 1996). In some cases, the vocabulary of political science is subordinated in favor of the language of affect and emotion. Emotion is also fashionable in research now with such concepts as "emotional intelligence" (Goleman, 1995) and "feeling power" (Boler, 1999), so it is not surprising that emotions play a part with third-way thinking and solidarity in the constitution of community for education.

The recent trend that constructs community on the basis of emotional appeals raises four contentious points: the dichotomization of reason and emotion, the universality of emotions, the construction of enemies, and the modern separation between individual and society. I address the problems of each of these points in turn.

Reason/emotion dichotomy. To argue that emotion and affect need to be included in rational debates is to assume that rationality is not already shaped by emotion. When researchers normalize the terms and criticize communities for being too *gesellschaftlich*, they perpetuate a very old dualism of mind and body, cognition and emotion. Many writers recommend that affect and emotion be brought back into social relations and understandings, as if it were possible to isolate thinking from feeling. However, as critical histories clearly argue, systems of reason and rationality have always been shaped by emotion, religion, belief systems, and power dynamics: "The archaeology of the human sciences has to be established through studying the mechanisms of power which have invested human bodies, acts and forms of behaviour" (Foucault, 1980, p. 61; see, also Rose 1989, 1999). The separation of reason and affect perpetuates the assumption that reason is somehow objective and impartial; the separation does not recognize that systems of reason have been produced as the effects of culturally and historically specific power relations that always entail an array of human faculties.

Universal emotions. The feelings that are identified as aspects of the affective domain – trust, caring, safety – have also been constructed by historical power relations. To essentialize these affective aspects is to assume the universality and naturalness of feelings that are culturally and historically specific. In other words, comfort has no essential meaning; there is no reason to assume that an atmosphere that feels safe, welcoming and caring to one person will feel that way to another person. More importantly, when people acknowledge difference in anything but trivial ways, those differences are precisely unfamiliar. Unfamiliarity is therefore likely to engender uncomfortable and disconcerting feelings. People who face systematic injustices daily generally recognize that feelings of trust and safety are not prerequisites of participation, but privileges endowed by existing hierarchies. Therefore, it is misguided to require a sense of caring or safety as a basis for community because these dimensions are neither universal nor natural. People learn to recognize when they are supposed to feel safe and when they are not as discourses of community are circulated and reiterated.

Some researchers call for a community in which such things as participation and safety are negotiated among members. For example:

> *Democratic community is aimed not just at improving student behavior but at creating the kinds of ties that bond students together and students and teachers together and that bind them to shared ideas and ideals. When students share the responsibility for developing norms and when their commitment to these norms is expected, they know they belong. They get the message that they are needed. They experience community.*
> (Sergiovanni, 1994, pp. 120-121)

However, systems of negotiation or dialogue are not neutral or immune from cultural bias, so the form of interaction will always favor some and exclude others. Even when norms of behavior are stated in such seemingly innocuous terms as "respect," those norms generally remain unspecified: Under what circumstances are humor and laughter considered respectful? How much time between conversational turn taking does courtesy require? How loud can voices be? What terms of address are acceptable?

What observations should remain politely unspoken? What vocabulary is uncouth? What rhythm of eye contact feels impertinent? What body postures appear offensive?

More importantly, even when communities ostensibly establish their own norms, they fail to recognize the power that circulates as socialization or governmentality. Negotiations about norms are shaped by a variety of expectations that include reliance on modern expertise. As Rose has argued extensively:

> *Yet our conceptions of normality are not simply generalizations from our accumulated experience of normal children. On the contrary, criteria of normality are elaborated by experts on the basis of their claims to a scientific knowledge of childhood and its vicissitudes.... [E]xpert notions of normality are extrapolated from our attention to those children who worry the courts, teachers, doctors, and parents.* (1989, p. 131)

What we understand to be respect is a conglomeration of expert advice, television images, intimate encounters, stereotypes, and ethical commitments.

Making enemies. Communities construct enemies as they attempt to prevent extremism, fragmentation, and alienation. Often, the products of community-negotiated norms are articulated in terms of "don'ts" rather than "dos"; for some reason, undesirable behaviors are more easily recognized and enumerated than "normal" behaviors. One corollary of this economy of community is the simultaneous construction of ally and enemy, same and other.

The prospects of building community in response to an enemy threat are not new. Nations, gangs, tribes, and movements have typically established their unity and identity not on the basis of what they support but on the basis of what they oppose. Especially in the United States, this aspect of community rhetoric has been particularly salient since October 2001. In his provocatively titled book, *Democracy Without Enemies*, Ulrich Beck (1998) points out the ways communities create enemies:

> *In all previously existing democracies, there have been two types of authority: one coming from the people and the other coming from the enemy. Enemy stereotypes empower. Enemy stereotypes have the highest conflict priority. They make it possible to cover up and force together all the other social antitheses. One could*

> *say that enemy stereotypes constitute an alternative energy source for consensus.* (p. 143)

After historicizing the relationship between communities and enemies, Beck argues that the current historical milieu, "after postmodernity," is comprised of a new constellation of social relations.

Individual/society dichotomy. Like Nikolas Rose, Beck argues that it does not make sense any more to talk about an agonistic or dichotomous relation between the individual and the collective: "Individualization therefore, to pick out one peculiarity, is a collective fate, not an individual one" (1998, p. 34). Beck uses problematic terms such as "imposed freedom," "programmed individualism," and "do-it-yourself biography" to convey the thought that the idea of a modern autonomous individual is anachronistic:

> *But what drives millions of people in all the countries of the globe, seemingly as individuals but actually following a generally shared dream, to break out of marriage and live together 'in sin' outside of the comfortable legal safety net? Is this a type of 'ego fever' that can be treated by hot compresses of 'us'? Not likely. A new relationship between individual and society is announcing itself here.* (p. 35)

The simultaneous construction of community and enemy is analogous to the simultaneous processes of inclusion and exclusion. The discourse creating communities/enemies entails appeals to nationalism, pride, and a sense of belonging. Insofar as community is constructed as an emotional bond, the discourse of psychology, which is the domain of affect, gets folded into the meaning of community.

Educational psychology generally bases discussions about community on assumptions about identity. For example, Wenger's (1998) communities of practice are delimited by participation and non-participation:

> *when communities define themselves by contrast to others – workers versus managers; collaborating versus rebellious students; or, more broadly, one ethnic, religious, or political group versus another – being inside implies, and is largely defined in terms of, being outside. This situation makes boundary crossing difficult, because each side is defined by opposition to the other and membership in one community implies marginalization in another.* (p. 168)

This construction of community is infused with assumptions about identity, which usually connotes coherence, individuality, or ascription. "In a landscape defined by boundaries and peripheries, a coherent identity is of necessity a mixture of being in and being out" (Wenger, 1998, p. 165). When identity is assumed to be coherent, then community membership becomes the problematic issue: "we define who we are by the ways we experience our selves through participation as well as by the ways we and others reify our selves.... We define who we are by the ways we reconcile our various forms of membership into one identity" (Wenger, 1998, p. 149).

Modern identity is commonly understood in terms of populational ascriptions – like race, class, and gender – that rely on sociological and demographic categorical unities (Popkewitz, 1998; Castel, 1991; Hacking 1990). Most educational research on community understands difference in those terms. But other, more nuanced versions of diversity have become available in postcolonial literature. Cameron McCarthy, for example, has advanced theories of race in terms of "nonsynchrony" (1990) and "counterpoint" (1995) that disavow unities of race and identity:

> *I offer a critique of essentialist theories of race. I suggest that such theories have limited explanatory and predictive capacity with respect to the operation of race in education and in daily life. Further, I argue that one cannot understand race, paradoxically, by looking at race alone.* (1990, p. 246)

When constructions of identity are problematized, constructions of community, otherness, and inclusion are also disrupted. In recognition of the theoretical difficulties inherent in the term community, Lynda Stone (1993) proposes the term "heteromity" saying, "I think the time has come to disavow community because the concept itself carries the historical and ideological baggage of the failures of western liberal association" (p. 98; italics in original). She characterizes heteromity as being fluid, decentered, and differentiated.

Conclusion

The deployment of community as a way to think about relations in educational research is bolstered by compelling appeals to third-way moderation, solidarity for empowerment, and emotional comfort. Through these discursive practices, community has become a mechanism of governance and a forum for specifying norms and rules of participation. The connotations of the word community and its associations with moderation, empowerment, and caring open new doors of research and analysis. For example, qualitative studies in education are designed to measure the degree of emotional attachment among working groups of teachers; policy research contrasts "successful" schools with "failing" schools and concludes that success is both correlated with and caused by a feeling of intimacy between school and community; trust and friendship become quantifiable and calculable in case studies of mentor teachers' relationships with their apprentices; and textbooks of teaching methods provide rubrics that evaluate the degree to which a lesson on punctuation contributes to a sense of belonging in the classroom. The ideal of the educated person constructed through the discourse of community becomes one who takes on personal responsibility for regulating his or her moral welfare as a member of a community. Rose writes:

> *Those who refuse to become responsible and govern themselves ethically have also refused the offer to become members of our moral community. Hence, for all of them, harsh measures are entirely appropriate. Three strikes and you are out. Citizenship becomes conditional on conduct. The counterpart to the moralism of these community-based programs is the enhancement of the powers of the penal and psychiatric complexes and the transformation of social workers and other caring professionals [e.g., educators] into agencies of control concerned with risk management and secure containment.* (Rose, 2000, online version)

Iris Marion Young (1990), whose work focuses on the politics of difference, argues that community aspirations are fraught with dead ends. She writes:

> *Too often contemporary discussion of these issues sets up an exhaustive dichotomy between individualism and community. Community appears in the oppositions of individualism/community, separated self/shared self, private/public. But like most such terms, individualism and community have a common logic underlying their polarity, which makes it possible for them to define each other negatively. Each entails a denial of difference and a desire to bring multiplicity and heterogeneity into unity, though in opposing ways.* (Young, 1990, pp. 228-229)

Community debates in educational research are not only about political theories of justice and inclusion. Community carves out a space for discussion that feels politically neutral, and therefore less alienating, less threatening, and less divisive. The idea is to "bring people together," so third-way thinking appears to be moderate and centrist. Solidarity provides a sense of security in the face of enemies, and a sense of identity in encounters with others. At the same time, the rhetoric of community can serve as sheep's clothing for the wolves of exclusion, normalization, and antagonism. Community discourse practices can glamorize third-way thinking, disguise culturally specific sensibilities as universal human emotions, and justify chauvinism in the name of empowerment.

References

Beck, U. (1998). *Democracy without enemies* (M. Ritter, Trans.). Cambridge, UK: Polity Press.

Boler, M. (1999). *Feeling power: Emotions and education.* New York: Routledge.

Castel, R. (1991). From dangerousness to risk. In G. Burchell, C. Gordon, & P. Miller (Eds.), *The Foucault effect: Studies in governmentality* (pp. 281-298). Chicago: University of Chicago Press.

Etzioni, A. (2000). *The third way to a good society.* London: Demos.

Foucault, M. (1980). Body/power. *In Power/Knowledge: Selected interviews and other writings, 1972-1977* (pp. 55-62). New York: Pantheon.

Goleman, D. (1995). *Emotional intelligence.* New York: Bantam Books.

Hacking, I. (1990). *The taming of chance.* Cambridge: Cambridge University Press.

Laclau, E. (1992, Summer), Universalism, particularism, and the question of identity, *October, 61,* 83-90.

Lave, J., & E. Wenger. (1991). *Situated learning: Legitimate peripheral participation.* New York: Cambridge University Press.

McCarthy, C. (1990). *Race and curriculum: Social inequality and the theories and politics of difference in contemporary research on schooling.* New York: Falmer Press.

McCarthy, C. (1995). The problem with origins: Race and the contrapuntal nature of the educational experience. In C.E. Sleeter & P. McLaren (Eds.), *Multicultural education, critical pedagogy, and the politics of difference* (pp. 245-268). Albany: SUNY Press.

Mouffe, C. (1992, Summer). Citizenship and political identity. *October, 61.* 28-32.

Nieto, S. (1995). From brown heroes and holidays to assimilationist agendas: Reconsidering the critiques of multicultural education. In C.E. Sleeter & P. McLaren (Eds.), *Multicultural education, critical pedagogy, and the politics of difference.*

Nisbet, R. (1953/1990). *The quest for community: A study in the ethics of order and freedom.* San Francisco, CA: Institute for Contemporary Studies Press.

Popkewitz, T.S. (1998). *Struggling for the soul: The politics of schooling and the construction of the teacher.* New York: Teachers College Press.

Popkewitz, T.S., & Bloch, M. (2001). Administering freedom: A history of the present: Rescuing the parent to rescue the child for society. In K. Hultqvuist & G. Dahlberg (Eds.), *Governing the child in the new millennium* (pp. 85-118). New York: Routledge Falmer.

Rose, N. (1989). *Governing the soul: The shaping of the private self.* New York: Routledge.

Rose, N. (1999). *Powers of freedom: Reframing political thought.* Cambridge, UK: Cambridge University Press.
Rose, N. (2000). Community, citizenship, and the third way. *The American Behavioral Scientist, 43,* 1395-1411.
Sergiovanni, T. (1994). *Building community in schools.* San Francisco: Jossey-Bass.
Skunabb-Kangas, T. (1990). Legitimating or delegitimating new forms of racism – the role of researchers. *Journal of Multilingual and Multicultural Development, 11*(1-2), 77-100.
Stone, L. (1993). Disavowing community. In H. Alexander (Ed.), *Philosophy of education: 1992. Philosophy of Education Society 48th Annual Meeting* (pp. 93-101). Normal, IL: Illinois State University. (Philosophers Index, 1993)
Tierney, W.G. (1993), *Building communities of difference.* Toronto: OISE Press.
Wenger, E. (1998). Communities of practice: Learning, meaning and identity. Cambridge, UK: Cambridge University Press.
Young, I. M. (1990). *Justice and the politics of difference.* Princeton, NJ: Princeton University Press.